# COLLEGIAL PROFESSIONALISM
## The Academy, Individualism, and the Common Good

by
John B. Bennett

AMERICAN COUNCIL ON EDUCATION ★
ORYX PRESS ★
Series on Higher Education
1998

*The rare Arabian oryx is believed to have inspired the myth of the unicorn. This desert antelope became virtually extinct in the early 1960s. At that time several groups of international conservationists arranged to have 9 animals sent to the Phoenix Zoo to be the nucleus of a captive breeding herd. Today the oryx population is over 1,000, and over 500 have been returned to the Middle East.*

© 1998 by American Council on Education and The Oryx Press
Published by The Oryx Press
4041 North Central at Indian School Road
Phoenix, Arizona 85012-3397

Published simultaneously in Canada
Printed and bound in the United States of America

∞ The paper used in this publication meets the minimum requirements of the American National Standard for Information Sciences—Permanence of Paper for Printed Library Materials, ANSI Z39.48-1984.

*Library of Congress Cataloging-in-Publication Data*

Bennett, John B. (John Beecher), 1940–
    Collegial professionalism : the academy, individualism, and the common good / by John B. Bennett.
        p. cm.—(American Council on Education/Oryx Press series on higher education)
    Includes bibliographical references and index.
    ISBN 1-57356-093-6 (alk. paper)
    1. College teachers—United States—Attitudes. 2. College teachers—United States—Professional relationships. 3. College teachers—Professional ethics—United States. 4. Education, Higher––Aims and objectives—United States. 5. Universities and colleges––United States—Departments. I. Title II. Series.
LB1778.2.B46 1998
378.1'2—dc21                                                    97-37069
                                                                         CIP

# CONTENTS

# PROLOGUE

This essay had its genesis 14 years ago. As a junior staff member at the American Council on Education (ACE), I was charged with organizing a Wingspread conference on post-tenure review to be cosponsored with the American Association of University Professors (AAUP). The assignment became a significant learning experience as I was brought to realize how difficult it is for the academy just to discuss an initiative that threatens its traditional routines and prerogatives.

Before the conference, it seemed that judicious use of post-tenure review—better termed periodic evaluation of senior faculty—represented an obvious value for individual professors, the academy, and the broader public. It promised to advance rewarding forms of academic collegiality as well as the common good. It would promote discussion of teaching and research activities and assure the public that the academy pays serious attention to ongoing professional development. Drawbacks could be identified and effective safeguards devised through thoughtful discussion. Three days with insightful and articulate colleagues, in a wonderfully hospitable environment far from work distractions, would surely produce a balanced understanding of both the advantages and shortcomings of the concept.

To my dismay, the yield was low. Some prominent academics were invited by the AAUP; the ACE participants turned out to be less well-known but more representative of the diversity of higher education in the United States. For weeks, though, even a list of participants was unavailable because the AAUP objected to several ACE-invited participants and for a period simply withdrew from planning the conference. When the conference finally began, it was marked by tense discussion and resistance to open self-examination. Several initial statements framed the idea as another impediment to academic freedom, obviously designed to overturn original decisions to award tenure. Some participants simply asserted that the concept of review had no merits and urged its immediate dismissal, their fallback position being that it was not needed since enough review already occurred. Respondents spoke of faculty arrogance and bad faith, implying professorial self-absorption and neglect of common structures for promoting professional responsibility and the common good.

Throughout, the conference failed to exhibit the patient and disciplined inquiry that the academy claims for itself. Uncharitable constructions were put on proposals and personal motives, and rhetoric polarized rather than advanced constructive communication. The discussion was characterized by posturing and little effort to understand one another. I was reminded of the conference years later when I read Julius Getman's characterization of the debate he often observed at faculty meetings—it "resembles one-on-one schoolyard basketball . . . . the level of competition is high. There are a variety of standard moves by average players and tricky moves by the very good ones" (Getman 1992, 92). Instead of demonstrating that the academy supported professional development and growth, conference speakers left the impression that true professionals took care of these things on their own. Rather than assuring the public that academe could manage itself, and that structures for continuing and mutual education were embedded in the organization, the discussion conveyed just the opposite.

Subsequent events were equally disappointing. The AAUP reported the conference as a victory for the autonomy of the professoriate, and concluded that no change was warranted. Indeed, the AAUP officially declared that "periodical formal institutional evaluation of each postprobationary faculty member would bring scant benefit, would incur unacceptable costs, not only in money and time but also in dampening of creativity and of collegial relation-ships, and would threaten academic freedom" (AAUP 1995, 49). The ACE disagreed and conducted a few workshops in the following months to promote better understanding of the multiple values of effective periodic evaluation of senior faculty, but then ceased its efforts.

Only in recent years has the concept reemerged as a resource for the academy—ironically, one now embraced by the country's two largest faculty collective bargaining units as essential to protect tenure from a suspicious public. The conference came to symbolize for me the ineffectiveness and protectionism for which the academy is increasingly criticized. Truly thought-ful discourse on a topic of importance both within and without the academy simply did not occur, despite an environment unusually conducive to civil intellectual exchange. Instead, the issue was put to the side and postponed until more than a decade later. Rather than moving assertively and proactively to advance its interests and those of the public, the academy dawdled until the public began to demand that the academy explain itself or surrender its prerogatives.

The intellectual stewardship of the academy, and the expert knowledge of its members, ought to make a difference in both character and behavior. Members of the academy enjoy conditions that should promote fair and patient inquiry, thoughtfulness, mutual respect, and hospitality—rather than the self-absorption, suspicion, and disconnection that the conference illustrated. I left the conference wondering why the academy cannot employ its many freedoms to devise better and more satisfying forms of togetherness, ones that promote the common good rather than pit individuals against each other in diminishing ways, modeling abusive rather than fulfilling uses of power.

## THE QUESTIONS

Most members of the academy do enjoy a privileged life and special prerogatives, once the rigor and anxious uncertainties surrounding the award of tenure have receded. They have remarkable control over when and how they conduct their work, they own large portions of the calendar year when they have no institutional obligations, after the probationary period they may go for years without significant formal performance evaluation, they are on the whole adequately compensated, and to date they have been largely immune to the savage downsizing and corporate reengineering that have affected many others. No one is drafted into academic service. Those in the academy enter voluntarily and are by choice intimately involved in what should provide exceptional rewards—guiding the learning of others in fields they have been able to cultivate over extended periods of time and in the company of colleagues with similar interests and abilities. Almost a century ago Timothy Dwight summed up the academic calling as "the most desirable of all kinds of life" (Vesey 1965, 419).

Yet many academics today seem almost indifferent to the benefits of their chosen profession, and some even display a moody defensiveness if not outright unhappiness. Recent studies point to growing faculty malaise, alienation, and a longing for earlier, better days. Some analysts say academic neutrality and professionalism are to blame, as they work against the integration of faculty professional and personal selves. Others claim the academy has been relativized philosophically and needs to recover earlier traditions and narratives that provide an overall context of meaning and standards of excellence. Many suggest that a perceived decrease in public esteem and standing for both institutions and the professoriate is a significant factor. Overall, most analysts agree that the health, wholeness, and attention to the common good of higher education—its ethics and what some would call its spirituality—are in jeopardy. For many educators, the college or university has become a job site and no longer an academy.

In this job, a number of mid-career and senior faculty report they are in repetitive activities, teaching the same courses but finding little room for personal or professional growth. Demands on their time, they say, restrict opportunities to pursue activities that might reinvigorate. Fatigue and curricular demands combine to create doubts about the value of work they *are* able to complete—doubts that easily spill over into insecurity about self-worth. Those who remain productive and satisfied often appear to monopolize opportunities and to take their status as reflecting entirely their own merits, deepening the self-doubts of colleagues. Facts and perceptions of racism and sexism continue to disrupt. And almost everywhere the departmentalized structure of inquiry fosters isolation and fragmentation rather than the wholeness and liberation commonly attributed to pursuit of knowledge. In this light, perhaps it is not surprising that the workplace contributes to a malaise and alienation expressed in uncivility and aggression.

Conflict occurs in many quarters—among faculty, between faculty and administrators, and between faculty and students. Academics are known to tolerate celebrated rifts between colleagues, with faculty sometimes refusing to cooperate or even speak to one another, perhaps for years. Other faculty regard colleagues who become administrators with suspicion, even contempt; a "regard" sometimes returned in full measure. And many instructors increasingly complain about student abilities and accomplishments in ways that demean the very ones they are to teach, and abate the possibility of instruction and learning.

Has the academy deteriorated as an intellectual, moral, and spiritual enterprise? Why would those committed to the life of the mind exempt themselves from the searching examinations to which they subject others? Why is it when there is self-scrutiny, disciplined standards of conduct and consistency applied to others are often relaxed? What are the grounds for claiming professional authority and what ought to be their impact on personal conduct and the conduct of the institution? In short, where are the ethics of the academy? These are large and vexing questions. This work explores some possible answers.

## OVERVIEW OF THE CONTENTS

Chapter 1 reviews suggestions that there *is* growing unease, that faculty uncertainties about their relation to the academy or even their own worth are being expressed with increasing force and poignancy. As the context within which faculty and students do much of their work, institutions are receiving increasing public scrutiny and criticism. Costs continue to increase at the same time that quality is alleged to be slipping. Colleges and universities appear to be disengaged and heedless. The chapter explores several recent critiques of faculty and institutions. Critical comments from within higher education are given special attention.

The second chapter is central, for it develops two contrasting models with large capacity to account for malaise and to provide hope for the future. First, a model supporting insistent individualism, privatism, isolation, and fragmentation of effort with resulting diminishment of intellectual community is constructed and explored. Reasons are presented for its prevalence, and its disadvantages discussed. Individualism comes naturally in academe, but often at a price. Little guidance for pursuit of larger educational and moral principles or goods seems available in this model. The academy's ability to regulate itself is marginal and conditions for perduring individual satisfaction seem elusive.

An alternative model emphasizing relationality is then proposed as more adequate and appropriate to the larger objectives of the academy. This model stresses intellectual community as essential to the mission of higher education as well as to individual satisfaction. It presents selves as relational and communities as mutually enhancing forms of togetherness. The model receives full expression in the concept of the collegium, which is rooted in academic traditions and remains a source of hope for the present and future. Essential to the collegium is an ethic with potential to structure realization of this hope and promotion of the common good. Hospitality and thoughtfulness are central virtues, reflecting the ultimate inseparability of the intellectual and the moral.

Chapter 3 returns to an examination of the unease reported to afflict faculty. Ways in which academics can properly be termed professionals are discussed; then a recent critique of academic professionalism is explored. The alienation it describes among faculty is correlated with the disconnectedness and lack of personal integration fostered by insistent individualism. Various problematic behaviors are identified as reflecting this model. Relations of academics to colleagues, students, and institutions are examined, as is the inability of many faculty to find continued personal satisfaction in their identity as educators. Contrasts are drawn with collegial professionalism. The malaise in which many academics are reported to dwell seems related to isolation and insufficient interest in affirming the worth of colleagues, students, and the academy itself—behaviors influenced and reinforced by the first model.

Chapter 4 looks at insistent individualism in organizational structures. Institutions commonly labor under the burdens of a rigid academic departmental structure, a century-old structure that fosters the professional isolation and disconnection associated with insistent individualism. Curricular fragmentation is a natural consequence of departmental balkanization. Faculty collective bargaining can add to fragmentation, and the relative absence of effective codes of ethics eliminates a potential source of help. Nor does the academy have many traditions that commend and celebrate leadership, preferring instead a mythology that depreciates its value. Institutions can also be excessively private. Accurate admissions and enrollment data can be difficult to secure and are sometimes exaggerated in public statements. The meaning of accreditation is often unclear, and most reports are confidential. Many institutions neglect the broader education of their publics and are disconnected from other needs of their environing communities. Instead, most institutions are preoccupied with competing with other colleges and universities for prestige, students, and other resources.

Chapters 5 and 6 return to the relational model as a source of hope for the work of the academy. Chapter 5 considers the import of the model for teaching and scholarship—activities often understood in more individualistic terms. Alternative descriptions are developed that delineate the public nature of both teaching and scholarship as well as their intergenerational character. Teaching is presented as presupposing scholarship, and scholarship as requiring the public expression known as teaching. The relationship of the collegium to intellectual relativism is also explored. Without an element of transcendence, interpretive communities and academic departments risk diminishing and relativizing knowledge claims. The capacity of the relational model to provide satisfaction and hope is examined throughout.

Chapter 6 explores resources within the academy for promoting the intellectual community envisioned in the relational model. Every institution has a large number of untitled but influential colleagues. Without them, academic leaders can do little. With their assistance, department chairs and deans can help advance the integrity and authority of the collegium. Chairs have the challenge of converting the department from an aggregation of insistent individualists into a collegium. Deans must address a collection of departments that can be insistently individualistic themselves. Considerable attention is given to ways that chairs and deans can cultivate and reinforce the value and appeal of the collegial ethic.

We must attend to these dimensions of our collective being even as we approach what may be the twilight of our corporate existence. For rapid globalization, government deregulation, and the telecommunications revolution are bringing sweeping changes to higher education as they have to other industries. We may be at the dawn of a newly configured corporate life with fresh challenges to the authority of the professoriate and institution, perhaps even to their traditional existence. The epilogue looks at these possibilities.

## READERSHIP

Currently an academic administrator who also teaches and writes, I present several issues in terms of faculty roles in teaching and learning—the very heart of the academy. Accordingly, fuller attention to the roles of the president or provost requires another book. Faculty who have not also had administrative experience may want to say some things differently. Personal experience certainly informs one's perspective, but I believe our commonalities are substantial. My aim in writing is to invite reflection and debate, and to strengthen our collective dispositions to address the problems identified. Deans and chairs may wish to use the text as both a catalyst and a focus for discussion with colleagues at other institutions, and with faculty and others on their own campuses.

The role of the professor is often complex and difficult. It requires intense effort and skill to work simultaneously with undergraduate and graduate students, often of widely differing academic preparation and skills, while staying abreast of what can be a rapidly burgeoning body of scholarship and attending to colleagues and to institutional needs. Insistent individualism adds to the burdens. In this context the collegium and the collegial ethic are resources that can provide greater satisfactions, ones commensurate with the demands and challenges of the calling.

The issues are much more urgent at some institutions than others. Malaise, alienation, and excessive fragmentation and disconnection are certainly not the whole story. Many faculty are exemplary educators, hospitable and thoughtful to the core—and quite satisfied in their roles. And many institutions are strong and vigorous. Yet no faculty member and no institution is exempt; all are implicated, if only indirectly. The purpose in noting these unattractive features of academic life is to identify the values at stake and the grounds for assurance. Unfortunately, much of the academy has taken its time in applying its moral sensitivities to itself. But when it does, there are good reasons for understanding the academy to be preeminently a moral enterprise and to possess ample resources for a better future.

The tentative ideas of excellence we already possess provide one such resource—ideas that can be enlarged and refined through exchange and debate. We can look at what we are doing and, through discussion, identify ways to improve and to resolve unsettled and unsettling practices and issues. Through collegial exchange the vague can become clearer, nagging doubts about concepts and practices sharpened, and possible resolutions identified. The process is continuous, and depends on the willingness of members of the academy to engage collectively, to practice civility, and to expect reciprocity—to be hospitable and thoughtful.

## ACKNOWLEDGEMENTS

Having spent almost forty years in and around the academy as student, professor, and administrator, I have often sought answers to the troubling matters of individualism in the academy. Writing this book provided an opportunity to bring discipline to my reflections. Once pen was put to paper bigger questions reappeared and I found it difficult to proceed without some attention to fundamental issues of the self, power, and meaning. Readers may recognize in a number of places the influence of Alfred North Whitehead and features of the process philosophy of which he was a major proponent. When persuasive, my use of this resource constitutes support for its applicability and adequacy. However, I have not mounted major arguments in its defense and this work does not presuppose a judgment on Whitehead or on metaphysics, though broad and deep philosophical issues are at stake.

Along the way, I found others pondering these issues and trying to distinguish between the foibles of the human condition and what we in the academy have created for ourselves. A literature that addresses various ethical issues is now beginning to appear. Increasing interest by academics in business, legal, and medical ethics has been evident for a couple of decades. But there has been a paucity of attention to ethics in the academy. Faculty members Robert and Jon Solomon note that for years "one could find only a handful of titles referring to academic ethics. This is a humiliating revelation. Instead of taking on the necessary self-examination ourselves, we waited for outsiders—bitter ex-academics, politicians, and journalists—to force the mirror before our faces" (Solomon and Solomon 1993, 49). This tendency of academics to remove themselves from moral examination is now being challenged from within the academy. I have found particularly helpful works by Charles Anderson, David Damrosch, Julius Getman, Mortimer Kadish, Parker Palmer, and Mark Schwehn.

My perceptions have also been informed by conversations with hundreds of colleagues and by firsthand observations of the academy. I have drawn on earlier experiences at the American Council on Education of consulting and working with scores of institutions from all sectors of higher education and in all parts of the country on topics of academic leadership and effective self-regulation. In virtually every conversation, people spoke of being troubled by the chronic problems this book addresses. More recently I have found encouragement in conversations with colleagues from other institutions in a nascent movement called the Associated New American Colleges—a movement explored later as one possible model for the future. I have benefitted as well from experiences and conversations at the four colleges and universities where I have worked. I am grateful to all these colleagues, several of whom have commented on parts of the manuscript. My greatest source of help has been my closest colleague and spouse, Elizabeth A. Dreyer, who displayed the highest form of hospitality and thoughtfulness in her extraordinary responsiveness to the various requirements of this work. I dedicate it to her.

# CHAPTER 1

# Assessing the Academy

A ssessments of the American academy range from glowing to grim. Its reputation abroad is in general stellar, its lead over the academies of Europe and the East substantial. At home, however, its standing is often judged to be eroding. Cynicism is growing, both within the academy and among the broader public. How can we reconcile these two realities?

Globally, our major institutions of higher education and our system of self-regulation and voluntary (rather than governmental) accreditation are admired. The research capacity of our leading institutions is regarded by many as second-to-none, and our record in extending higher education to the masses is widely studied. Reflecting on these phenomena, Derek Bok observes that "most experts here and abroad believe that our universities surpass those of other industrialized countries in their capacity for first-rate research, the quality of their professional education, the degree of innovation in their educational programs, and their success in opening higher education to...the differing needs and abilities of a huge student population" (Bok 1986, 31). Others also point to the record of college and university service to the larger community as well as to the pluralism of American institutions and the choice this diversity represents for prospective students (Kerr and Gade 1989, 7).

Things are not perfect, for many of the same experts also comment on the unevenness of self-regulation and the inefficiency of relatively uncoordinated institutional activities. But on the whole, the judgment is certainly favorable. The relative freedom and autonomy of American institutions stands in clear contrast to the typical governmentally regulated foreign institutions. In the United States, faculty appointments, program development, admission of students, and fundraising strategies are institutional, not governmental, decisions. Competition among institutions for faculty, students, grants, gifts, and prestige expresses and reinforces individual institutional autonomy; the competition tends to promote creativity and greater responsiveness to different constituencies; increased quality is often a result. The excellence of some of our educational activity as compared to European and Asian counterparts seems directly related to these traditions of autonomy, self-governance, and self-regulation. We are fortunate in having local and regional control rather than a centralized, national ministry of education.

Domestically, however, a different formula seems to predominate and the mood is more somber. In fact, the very things that make us attractive from abroad may be working against us at home—our traditions of autonomy, self-governance, and self-regulation. Are they adequate now and will they be up to the demands of the twenty-first century? Some argue that our penchant toward individualism rather than community has gone too far. By common report, many faculty are already disposed toward self more than others— toward aggressive pursuit of individual interests rather than a common good. As Parker Palmer observes, "we have a hard time talking to each other without falling into competition and even combat, into an unconscious rhythm of defense and offense that allows for little openness and growth" (Palmer 1993, 13).

Other factors magnify this tendency. Institutional competition for faculty "stars" increases individual self-preoccupation and diminishes faculty loyalty to institutions, colleagues, and students. The lure of greater prestige and standing in popular polls pulls both faculty and institutions away from service to others and cooperation with them. Pursuit of federal funding leads faculty and administrators to seek special political arrangements, by-passing established peer-review processes. Overall, academe has been reluctant to demand more individual and institutional accountability to common educational goods. As a consequence, public concern about both the quality and the cost of higher education is growing. Critics outside and inside the academy are multiplying, and many charge that institutional standards as well as performance are slipping. Repeatedly, these voices have been amplified by the media, sometimes sensationally so.

## CRITICISM FROM WITHOUT

At the close of the twentieth century, the sheer scope and magnitude of higher education in the United States mean that academe and the work of the professoriate are too important to the rest of the country to be left unexamined.

A number of sharp-tongued critics argue that the core integrity of higher education has diminished.

## Public Concerns

The critics speak of a growing suspicion that teaching is neglected by institutions and professors alike. Too much is delegated to graduate assistants, and yet the cost of higher education has increased far more rapidly than average American family incomes. They complain of college graduates with inadequate communication skills and scientific or historical competencies. Some critics point to the vastly increased amount of research generated and published in academe—but research whose relevance, accessibility, and even quality, they allege, has declined. Faculty are coming under the gun for being disconnected, even self-preoccupied, educators. And institutions are blamed because they are not paying attention to these problems—they may even be abetting them. They certainly are not doing much by way of educating the public about these or other elements of their mission and work.

These broad public concerns about neglect of teaching, the cost and inadequacy of instruction, and the quality of research are substantial matters to which the academy must attend. They may be less colorful and arresting than recurring scandals in intercollegiate athletics or periodic exposures of indirect cost abuses, plagiarism or outright fraud, but they are of no less immediate importance and they point to more fundamental challenges. They speak to the very standing of the academy and whether it has adequate self-regulation and appropriate concepts of professionalism.

## Specific Problems

The most recent national commission report suggests part of what is at stake—"a disturbing and dangerous mismatch exists between what American society needs of higher education and what it is receiving . . . . society must hold higher education to much higher expectations or risk national decline." Among the areas of concern is inattention to student learning. "The simple fact is that some faculties and institutions certify for graduation too many students who cannot read and write very well, too many whose intellectual depth and breadth are unimpressive, and too many whose skills are inadequate in the face of contemporary life" (Wingspread Group on Higher Education 1993, 1). The report also decries the disconnection between societal needs and educational attention to values and character, and the failure to develop an integrated and collaborative system of education from secondary through graduate school.

Other reports and studies point to the failure of higher education to educate the workforce for an information-based, global economy (Fairweather 1996). Rather than modeling what this education might mean, institutions and faculty are perceived as too removed from the rapidly changing world for which they are preparing students. Institutions seem unable to adjust curricula or standards to accommodate change—or to persuade the public that present curricula and standards are in fact adequate. Sheltered by tenure from the job-related anxieties and uncertainties of students and parents, faculty are seen as unsympathetic to the challenges of global competition and marketplace turmoil. Many are also seen to pursue trivial research at the expense of teaching.

For instance, Martin Anderson probably speaks for many when he deplores that writing for publication has become *the* standard by which academics judge their performance. A self-selected standard, not one fashioned outside the academy and foisted upon it, this writing for publication is a prime example of the personal privilege and prestige many faculty pursue. Since Anderson holds that the writing published is often trivial, he concludes that the standard is corrosive. When academics "pretend [as they do] that each other's work is important when it is not, that it is relevant when it is not, that it is a significant contribution to knowledge when it is not, they violate the integrity of who and what they are" (Anderson 1992, 102). Academics are able to persist in this practice, Anderson argues, because they are removed from the society that supports them. Because they can avoid the marketplace, academic intellectuals almost always write only for each other, an increasingly narrow group of like-minded people. They have a friendly arrangement, devoid of the cleansing forces of broader, open competition. At bottom, Anderson seems to argue, the academy lacks truly effective self-regulation because it is excessively privatized and isolated.

By all accounts, the academy has yet to provide an honest hearing for these concerns. Since the more polemical criticisms often excoriate academics as partisan political liberals, it has been easy for some in the academy to dismiss them as colored, if not manufactured, by political animus. Other academics have seen the need to respond, but consider it essentially a public relations task. A few seem determined to ignore the whole affair, holding that the academy has always had critics. These responses are badly mistaken. No enterprise is without flaws, and an enterprise as big and complex as American higher education is bound to have many. To dismiss critics out-of-hand suggests a degree of complacency that borders on arrogance. To remain indifferent concedes territory to those who may not have the long-term interests of the academy in mind. To suggest that the academy cannot learn from criticism conflicts with its mission to support learning and to pursue knowledge—through openly interrogating and assessing experience, including reports of its own deficiencies.

## CRITICISM FROM WITHIN

Within the academy, a number of respected scholars also express concerns. They point to increased faculty cynicism about the purposes of higher education and a correspondingly heightened self-preoccupation. They observe that traditional, reassuring understandings about the special charge and trust of colleges and universities are rapidly receding. One well-known president, Leon Botstein, is representative in concluding that traditional idealism about the mission and activities of colleges and universities "has given way to a sense of ordinary pragmatism and cynicism. The university, even in the eyes of its own constituents, is no different from any other self-interested sector or modern bureaucracy" (Botstein 1992, 50). For many educators, the academy has lost an earlier enchantment and has become simply a job. For others, ordinariness has replaced the heroism of the academy. However reluctantly, a large number would probably agree with Charles Anderson that "the average department has no more people of genuine intellectual zest and broad enthusiasm than one is apt to find at a convention of stockmen, charter fishing boat operators, city managers, or restaurateurs" (Anderson 1993, 26).

### Educators' Concerns

There is a growing disenchantment about the fundamental satisfactions of a career in higher education. The lost idealism extends to what one might call the internal morality and even the spirituality of the academy. The academic calling that over a century ago John Henry Newman called "arduous, pleasant, and hopeful toil" has for many in our time turned sour. Doubtless many keep to themselves their ambivalence or disappointment. But others convey an increasing lament about excessive individualism, isolation, and competition in the workplace, as well as sorrow at the malaise and pain that loss of community creates.

Julius Getman's reflections on his frustration and disappointment in higher education may represent the reflections and experience of others. He writes of entering academic life with the expectation that "universities provided an opportunity for caring relations, a sense of community, an atmosphere in which ideas were shared and refined, an egalitarian ethic, and a style of life that would permit time for family, friends, and self-expression" (Getman 1992, ix). However, in his experience hierarchy and competition dominated, teaching and scholarship seemed excessively removed from the concerns of humanity, and the marks of professional accomplishment were elusive. The personal meaning he had expected to find in academe was often beyond his grasp.

Getman's academic experience has been in a professional (law) school and incorporates service at Ivy League and large public institutions; but faculty of all kinds seem uncomfortable. Directing a special national project on faculty work and rewards, Clara Lovett reports that at every type of institution she visited, "faculty express a longing for an older and spiritually richer academic culture, one that placed greater value on the education of students and on the public responsibilities of scholars, one that nurtured community and collegiality instead of promoting competition for resources and prestige" (Lovett 1993, 3). Certainly many faculty feel more isolated now and their connections with colleagues and students are more frayed, or at least less fulfilling. Writing of her increasing restlessness and dissatisfaction with life in the university, Jane Tompkins laments that she is "hungry for some emotional or spiritual fulfillment that it doesn't seem to afford. I crave a sense of belonging, the feeling that I'm part of an enterprise larger than myself, part of a group that shares some common purpose" (Tompkins 1992, 13).

Long-time professor Ejner Jensen is even more blunt. "Many faculty members in our colleges and universities are embittered to a quite surprising degree and...the very real losses caused by their feelings of regret, envy, frustration, betrayal, and isolation constitute one of the continuing unresolved problems in higher education." Disaffection and cynicism are widespread, Jensen reports, and often expressed with unusual skill and power by faculty because of their highly developed rhetorical abilities. The more virulent forms of this disaffection and alienation include "mean-spiritedness toward colleagues, contempt for students, and a strong condemnation of the whole academic enterprise" (Jensen 1995, 8). These expressions then have a multiplicative effect and a corrosive impact on other faculty, administrators, and students. A "pall of negation" settles over institutional activities.

## The Special Role of the Research Institution

Jensen's comments are troubling. While his descriptions are certainly rooted in various academic realities, they are probably better understood as reflecting pitfalls for most academics rather than widespread inevitabilities. That is, they indicate what *could* happen rather than what *has happened* everywhere. The best mode of prevention, as well as the best cure, resides in the relational community described in the next chapter.

Jensen is describing the research institution, not other sectors of higher education, and he grants that some disciplines are more prone than others to express disaffection. Further, he acknowledges that not everyone who complains loudly is constantly unhappy. Yet the research institution has become a major model for much of the rest of higher education; and Jensen argues that the bitterness he is describing is quite real and authentically felt, "almost endemic to academic life," not simply a matter of show or faculty gamesmanship. Self-preoccupation, mean-spiritedness, and contemptuousness toward students and academe are more than isolated, random foibles. These behaviors are too widespread and occur too frequently to be dismissed as oddities of particular individuals who happen to be professors. They are significant failures in professionalism and they have moral and spiritual overtones. They threaten the health of academic life. Why do they appear in what is surely an environment of extraordinary privilege and security?

Jensen attributes much of the alienation and bitterness he detects to a reward system that emphasizes publication as key to status, money, and perks. This elevation of publication over teaching has a deleterious impact on faculty self-worth and financial standing. Almost by definition, truly substantial scholarly eminence can be claimed by only a few. The rest must confront what they take to be a secondary status—a kind of failure—despite what may be their own quite significant scholarly accomplishments. And those who have chosen to concentrate their energies on teaching almost always have less status, money, and fewer perks for their efforts.

Does Jensen exaggerate? Common sense suggests that expectations for national recognition are set too highly if they extend beyond a narrow range of research institutions. Yet smaller, non-research institutions send external reviewers materials for tenure cases, asking whether the applicant ranks in the top 10 percent of scholars nationally! In these cases, faculty disappointment is inevitable, and institutional expectations are ludicrous. In other institutions, though, expectations are less elevated. Most institutions do not require significant and extensive publication, though they will reward it. In the past, it was normal for their faculty to receive tenure and promotion without any substantial scholarly productivity.

Yet studies show that the trend at institutions of all types is toward more research (Fairweather 1996, 67); and the cultures at many institutions suggest that faculty have internalized these expectations. The Solomons may be correct in saying "for every Mozart out there, there are hundreds if not thousands of Salieris, burning with envy, taking it out on their classes, and waiting with a dose of poison" (Solomon and Solomon 1993, 208–209). Other faculty, who do not publish at all and have no intent to change, may for years have been laboring "with a bad conscience" for having failed to meet expectations laid on in graduate school (Schwehn 1993, 73). In either case, faculty disaffection is a natural consequence. Although Jensen does not comment on it, the very organizational structure of the university or college may also contribute to the bitterness and alienation he describes. Later chapters will consider the role of the academic disciplines in reinforcing faculty separation and isolation—and thereby alienation from common purposes. Trivial writing, to the degree it exists, may be an expression of this disconnection from the common good.

Also contributing to faculty disaffection and cynicism, according to Jensen, is the difficulty faculty experience in being intellectuals within a society that values action over reflection. We can add to Jensen's observation by noting that in a culture of activism, professors are often described by critics as underworked and unproductive, if not also lazy and parasitical. Former Harvard Dean of the Faculty Henry Rosovsky makes a point similar to Jensen's in commenting on the prevalence of envy in the academic world. The trait is rooted in a "deep conviction concerning our own worth and resentment at lack of recognition by 'others': i.e., university administrators, the public, the government, students, nearly everyone" (Rosovosky 1990, 218). Retaining inner equanimity while fully conscious of being outside the national mainstream requires substantial and unusual personal resources, not generously distributed in any population. "Very few are fitted by temperament and talent to derive full and lasting satisfaction from the scholar's life," Jensen observes. In earlier times, smaller faculties were more likely to include those with the necessary personalities. In the larger faculties of today "bitterness is the inevitable product of a situation in which many are called but few are chosen" (Jensen 1995, 10).

## GROWTH AND CHANGE IN THE ENTERPRISE

Many faculty have been "called," their number having swollen enormously since World War II. Higher education enjoyed extraordinary growth in these decades. From 1940 to 1960 the number of faculty in the United States almost doubled. In the next decade, faculty ranks more than doubled again (Sloan 1994, 180). Surging student enrollments led the way, creating the need for more faculty. Thus, most of today's older faculty started their academic careers in a setting of unparalleled change and growth, and in a time of public enthusiasm for higher education. The growth and esteem that higher education enjoyed in those decades has now plateaued; faculty hirings have been considerably restricted, the competition for academic positions much more intense, and the credentials of successful finalists typically far more impressive.

As a consequence, the academy today contains faculty with quite different perspectives on higher education. Most older professors have little recent experience of struggling to enter a sluggish or contracting market. More recent faculty often report an exhausting battle to locate the entry-level position that appears to them to have come so easily to their senior colleagues. After years of underemployment and migration among part-time or temporary positions, some newer faculty find their elders simply unable to understand the personal meaning of these vastly changed circumstances. Even though these senior faculty may report earlier periods of deprivation and uncertainty and some claim now to be stuck in their careers, they have enjoyed decades of employment in their chosen areas, even if not at their preferred institutions. Reconciling these different faculty experiences is difficult and surely contributes to the bitterness and malaise that Jensen and others report.

## The Growth Period

It is in the growth period of the 1960s that Clark Kerr dates the beginning of ethical decline. "I once looked upon the colleges and universities as the purest ethical institutions on earth. I regret to say that I have observed what I consider to be a partial disintegration since about 1960" (Kerr 1994a, 15). Not surprisingly, the major area of ethical disintegration in Kerr's assessment is citizenship. In these recent decades faculty have become more self-preoccupied and less interested in the common good. Kerr describes this change for the worse in terms of a transition "from a traditional to a postmodern paradigm in academic life. In the traditional paradigm most faculty members were part of a particular academic community as the center of their lives, and they took their on-campus citizenship responsibilities very seriously" (Kerr 1994a, 9). There was substantial faculty presence and activity at each campus. There was also significant peer pressure to participate—pressure not easy to ignore.

By contrast, in the new era faculty feel less commitment to the local academic community and obligations of citizenship within it. They "have more attachments to economic opportunities off campus [and] the campus is more of a means to nonacademic ends." Private pursuits and individual advantage are far more common in the new situation and the older "implicit contracts governing behavior and informal means of enforcement are less effective" (Kerr 1994a, 10). Informal peer pressure in support of overall institutional values and welfare is less evident and the voluntary impetus is greatly diminished. Centrifugal forces have mounted and bonds among colleagues have weakened. The external attractions are great. "Knowledge is not only power, it is also money—and it is both power and money as never before; and the professoriate above all other groups has knowledge" (Kerr 1994a, 9).

The concern Kerr expresses about academics covers the same period in which professionals of all kinds have come under increasing suspicion. Those who are traditionally pillars of respectability in the community have in recent decades been viewed with growing public distrust as self-aggrandizing professionals. William Sullivan reports a widespread sense that in all professions commitment to social values and responsibility has deteriorated. At the very time that the technological competency and economic importance of professionals has increased, their contribution to a larger common good has diminished (Sullivan 1995, 124).

### A New Situation

This new situation raises significant ethical and spiritual questions about the professoriate and the academy. An earlier balance between private and public goods has deteriorated. The individual professor and the individual institution are often seen now to pursue excessive private advantage at the expense of the public good. In its implicit compact with society, the academy is expected to educate others and prepare them for lives marked by competency and concern for the larger social good. Unless its own house is in order, the educational institution is scarcely in a strong position to model the values it is assigned to promote.

Perhaps unwittingly, the Solomons illustrate the complexity of the problem. On one hand, they note the extraordinary accomplishments of the modern university—its remarkable success in educating large numbers of students who in earlier decades would not have attended college at all. And these students *are* being educated. It is true that teaching "has rarely been better, and it has almost always been much worse" (Solomon and Solomon 1993, xvi). The university, they argue, has not failed. On the other hand, in the Solomons' judgment there *is* a crisis—education is no longer the center of institutional attention and activity. There are too many competing and compelling attractions in the research, sports, entertainment, and corporate activities that constitute the contemporary university conglomerate. Educators themselves have contributed to the crisis through polarizing attitudes of superiority and unacceptable academic politics. Indeed, "the most horrifying fact about academic life is the abuse of academic power and the contempt so often evident for one's colleagues and students" (Solomon and Solomon 1993, 219). Reflecting on their many years of experience in the academy, the Solomons conclude that "the viciousness and corruption of academic life are a match for all but the most brutal corporations" (Solomon and Solomon 1993, 49). As they see things, education is short-changed by both administrators and faculty.

## CONCLUSION

This picture suggests that there are serious problems in higher education. Professors and academic institutions need to turn the lights of inquiry back upon themselves and be open to correction. Providing the public a better and clearer accounting, rendering public what too often has been left private, is in order. The academy also needs to pay more attention to the ethics of higher education—to the forms of togetherness we create and the ways they advance the common good. This can demand major changes in attitudes and behaviors. Some of this need for change stems from what Parker Palmer has called "the pain of disconnection"—the sense "on the part of faculty of being detached from students, from colleagues, from their own intellectual vocation and the passions that originally animated it" (Palmer 1992a, 3–4).

The next chapter examines two contrasting models at work in higher education. The first model generates disconnection among faculty and within institutions. It emphasizes competition and isolation, and results in diminishment of intellectual community. This model of insistent individualism is solidly rooted in many academic self-understandings as well as in disciplinary and organizational arrangements. Then a second, relational model is identified and examined. It too resides deep in our traditions, supports many of the best dimensions of life in the academy, and offers hope for the future. Implicit within this second model is an ethic that calls for greater collaboration and openness within the academy, holds up hospitality and thoughtfulness as essential collegial virtues, and promises a more satisfying and effective professionalism.

# CHAPTER

# Self and Community
# in the Collegium

Obviously, faculty and institutions of higher education have contributed to their difficulties. Some have graduated too many poorly prepared students. Many have failed adequately to regulate themselves, define carefully their mission, or attend to unproductive colleagues. Almost all have paid insufficient attention to educating the public as to what the academy is truly about, and some have oversold what they can offer.

Spawning and reinforcing these problems is a questionable model of the academic self—one that emphasizes separation, individual autonomy, privacy, fragmentation, and self-sufficiency. This model of insistent individualism generates undesirable behaviors and diverts attention from the prior, more basic, and more fulfilling model the academy already possesses. This more basic model emphasizes connectedness, collegiality, and attention to a common good. This relational model is deeply embedded in our traditions, more adequate to the present situation, more penetrating in its ability to analyze teaching, learning, and scholarship; and, together with the concept of "collegium" toward which it points, more productive of a viable future. We need to recover and reappropriate this relational model and the collegial ethic it embodies.

A model is a subtle thing, more suggestive than precise—a matter more of nuance than of overt clarity, yet influential for that very reason. Models suggest images that inform individual and collective self-understandings. There is not *a* model of academic community clearly fixed in our thinking. Our history is too complex and our institutions too varied for that. But there are in the academy wide-spread dispositions to behave in certain ways. Models are derived from these behaviors, and used to reinforce and extend them. At issue in the two models explored below are the relationships of an individual to self, to others, and to one's community as a whole. Also implicated in the models are specific concepts of power and of virtue. The models have multiple iterations and variations, but there are some central features we can identify.

## THE AUTONOMOUS SELF

The academy can dispose one to isolation, fragmentation of effort, and neglect of a common good. Consider the highly differentiated subject matters within traditional academic disciplines and departments. It is commonplace that over time the typical focus of inquiry becomes deeper and narrower. Faculty attitudes of individualism and isolationism are both cause and consequence. Separation rather than connection predominates, and an exaggerated sense of self-containment and even self-sufficiency may follow. The model of the insistent individualist is converted into the image of the rugged individualist, a solitary laborer tenaciously cultivating and defending his or her small plot of truth. When we view the college or university through this model, it is no wonder that professors appear as autonomous individuals working in separate spheres.

### Insistent Individualism

To be sure, faculty and departments can be eloquent in endorsing collegiality and community. But actual practice often suggests contrary values and commitments. Consider the only somewhat exaggerated claim that members of the same field are unqualified to assess and evaluate each other's special accomplishments and competencies (unless they have almost exactly the same set of credentials, and then they may be deemed hostile opponents). William R. Brown argues that what we are calling insistent individualism means that "an individual can be evaluated only on his own merits....A scholar's worth is absolute and intrinsic; it cannot be assessed against the relative performance of other faculty members, particularly if they are concerned with dissimilar disciplinary pursuits" (Brown 1982, 25). Even medieval Slavic studies is so distinct from early modern Slavic studies, it seems, that the specialist in one may not be able to comment about the other.

Reflecting on their many years of experience with disciplinary segmentation and control, Robert and Jon Solomon are even more direct in their criticism of faculty autonomy, observing that because of "such specialization, professors are hesitant to make a statement that lies even slightly outside their realm and become ferociously indignant when someone else lays claim to their turf" (Solomon and Solomon 1993, 215). The concepts of general academic citizenship and common responsibility to speak about teaching and learning in a wider and more accessible vocabulary are shunted. Differences rather than commonalities are stressed and genuine intellectual community is attenuated.

Further examples of academic separatism and insistent individualism present themselves. A familiar one on many campuses is the tenured full professor who behaves as though beyond any need to secure approval, evaluation, or even comment by others. Many institutions have traditions and governance structures that encourage such behavior. Most institutional evaluation is front-loaded and focused on the probationary period—reinforcing the impression that the tenured full professor is the measure of his or her own value, possessed primarily of rights rather than also of responsibilities. The aloof, self-absorbed, and controlling individual is not far away. One specimen is the "star"— supposedly too busy with research, consulting, or both to attend department meetings, serve on committees, or be available to colleagues or students. Stars are often in demand elsewhere, or expect to be. David Damrosch terms such peripatetic scholars "resident aliens" (Damrosch 1995, 41). Some seem almost permanently in exile. The academic community to which these nomads are present is somewhere else, if it exists at all.

Another familiar figure is the fiercely combative soul who follows his or her own private drummer in constructing course and evaluation objectives, despite departmental or school guidelines. Cooperation or collaboration with others is a foreign concept. This person specializes in "academic freedom" and is rarely moved by entreaties to observe community standards. Then there are the chronic malcontents, impossible to satisfy respecting almost anything, who have mastered the rhetoric of polarization—a mode of discourse that leaves no room for compromise. Nothing is right, the barbarians are constantly at the gate, and even innocent efforts at friendly engagement are returned with an edge that evaporates charity quickly. Most campuses also have the monumentally disengaged or withdrawn individuals, dwelling in self-imposed isolation, supposedly nursing old wounds unjustly suffered. These world-weary individuals have become absentee voters and detached spectators.

Some insistent individualists become curmudgeons whose ways are so difficult to challenge that colleagues have grown tired of trying. They seem oblivious to the discomfort they engender. Other individualists are slick, evasive individuals who are commonly regarded as calculating egoists. However, many are ordinary individuals who simply insist on going their own way. Rarely do disagreements turn on the intellectual adequacy of ideas. More often the difficulty is their lack of interest in colleagues and in working with them. They present an excess of self-preoccupation and, frankly, a problem of character. John Gardner speaks of the illusory values of their behavior: "Self-preoccupation is not without its attractions. Selfishness pays dividends; self-indulgence has multiple rewards; self-pity is deeply satisfying; even self-castigation can yield pleasure. But they are toxic joys. Self-absorption is a prison" (Gardner 1976, 60).

Departments, divisions, schools, and colleges function for the aggressively insistent individualist as secondary communities that exist more for his or her convenience—as places to receive mail and paychecks, for instance—than as informing significant self-understanding. An important exception is the status and prestige associated with the relative ranking of one's institution, a source of continuing anguish to many at institutions in the second or third tier. Otherwise, where one is located seems incidental to one's "real work." As many have noted, academic language betrays some of this independence from our setting when we contrast our "load" with our "own work." The one is assigned from without; the other, assumed from within.

### Failure to Collaborate

William Massy and others have identified academic departments as potentially important contexts for collaborative faculty work that ought to counteract this atomization and isolation. The authors identify five major elements that contribute to the failure of faculty collaboration. In addition to excessive specialization and tendencies to work alone, Massy and his colleagues point to the roles that generational differences and personal politics can play. Generational differences reflect workload inequities between young and old and their different interests in disciplinary developments. Personal politics include divergent ideological commitments as well as clashes in individual "chemistry." Both generational and ideological differences can generate considerable resentment and conflict, reinforcing faculty in working alone rather than collaboratively. The fifth factor they cite is civility—but as a veneer established to prevent pursuit of issues that might provoke division, not as a means to work through differences in order to establish, reinforce, and extend community (Massy et al. 1994). Competition for funding and students and increasing pressures on time are additional factors that work against faculty interaction and collaboration within departments.

Clearly these are challenges to community, not insuperable obstacles. However, they add to the difficulties facing chairpersons and faculty who want to collaborate. For overall, the academy celebrates and honors the "independent mind" and often wonders about the depth of those who are too collaborative. The point is not simply that one is to govern oneself, but that one's ideas, writings, and teaching are most valuable when most distinctive. This often leads to an emphasis on research, defined and executed independent of others. But it can apply to teaching as well, where the outcome, if not also the objective, becomes securing one's own following of students rather than collaborating with colleagues.

## Ambivalence about Peer Review

There is a natural connection between this model and the ambivalence faculty sometimes feel about peer review. On one hand, insistent individualism regularly generates distrust of colleagues in peer review activities. Turf must be defended. The Solomons argue this position: "Given the bitter competitive and political atmosphere of the university and the dramatic differences in styles and approaches, not to mention ideological differences concerning the same subject matter, 'peer review' is a notoriously undependable form of evaluation" (Solomon and Solomon 1993, 130). An alternative view is that peer review is undependable because it is in fact toothless. Despite the appearance of vigor, or even of viciousness, the tendency of faculty is really to go lightly on peers since roles will likely be reversed at some point.

Both positions are deeply troubling. Peer review has to be associated with the greater authority of the scholarly community. It is a fundamental repudiation of privatism. Peer review means that others are recognized as competent to judge and evaluate one's academic work—teaching and scholarship. These others have credentials equal to one's own and the judgments they make are rooted in intellectual, not political, authority. Rather than an exercise in partisanship, peer review incorporates critical distance as an essential part of assessment. But it also illustrates thoughtful, civil, and responsible evaluation rather than conviviality. Those who argue against external regulation of the academy must rest their case squarely upon the appropriateness and efficacy of faculty and institutional self-regulation by peers. This self-regulation is not easy and the fragility of the peer review mechanism is the Achilles' heel of personal and institutional independence. When peer review fails, other agencies of society will take its place.

## Unilateral Power

Reinforcing difficulties in peer review is the autonomous concept of power implied in this model. Bernard Loomer's analysis of power is helpful. What he calls unilateral power is "the strength to exert a shaping and determining influence on the other, whatever or whoever the other might be" (Loomer 1976, 6). It is the ability to determine and to resist being determined. It means success in attaining one's objectives and goals in contest with others. It signals, and defines, winning at the expense of others. Unilateral power relates to value, for one's sense of worth and importance is correlated with ability to shape and control others while being only minimally shaped by them. The aim is to maximize the desired effect on the other and to minimize influence from the other. The more the other can be blunted and overcome, the greater one's status or importance and the more satisfying one's sense of standing.

In addition, Loomer correctly observes that "our universities have become major training grounds for the practice of this kind of power" (Loomer 1976, 16). It is, he notes, particularly associated with the pursuit and possession of specialized knowledge. The pecking order reflects—and is created by—skill in the exercise of unilateral power. A commanding figure is one who commands, not follows—one who confounds opponents, not learns from them. Autonomous selves frequently cope with feelings of vulnerability, insecurity, and insufficiency by attacking, by countering the influence of the other rather than absorbing it. The attack may be frontal or passively aggressive, but the objective is control. This impulse affects activities throughout the academy, but its impact on teaching is particularly troubling. Student dependencies are created when the instructor attempts to control the process of learning. Decisions about learning are taken out of the hands of students. The professor decides for them, instead of cultivating confidence in their own skills and abilities. In research and service as well, perceptions of self-identity and self-worth are often based on assessments of relative strength. These struggles for control can be fatiguing and the victories precarious, but unilateral power seems deeply entrenched. Insistent individualism is both a consequence and an expression.

### Inequitable Distribution

Unilateral power is almost always inequitably distributed. Gain by one professor requires loss by another and the loss extends to status and importance, even if only in one's eyes. This kind of competition easily becomes destructive. Students and faculty colleagues suffer. No doubt this familiar investment in unilateral power helps engender the alienation, aggression, and bitter politics that Jensen thinks plague academe. But what appears initially as the strength of unilateral power is actually a weakness. For insistent individualists deprive themselves of the gifts and richness that others could provide if they were respected as colleagues. Only those who feel respected can be expected to reciprocate. Ironically, educators captured by this concept of power risk impoverishment. Remaining external to and unaffected by the other, these educators direct a process of enrichment from which they are excluded. The flow of value is only one way. Yet many in academe judge this loss and estrangement an acceptable expense. Viewing professional maturity and success as involving substantial independence and separation from others is widespread. Self-fulfillment requires individual self-realization, and community appears to be simply a means.

When power is understood in these ways, the institution is reduced to providing financial resources and setting limits to conflict and exploitation. It is banker and regulator, ideally more of the one and less of the other. Since individuals appear as independent contractors and private entrepreneurs, conflict among them seems inevitable. The good of each autonomous and isolated self is in principle a private good. Happiness is individual in nature; communities are but instruments to achieve this individual happiness and freedom (academic or otherwise) becomes important in protecting each self from others—preventing their interference and holding at bay unwelcome external authority. This emphasis upon rights rather than responsibilities, upon unilateral power rather than interdependence, reinforces the centrifugal forces and fragmentation that isolate rather than empower individuals.

### A Special Irony

The irony is that this concept of power as competitive success at the expense of another suggests a realm of value broader than the autonomous self. For competition logically presupposes a common understanding that individual worth is achieved through competitive acts—that personal identity and status are fundamentally relational. There needs to be an appreciative audience, no matter how small. Thus, truly autonomous power has no cash value independent of prior social value. The very conditions of its effectiveness attest to its ultimate descriptive inadequacy. It presupposes a social concept and is dependent upon it. But the understood concept of community is hardly compelling since its function is primarily to protect the individual from violations of his or her rights. It is a concept of community devoid of any substantive notion of a communal good.

In this model, the academic community is an aggregation of self-contained and self-regarding souls with minimal internal connectedness and mutual influence. It is less than the sum of the individuals who are its parts and is a community only in the thinnest of senses. In this radical nominalism, the academy is simply a heap of folk bound by superficial bonds or commonalities. Their privatized experiences lead ineluctably to the devaluation of genuine community and only an "invisible hand" could assure that any collective public good results from these private, individualistic pursuits. It is a surprise and a mystery that there is any collective good; it is no mystery that there are poorly prepared students, unhappy faculty, and inadequate self-regulation.

## The Appeal of Individualism

There are significant reasons for the academy's individualism. Consider the attraction of the professoriate. Free from routines and details that entrap others, professors enjoy considerable flexibility in their calendars. In addition, they have extraordinary control over what they actually do and how they do it. Selection of research areas, choice of methodology and approach, determination of pace and intensity—all are largely decided by the individual. Parallel freedoms exist with respect to teaching responsibilities—symbolized, reinforced, and extended by the separate classrooms into which colleagues or outsiders are rarely invited.

Such freedom and discretion attract those already disposed to be insistent individualists. And graduate programs are likely to favor these applicants, for the odds are they will complete them. Once in graduate school, they find themselves further socialized as individualists. The very structure of graduate education engenders increasing separation and isolation; notes one observer, "students go from working in courses to working with a few professors for their doctoral orals, and then working alone in the library to complete a dissertation, often under the guidance of a single sponsor" (Damrosch 1995, 10). It is no wonder that many academic personalities contain a strong component of insistent individuality.

The values to be absorbed in graduate school are fairly standard: to study carefully and critically the received past with an eye toward challenging and revising the tradition, to develop and defend one's own distinctive ways of interpreting the data and phenomena of the discipline, and "to make a name for oneself." Almost always, the major emphasis is disciplinary in character. Far less emphasis is placed on the ethos that supports the university as an intellectual and moral community committed to a common task. Indeed, this disciplinary emphasis at the very outset of the faculty career undercuts awareness that institutions need to be viable, strong centers of values. The university or college must then depend upon earlier traditions supporting a common good, traditions that may become weakened and even depleted as time passes.

These traditions include commitment to the value of broad, collective discussion of ideas; the wide-spread assessment of ideas on their merits independent of personalities or ideologies; rough agreement that criteria for assessment include not just coherence and consistency, but also a generous pragmatic dimension evident in the usefulness of one idea to another, to ideas in other communities of inquiry, and to issues of personal meaning for individuals; and agreement that review is never concluded, that each idea is tentative, however firmly supported at present. These traditions are far more clearly implicated in what we will call the relational model than in insistent individualism. They point to the importance of hospitality and thoughtfulness in the work of the academy and we will return to them in due course.

The consequence of much graduate education is that individuals are encouraged to be insistent, even aggressive, individualists. Hiring practices often perpetuate this individualism, since departments usually look for those with similar values. Typical academic reward systems also reinforce insistent individualism. They may not create the phenomenon, but they do little to check it. Young faculty learn early the values assigned to publication and that the academy almost always rewards the individual, not the collective, accomplishment. Better to be first author than second. Collaboration is not a primary value. As a result, faculty become uncomfortable even in agreeing too much, and search for some fine point of difference and distinction. Hence the common definition: "Faculty are those who think otherwise."

In part, the academy fosters insistent individualism because it does value the particular accomplishment and the distinctive competency. The heroic ascetic pursuing truth at the expense of everything else may be the rare creature, but the image pulls on all of us. After all, the business of the academy includes credentialing individuals and attesting to their knowledge and skills. So academe creates outstanding teacher awards, research and publication prizes, student scholarships, and other ways to recognize individual initiative and tenacity. It is easier to identify and hold up the specialist and the expert. It is much more difficult to celebrate the accomplished generalist. And rarely are there celebrations of collective or collaborative effort.

## The Flaws of Autonomy

However natural these ways of thinking and behaving seem, they weaken the academy. Insistent individualism does not enhance common life; it cannot even stand alone. Behind the extreme, unqualified expression of insistent individualism lurks the unfortunate philosophical notion of an enduring, substantial self—one only externally qualified by knowledge and essentially unaffected by relationships with others. External relatedness means reception and transmission of external influences with little internal impact, hardly the mark of a rich, thoughtful, and hospitable person. Obviously there will be some communal interaction, but the unqualified model suggests that in the main this is to be transcended. The truly insistent individualist may seek authority and validation from peers, but in the end he or she is not prepared to allow them entrance to the self. Significant relationships smack of dependence. The contributions others make are held at a distance and valued only instrumentally. They are kept external to the self rather than internally absorbed and cherished.

Paradoxically, the insistent self must be ever alert to attack, ever anxious about the security of his or her accomplishments in this Hobbesian world of academic competition. Without confidence in mutual support and shared values and tasks, the autonomous individual can never rest easy. Since the commanding and controlling person exercises power by excluding the influence of others, eventually he or she will probably be seen as bland, empty of diversity and integrity, and perhaps even fearful of others. The poignance of insistent individualism is its loss of the supporting, affirming, and nourishing community with which one can feel a larger identity and sense of common purpose. Surely Jane Tompkins is criticizing just this failure of the academy to create and sustain effective collegia when, as noted above, she speaks of craving a sense of belonging to a larger group bound by a common purpose.

It is ironic, therefore, that in addition to inhibiting people from working together, this model also hides the ways in which thinking can be a kind of group thinking. There is an insistent individualism of the group as well as of the person. As David Damrosch observes, "the myth of the scholar as isolated individual...conceals the extent to which individuals do bear the marks of the disciplines and departments in which we live. A herd of independent thinkers is still a herd" (Damrosch 1995, 188). To overcome the shallowness and insularity of the group-thinker, experience available to all must be the ultimate court of appeal, not that confined only to specific races or genders or seen only through specific ideological frames. Independent thought reflecting on common, not privileged, experiences is essential.

We saw that one reason for the inadequacy of this model is its inability to account for the conditions of its own applicability. It cannot stand alone, since logically and practically it requires a common life. Even academic individualism presumes that knowledge is a social achievement, not a private accomplishment. Rules govern and constitute the achievement of knowledge. And rules are community achievements and possessions, not individual artifacts. Language itself—the means by which knowledge is expressed and communicated—is preeminently a public phenomenon. Any private use presupposes its common character. The point of constructing the individualistic persona may be to protect oneself from the demands and intrusiveness of others—but to be effective, this very persona also requires acceptance by others.

As Charles Taylor reminds us, community is already present. Each individual achieves self-identity only in dialogue with others (Taylor 1991, 33); selves emerge only through discourse. Each of us is inducted into preexisting languages. We do not create the languages on our own, and conversations with ourselves alone will not suffice. This holds for all inquiry, from rudimentary to advanced. It is true not only for early stages of personal or intellectual self-understanding, but throughout our lives. There must be discourse, dialogue, and conversation at the outset; and it must perdure. Even if internal-ized, it is constructed to meet anticipated objections from others. Solitary reflection is incomplete without an "other." As Loomer notes, "we are at once both communal and solitary individuals. But the solitariness of individuality is lived out only in the midst of constitutive relationships" (Loomer 1976, 20).

The autonomous, independent, discrete self of the full professor is at best a rough abstraction. It fails to account for the interchange within the collegium that provides academic life with growth and development, refreshment and delight, as well as challenge and rigor. It is just these interchanges with others within environments of significance that constitute things that matter. To search for meaning and yet to stand back from engagements and relationships with others is self-stultifying. Even though they associate worth and self-value with independence, most faculty become uncomfortable when the model of insistent individualism is pushed to the extreme. They sense that intellectual stature and leadership should mean neither domination nor isolation. What was initially appealing becomes problematic. "To shut out demands emanating from beyond the self is precisely to suppress the conditions of significance, and hence to court trivialization" (Taylor 1991, 40). Insistent individualism is both impoverished and, in the end, impoverishing. In Whitehead's terms, the notion of the autonomous self commits the "fallacy of misplaced concrete-ness." It takes as real what is only an abstraction from the real.

## THE RELATIONAL MODEL

However influential the model of the autonomous self, it is very much in tension with other parts of our heritage—parts that emphasize the lively community of scholars. To be sure, suggestions that this community was more vigorous in the past may be wistful projections of a nostalgic present; but not all is projection. Robert Secor, for instance, provides an intriguing look at the historical record of the English Department at Penn State, disclosing that at the turn of the century it was "a department that reads, teaches, and discusses together" (Secor 1995, 3). Closer to our own time, Jack Schuster reports on his interviews with senior faculty and their frequent, moving expressions of regret at the loss of an earlier "sense of community and shared purpose within the academy"—regret for an era characterized by "images of a simpler and (it would seem) happier time, with faculty colleagueship perceived as having been more genuine than illusory" (Schuster 1991–1992, 1). Of course, institu-tions in the middle fifties were smaller, the faculty was more compact, both faculty and students were far more homogenous, and the nature of knowledge was far less complicated. Since then, Schuster notes, the scale of things has increased enormously and become less manageable. Common ground has receded with increasing specialization, market pressures for widened salary differentials, broader ethnic and gender representation, and growth in numbers of adjunct, part-time, or temporary faculty. That earlier, simpler past is gone. But the model of common purpose it incorporated is still available.

Not many of us need arguments that the insistent individualist model is unhelpful, for we know that it is unfaithful to the ultimate realities of our own experience. What we need instead of arguments are periodic reminders of its inadequacy, and a relational model that preserves appropriate individualism. We need a balanced model, one that includes the solitary and the communal, virtues of self-reliance and enrichment by others.

## The Relational Nature of Individuality

Recall that at most institutions it is academic groupings (departments, divisions, or schools) that provide the setting for individual faculty and the context within which nuances of freedom, responsibility, and personal identity are established. It is within these settings that entering faculty members receive answers to their questions about teaching performance, scholarly productivity, and service contributions. It is from their colleagues in these groupings that mid-career faculty get clues about their own stature respecting teaching prowess, scholarly depth, and citizenship—clues that enhance self-esteem or reinforce self-doubts and unhappiness. And it is out of reputations forged within these settings that senior faculty are known and cherished (or avoided) for their idiosyncrasies and accomplishments. Rather than a solitary agent independent of institutional colleagues, the individual is in many respects shaped and formed by them. Conditions for teaching and research are established through relationships of teachers and scholars with one another, as are measures for determining success and for evaluating citizenship. The relational model takes these facts of connectedness with others as basic, and their incorporation into self-understanding as essential for personal satisfaction.

Rather than celebrating independence from others, this model emphasizes values that accrue from openness to others. Bernard Loomer is again helpful: "Our openness to be influenced by another, without losing our identity or sense of self-dependence, is not only an acknowledgement and affirmation of the other as an end rather than a means to an end. It is also a measure of our own strength and size, even and especially when this influence of the other helps to effect a creative transformation of ourselves and our world" (Loomer 1976, 18). Insistent individualism reduces relationships with others to instrumental values—they become only means whereby private ends are pursued and advanced. The relational model not only observes the Kantian imperative that others never be regarded only as means, but it also extends the value of others as ends. The relational model presupposes self-confidence in one's worth, but insists this worth is not only reinforced but expanded and perhaps even transformed by the diversity of experience represented by others.

Challenged by insights of others, rather than isolated from them, the individual absorbs and evaluates these perspectives and finds they may enhance his or her own freedom and creativity. Others are no longer just associates, but companions and colleagues. They disclose elements of one's own selfhood. Self-understandings and new perspectives on self-identity not previously available are gained. Possibilities for new understandings and discoveries emerge out of these relationships, and are even created by them. Further, the possibilities extend in both directions. Sufficiently secure, one is able to provide others with the conditions that enable them to grow in their diversity and uniqueness, even as they provide these conditions for oneself. Educators influenced by this model are known for supporting others, students and colleagues alike. They know that only by providing respect to others is respect created for self. One becomes enriched through enriching others.

Whitehead provides help in conceptualizing the relational nature of individuality (Whitehead 1978). He suggests that we understand each self at any "now" as the immediate present experienced in that longer series of moments of actions and decisions we identify as a person. In this series the past is continuously presented to each now. Structures of personality, the deliverances of bodily experience, and the influences of physical and cultural environments press in. The present receives or undergoes its past, unifies it into the present immediacy, and in deciding how to proceed contributes its legacy to the future—its own and that of others.

Whitehead is a resource because his systematic thought elaborates internal relationships (that individuals are internally constituted or created by their relations with others) and individual freedom and agency (that individuals always enjoy some elements of self-determination in working with these elements of relatedness) as key notions. And Whitehead avoids overemphasizing intellectuality and self-consciousness. Self-identity, for instance, is a function of a multiplicity of connections and relationships whether or not one is aware of them. Consciousness itself is highly selective. There is always far more to who one is than the heightened self-consciousness of the individualist suggests. The Cartesian tradition in which we still dwell is unhelpful, for intellectuality can distort and deceive, leading one to overlook the influence of community and colleagues, of emotional ties, even of one's very embodiedness. As Bruce Wilshire observes, "Descartes' equating of self and self-reflexive consciousness only exacerbates the tendency to deceive oneself....The sharper and more brilliant is the focus on self in its own deliberate self-consciousness, the more obscured is the archaic background of experience which also comprises it—the background with its primal bodily attitudes, habitual orientations and moods, inherited communal patterns of living" (Wilshire 1990, 28).

## The Relationship of Self and Other

The next chapter examines how neglect of this background of experience creates seeds of scientism and ultimately of solipsism. For proper analysis of experience is crucial to an informed analysis of self. Understanding the world as external leads to the isolated and self-imprisoned individual, unconnected with others and unknown even to himself or herself. Divorced from this broader horizon, reason is reduced to utilitarian or instrumental functions, leaving no sure access to matters of value and importance. We usually ignore these philosophical implications, but the price can be lack of personal integration—of melding reason and experience. For experience anticipates a knowable (and thereby dependable) world with which one is connected, and in relationship with which one experiences value.

Accordingly, Whitehead insists that we attend to the epistemological importance of this vague but crucial background of experience. It provides the soil out of which the richness of personal experience is derived. For Whitehead, my past includes my experiences of others—of their ideas, and their reactions to my ideas. It includes the norms and expectations of the communities to which I belong, as well as my earlier appraisal and incorporation of their standards. I internalize selected elements of these communities—elements I may later judge differently with more awareness and deliberation. These experiences become part of me and require and enable me at each new moment to create myself in response. I create and express who I am in these decisions. My identity resides in my decisions, not in some entity separate from them. I pursue some directions at the expense of eliminating others. My decision to do *this* means that I cannot at that moment (or perhaps ever afterwards) do *that*. In this immensely complicated way, through others, I create my own identity and character, my own set of dispositions to attend to others and to a narrower or a broader set of goods and values.

### Personal Identity

This identity is laid on the present, conditioning and empowering it. The inheritance from the past is massive, but self-determination remains as do freedom and moral responsibility. The self is always an agent, however restricted the agency. And these decisions have consequences. In one way or another, my decisions further relate me to others. Others, in turn, absorb and evaluate what I have to offer them—which, of course, then has potential to influence me further. There is a strong existential element together with a social dimension in this concept. Who I am is what I, through others, have made myself to be—how I have chosen to decide and how others have influenced and empowered me to choose—in this long series of decisions. "Self" and "other" are correlative, mutually implicated, realities. One does not exist independently of, or prior to, relationships. Indeed, the very notion of self points to relationship, for to exist is to be in relation to others. One grows precisely in and through deepening these relationships and developing further ones. One's relatedness is always present and available for richer development and selective appropriation and enjoyment—if one chooses. It is acknowledgement of one's relationality that enhances personal authenticity and empowers future choices.

### Relational Power

The relational model suggests that *homo educatus et educans* is the basic, primordial capacity of humanity. Each self is created out of influence received from, and then given to, others. Educating is the development of a capacity present from the beginning, but overlooked or refused by many. This potential for creative relationality lies behind the capacities of making and of wisdom seeking—of *homo faber* and of *homo sapiens*. This relatedness is at the root of community and suggests another sense of power. As Loomer notes, the concept of "relational power, in contrast to power conceived as unilateral, has as one of its premises the notion that the capacity to absorb an influence is as truly a mark of power as the strength involved in exerting an influence" (Loomer 1976, 17). One is enriched through relationships with colleagues in the communities to which one belongs. Dwelling in this capacity to be strengthened through connectedness renders one less vulnerable to fear of the other and therefore less concerned to protect the self through the preemptive strikes and ugly polarizing rhetoric all too common in the academy.

It is the academy that ought to find the relational model especially congenial. For the academy rests upon its past, drawing nourishment from it. The more we are able to find in our traditions instances of persistent and engaging inquiry marked by intellectual reciprocity, of insight informed by and informing others, of rich and suggestive thought and service, the more enriched and sustained we are in maintaining these traditions. Power inheres in receptivity as well as agency. Rather than holding up as desirable the isolated individual struggling to protect him or herself against others, this model celebrates the contributions each self can receive from and make to the other. The truly and authentically relational self "makes his claims and expresses his concerns in such a style as to enable the other to make his largest contribution to the relationship" (Loomer 1976, 27).

Whitehead and Loomer remind us that individuals emerge from their defining communities and contribute to those communities. The communities of which we are part are significant aspects of who we are—both components and expressions of our identities. Each member of a community makes value possible for the other and for the whole. It is from the context of relationality that one abstracts the autonomous self—not vice versa. It is the dubious accomplishment of the insistent individualist not to take advantage of relatedness but to hold others at a distance and not allow them to know the self. Detached from others, the isolated self keeps the moat filled and the drawbridge raised. Otherwise one must be responsive to colleagues. We would have to acknowledge the other as not reducible to our particular, private needs and desires—to preestablished, comfortable, and perhaps self-serving values and images. That is, we would have to allow the other to challenge us and make an impact upon us, even potentially transform us. This is a risky form of togetherness, though a very rewarding one.

## THE COLLEGIUM

All this requires that we understand the academic community or collegium as relational, not autonomous. Connectivity, not separation, is basic. Be it the department, the school, or a wider collegium of smaller collegia, the collegium is the primary context of connectivity and reciprocity among its constituent members. As a context, a collegium is not simply a togetherness of individual creative souls having in common their particular disciplinary forms of creativity. Nor is it simply an outcome of their tacit agreement to a particular culture. The collegium is not simply a class name for various individuals associated spatially, sharing a corner of a building and sporting the same department or school letterhead. Those notions are entirely too passive and too much like the community as aggregation. Rather, the commonalities in question—the defining characteristics of the collegium—are themselves established and maintained through interactions of the members, and preeminently interactions effected through discourse. For discourse is the basic academic connection and means of mutual recognition and enrichment.

### A Collaborative Narrative

For instance, a collegium is in part created and defined by the telling, retelling, and amending of a common history with common values and commitments. It presents an interplay of change and of continuity that characterized the past and that in being recalled gives the past fresh momentum into the present. Lore about personalities, notorious escapades, and defining moments of triumph or conflict may figure prominently, providing elements of a common schema in terms of which other information is understood and interpreted. Narrative generates and conveys a reservoir of meaning and even a kind of grammar or set of rules for a collegium, providing it order and structure as well as possibility.

Each member of the collegium is inducted into this collective tradition and appropriates it in a unique way. Each also contributes to this shared inheritance—thereby making possible for colleagues new experiences and values. The collective inheritance is shared and passed on, the defining characteristics enhanced or muted by these new contributions. These defining characteristics also function as lures for the future—generating new, creative possibilities available for concrete realization. In effect, these inherited and enhanced traditions, symbols, and values function for individual members as a way of experiencing the future, not only as a way of ordering inherited experience. One experiences the satisfaction not just of shared customs and memories, but of shared hopes and contributions respecting the future—generating the possibility of deep fulfillment in experiencing oneself as one among many.

There is always the potential for discomfort, since the collegium is fragile and can deteriorate. Narrative sustains and recreates, but it can also create dysfunctionality, as when members of a fragmented and fractious collegium assure the public of their own harmoniousness and cooperative relationships—assurances that leave knowledgeable others in stunned and gaping silence. Recognizing contradiction between narrative and reality can serve as a goad to growth. It can also accelerate dysfunctionality. For this reason, collegia need periodic critical analysis to assess myths and expose conceits and distortions. Like others, faculty can dwell in imagined pasts and have highly selective recall. Distant moments of creativity or trauma can be retold and relived as though nothing in the interim had happened. Critical historical review is essential. Our past and how we understand it define, focus, and limit our future. With periodic and honest review, narrative and story can be rich and living symbols that, joined with rituals and ceremonies, provide individuals access to meanings not effectively conveyed in other ways.

Since discourse creates and nourishes the collegium, the actuality of the community must be regularly, even explicitly, reaffirmed—perhaps in retreats or other special meetings given over to self-renewal or reengineering. Reaffirmation creates something new as much as it renews and reinforces the values and activity of the past. Renewal also occurs when the collegium incorporates new members and their individual gifts and talents. Over time a vigorous collegium requires the induction of new members as well as continuing commitment to honest and civil discourse—maintaining the collegium and its corporate authority. In this fashion the collegium is both cause and consequence of the collective effort. It is apprehended as a distinctive unity by those inside and outside. It may become known for its uniformly high teaching, its special attention to advising and mentoring, its support of student research, or the affirmation members provide each other at seminars or colloquia.

However, without constructive activity by its members, the collegium inexorably fades into nonexistence. The routes are multiple. Since the collegium is created and expressed by its discourse, undisciplined rhetoric is destructive. Polarizing rhetoric, careless and self-indulgent discourse, being candid only when personally convenient, and dwelling in unchecked negative complaining, corrode the very foundation of a community. The collegium disappears when members are too abrasive, when aggressiveness dominates exchange, when learners are abused, or when the concepts insisted upon are isolating and obscuring rather than inclusive and illuminating. A constant threat to any collegium is individual insecurity and jealousy—diminishing community and generating isolation and insulation. Since the collegium is created in interaction among participants, to stand back from interaction and sharing renders one a mere observer. Failing to assume one's own share of the "overhead" burdens of a collegium weakens and reduces it to a medium for self-fulfillment. When enough of these behaviors occur, the collegium self-destructs, becoming a mere aggregation of individualists.

## A Form of Togetherness

Though more than the sum of its parts, the collegium has no agency apart from its members. Whitehead's technical notion of "structured society" helps make this clear (Whitehead 1978). The aims, values, and purposes of a collegium are advanced only through its members; it can be said to enjoy them only metaphorically, for it is not a center of experience, a super- or supra-individual above all other individuals. It is the constitutive individuals who enjoy and act. On the other hand, the healthy collegium does have a being and authority of its own, however much it is a being sustained only by the being of its members. It makes its impact through them. Individual faculty members are in some ways different from what they would otherwise have been precisely because of the specific collegia to which they belong and contribute. Therein lies the special efficacy of the collegium. The collegium is a form of togetherness for its members. The whole as such makes a difference because it is more than just the sum of its parts. Its properties or characteristics are not reducible to the features of the individual members taken in isolation. Instead, it is by and through faculty interaction that these properties of the collegium are in fact constituted and come to define subsequent relationships.

The relationships vary greatly, and diversity enhances the potential for mutual enrichment. The collegium is not properly understood as creating constraining commonalities or emphasizing lowest common denominators. The common form creating the collegium is individual commitment to a shared community of purpose and rough agreement on standards of excellence in teaching, research, and service—the commitment and agreement (periodically and explicitly reaffirmed) to work together in and through disagreements, to engage one another even amidst a plurality of substantive conceptions of the good academic life. As its etymology suggests, "colleagues" are those linked together. Most collegia need leaders, informal as well as formal, to enable and to strengthen these commitments—to push, cajole, arouse, and entice colleagues to greater linkage with each other. The linkages must reflect processes that reconcile destructive conflicts and promote the common good. Later chapters will explore further challenges and opportunities for leaders.

As professional educators we dwell within a collegium (in fact, many collegia), just as these collegia are also partly within us. It is these collegia that reinforce the concrete standards we invoke in our work. For collegia are marked by the common commitment that certain standards governing critical inquiry are at least provisionally warranted. And these warrants, by definition, have more than personal application. There are consequences and values to which we must appeal beyond those that advantage the individual. Otherwise we are talking about communities of convenience, not academic collegia. Without such commitment and genuine intellectual reciprocity among faculty, these collegia implode and disappear, taking with them the grounds of our professional authority and leaving us little better than late twentieth-century sophists.

The sadness of the insistent individualist is the loss of greater personal significance. Self-fulfillment requires refusal to define or assert self only in terms of self. Authentic individual freedom depends upon refusal to place oneself at the center. The healthy collegium is where individuals achieve maximum freedom and personal satisfaction—not in isolation or in a collective. In isolation, or in an aggregation of isolates, there is insufficient connectedness. In a collective there is insufficient diversity and colleagues often become boring, ironically reinforcing a kind of self-centeredness. In either isolation or a collective there is common failure to support and correct one another, to uplift and restrain, to expend the effort and energy on the discipline and attention to others required to maintain a collegium. The result is self-preoccupation with career, pursuits off-campus, or redirecting energies toward rebuking colleagues, administrators, or students. The effect diminishes both self and the collegíum.

Conversely, in the healthy relational community, individuals are neither swallowed up in the collective nor reduced to instrumental values for others. They have the possibility of transformation to greater personal depth and value. These are the gifts of enhanced freedom that members of the collegium provide each other—enhanced freedom to give and to receive. The feeling that one is part of an enterprise greater than oneself is crucial for a sense of fulfillment and satisfaction—and, as we have seen, it is a feeling that seems to elude many in the academy today. Instead of finding social and intellectual company, faculty like Tompkins and those interviewed by Lovett report experiencing the university as a lonely place. Rather than presenting an ideal combination of companionship and solitude, the institution is seen as lacking community.

To be sure, the isolation that becomes problematic is often initially sought— necessary for the reading and the writing that attracts one to the academy in the first place. Complaints of loneliness coexist with demands for autonomy in the academy—autonomy that often generates loneliness. Autonomy becomes a problem when it prevents the emergence of community that nourishes and supports, that affirms by promoting reciprocity and intellectual interchange, that invites respectful conversations. Autonomy becomes problematic when it interrupts and prevents the very community in which it would be strengthened and fulfilled.

We return to Jan Tompkins for a moving expression of her hopes for the academy. Though she is speaking of her own faculty experience at a research institution, her points resonate more widely. Universities, she writes, "should model social excellence as well as personal achievement—teach, by the very way they conduct their own internal business, something about our dependence upon and need for one another, something about how to achieve the feelings of acceptance and encouragement that community life affords, the sense of self-worth and belonging that keeps us all going on the inside" (Tompkins 1992, 19). She terms these institutional quality of life issues "housekeeping issues"—but adds that they cannot be delegated to an isolated group of custodians. Looking after relationships among colleagues of all kinds is a duty to which everyone in the institution must attend.

## THE COLLEGIAL ETHIC

Let us generalize the notion of housekeeping to speak of an ethic for the collegium and the academy. Two initial, connected points are important. First, the collegium is a form of togetherness within the academy, not in the home, the business workplace, or the neighborhood. The housekeeping issues bear on the cultivation and advancement of learning and knowing that academics pursue as the process and product of inquiry. The social excellence sought—the teaching of interdependence and the fostering of acceptance and belonging—is excellence that promotes educational ends and values.

Even so, much of what follows applies to housekeeping issues in other environments characterized by other distinctive purposes. For the collegial ethic highlights virtues important in a variety of situations and forms of togetherness where, in pursuing other objectives, we also teach and learn from each other. These virtues apply preeminently to academic life, for it above all ought to be characterized by inquiry in pursuit of learning and knowing. The collegial ethic and its virtues should characterize the classroom, laboratory and faculty office and extend beyond them to relationships with and among secretaries, groundskeepers, admissions representatives, financial officers, and all the other staff and administrators who together create an institution of higher education.

Second, the central mission of the academy is to serve its members and others through the advancement of learning and knowledge. Members of the academy have special obligations to establish, protect, and extend the conditions under which learning and claims to knowledge can be advanced and supported—the collective conditions wherein colleagues, students, and the broader public are enlisted in intellectual inquiry and learning as well as in the preservation of knowledge. These conditions are communal and connected—not marked by insistent individualism and fragmentation. We reviewed reasons for thinking that the self is more adequately understood as relational and that power is the capacity to be influenced as well as to influence. Within the academy these features of the self and of power remind us that inquiry is never solitary, despite the appeal of the private and the undisturbed. In the larger sense inquiry is always communal and characterized by growth. It is thereby in a context marked by connection with other inquiries. However narrowly focused, every inquiry is situated in a larger context and relates to other inquiries.

## Acceptance and Support

For both reasons, good academic housekeeping requires active interest in the work and insights of others and interaction with them—it requires the risk-taking that goes with sharing self and making oneself vulnerable to correction by others, to being called wrong, even to being ridiculed for one's own work. It requires risking rebuff and rejection by expressing genuine interest in others and expecting that they too make their work public. These are real ventures.

It is easier not to take these risks, but without them there is neither verified learning and knowing nor the vibrant collegium that accelerates further learning.

Housekeepers in the academy are in a community of reason and reciprocity, commitment to which entails vibrant peer review of inquiry, learning, and knowing—critical, constructive scrutiny. The primary commitment has to be to learning, not to unilateral power or friendship. Claims to knowledge and truth are always to be supported by arguments that embody reasons—not convenience, politics, or other personal advantage. And the reasons are public, not private, in character—available for consideration by others, not squirreled away and protected by obfuscation or inaccessible vocabularies. This commitment reflects no overbearing Enlightenment expectation of unattainable certainty. The arguments embodying these reasons are always corrigible, for better reasons may develop or new evidence found. But the best reasons at the time must be presented in support of one's position.

The many ways in which we pursue learning and knowing require that each of us support others (colleagues and students) in their own relevant pursuits. Each has an obligation to encourage the other by expressing interest and by providing critique as well as suggestion. The collegium provides for self-fulfillment but this achievement cannot be separated from the achievements of others. For the healthy collegium is the respectful collegium, characterized by both acceptance and critical judgment. Members accept and support others by attending with constructive criticism to their work. Without acceptance and support, relationships within the collegium become marked by indifference or carping; without critical evaluation, the collegium falls into excessive sentiment and intellectual flabbiness. Acceptance and critical judgment require interest in the work of others, and that in turn means knowledge of, and a modicum of care for, the well-being and growth of these others.

## Constructive Criticism

Linked to acceptance and support of colleagues is spending the time and energy to provide substantive critique of their ideas and work. Substantive critique often involves disagreement. Indeed, the academy thrives on difference and controversy. Advancement in learning and knowledge is purchased through dissatisfaction and disagreement with received positions. Questioning the authorized version of things is an engine for progress. Without constructive engagement with colleagues characterized by elements of challenge and possibilities of disagreement, there is little prospect of advance in learning. The health of the academy and its collegia requires openness to constructive tension and conflict. The key is how the differences are expressed—in ways that create acrimony and invite retaliation or, instead, present opportunities for exploring with civility and hope new possibilities and directions.

Parker Palmer observes that community is sometimes regarded simply as a supplement to the broader and prior work of cognition—as though the former were only a fringe addition to the latter. In truth, though, the former provides the context for the latter. Without adequate community, advances in knowledge come only with greater difficulty. "Our ability to confront each other critically and honestly over alleged facts, imputed meanings, or personal biases and prejudices—*that* is the ability impaired by the absence of community" (Palmer 1987, 25). These are the open, but civil confrontations necessary in the process of working together toward learning, correcting, or enlarging the stock of things known, solving relevant problems, and making appropriate decisions.

The point has epistemological import. A community does not create truths about reality, though it can hide and obscure those truths. A community helps its members discern, validate, and connect insights into reality. It provides ways of knowing that become ways of being. Openness to challenge and correction, for instance, generates both intellectual and moral value. Almost by definition a collegium points beyond itself and its boundaries to other communities, illustrating that it is not the measure of things any more than are its individual members.

Working in the collegium should remind us of resources we always have— our ability, refined in discourse and other interactions, to identify inadequate concepts and practices because of our grasp (however faltering) of better concepts and practices. However tentative and tenuous our hold on the ideal, it offers hope and direction. Even our awareness of the partial and limited character of our learning is an earnest of the better. Our sense of corrigibility provides glad tidings of the possibility of improvement both in general housekeeping and in specific pursuits of understanding. With the help of good citizens and academic leaders, collegia become places where intellectual and social virtue is acquired and exercised. The very ideals against which we judge ourselves become clearer.

## Rules and Virtues

Philosophically, an ethic can be expressed in terms of principles or rules. Traditionally, these include rules supported by deontological or by utilitarian arguments. The one set of arguments appeals to Kantian-like considerations, emphasizing duty and the rightness or wrongness of particular actions according to principles of universalizable generalization. For instance, I should evaluate your teaching and scholarship according to the same principles as I would have you evaluate mine. The other set of arguments enlists likely consequences as the key ethical consideration and holds that the rules must advance the overall welfare of persons. Thus, evaluation of teaching and scholarship, when done well, is desirable because it advances the common good.

The collegial ethic can also be presented in terms of dispositions and virtues rather than rules. A dispositional analysis draws attention to the importance of antecedent habits or proclivities to act in one way—to work in specific ways to promote the good with others. Virtues are propensities such that one can be expected or counted on, for instance, to be hospitable or thoughtful. Emulating models of virtue and practicing virtuous acts develops the habit of being virtuous. One does not first acquire the skill or ability of being hospitable or thoughtful and then resolve or decide to use it. Rather one becomes disposed to act in a hospitable or thoughtful manner. To view the collegial ethic in dispositional terms is to emphasize the complex of learned, cultivated, and shared motivations that underlie the very engagement with ethical principles and rules.

Rules seem inadequate without prior attention to character or virtue. There is no rule that governs in detail the use of rules. To require prior possession of a rule that would dictate subsequent selection and application of other rules seems to open up an infinite regress. The rule that would govern the application of other rules presupposes an earlier rule requiring still an earlier rule, etc. In addition to this logical point, rules seem partial, only part of the story. One can follow the rules and still be a pedant; tell the truth or serve the common good and still be vainglorious; scrupulously observe principles of obligation and still be manipulative of others. And in any case, the ability effectively to adhere to rules assumes habits both permitted and supported by the environing community. That is, the exercise of individual rights presupposes a virtuous community—one prepared to recognize and uphold the rights. So a dispositional analysis seems important.

Mature collegia nourish the dispositions and sensibilities that hold and sustain academic integrity. These virtues characterize communities and members intent upon cultivating and advancing understanding and knowledge as well as avoiding provincialism. They are acquired and developed. They are taught and learned through working with colleagues and are necessary for carrying out successfully the roles of the academic citizen in the classroom, in scholarship, and in service. They have cognitive significance. They are not mere expressions of feeling, but guides to behavior that correlate importantly with learning and the increase of knowledge. Hospitality and thoughtfulness are two encompassing virtues that seem essential to the collegium and to constitute the heart of the collegial ethic. Neither can be isolated and each incorporates other virtues.

## Hospitality

Hospitality is the willingness to consider, acknowledge, and attend to the strange and the new as well as to reassess the old and the familiar. It is generosity and openness in extending and in receiving—in sharing and in learning. It is both an ethical and an intellectual virtue, central to the increase of human well-being and of knowledge. The definition in the *Oxford English Dictionary* is suggestive—hospitality involves "the reception and entertainment of guests, visitors, or strangers, with liberality and goodwill."

Essential to hospitality is the act of listening to the other, suspending for the moment traditional boundaries, and expressing respectful and genuine—not intrusive or feigned—interest. The rituals of unilateral power—pursuing clever one-upmanship and self-serving assertions of privilege, scoring points and counting coup, avoiding defeat at all costs—are set aside. Hospitality means anticipating and meeting appropriate needs of others, letting them know they matter as fellow inquirers, and sharing one's own stock of insights and uncertainties. Hospitality is not chumminess; it is disciplined openness to treating others as at least initial equals. Usually one has to work hard at acquiring and cultivating this habit, paying attention to one's own psychological development and wholeness—attending to self in order to transcend self.

The liberality and goodwill to be displayed do not involve gullibility or uncritical acceptance. To be hospitable does not mean that one is at sea, devoid of well-founded knowledge, nor does it mean abandoning rigor for permissiveness or indulgence. Hospitality means envisioning and treating the other as potentially authoritative. Hospitality mandates the traditional suspension of judgment when faced with inadequate evidence, but it also points to the need to examine the very meanings of evidence, adequacy, and what seems obvious. Hospitality involves the recognition that overall one is possessed of few certainties, and that improvements and refinements are always possible and may come from unexpected, even unlikely corners. Hospitality presumes there is sense to be found in the other and there ought not to be quick dismissal without a thoughtful effort to learn and to evaluate. A rush to judgment expresses lack of trust, creating cynicism on all sides. Hospitality, though, assumes that the other is guided by intentions of intelligibility parallel to one's own, although effort may be required to see them. It involves refusing to enter a discussion, activity, or interaction with a judgment already fully and, more to the point, irrevocably formed. Clearly, hospitality must extend to the variety of issues that comes under the rubric of diversity and multiculturalism today. We must make room for common ground and that means transcending at the outset the narrow preoccupations that shield us from our commonalities.

Accordingly, hospitality repudiates the hierarchy and exclusivity associated with insistent individualism. It demands that meaning, truth, and knowledge not be automatically correlated with status, privilege, or personal position. Extending respect to others means willingness to work with the strange, the unsettling, and the eccentric in order to discover the learning and insight they may possess. That is, hospitality relates to charity, for goodwill means one is more likely to make progress through generously crediting and nourishing the germ of another's idea, however poorly expressed, than by ridiculing it. It entails honesty because the quest for insight and for corroborating evidence presupposes sincerity and openness in the presentation of evidence. In part this is what the need for replication in science involves, for one can claim knowledge only if others can replicate the results. Thus, the search for validated insight requires more than truthfulness and sincerity. It requires enlisting the other in a collaborative pursuit of learning. Writing of the virtue of "veracity," William F. May argues that it "expands beyond the duty to tell the truth, and includes the enabling act of sharing it" (May 1980, 231). It requires the conversion of the private into the collegial self. This empowering of others through the open, enabling sharing of truth is precisely the standard of excellence against which all teaching and scholarship should be measured. For this is at the heart of the relational self and the collegium.

Hospitality also entails allowing others to make claims upon *us*. It means openness to the possibility of transformation that can come only when we surrender control, but remain open to reason—when commitment to unilateral power is replaced by respect for relational power. Hospitality is hard for many professors, because insistent individualism is deeply ingrained. Suspicion and resistance come more quickly than openness. However well-funded, though, one's own experience can in principle always be extended. And that experience may even need fundamental challenge and change. This, after all, is the reason for and the heart of peer review—both to challenge and to validate.

Accordingly, closely associated with the virtues of hospitality, charity, honesty, and veracity is humility, the recognition that one's knowledge is not the totality, that others may and should function as peers. Humility requires self-denial and willingness to risk in order to grow—willingness to test treasured beliefs in order to penetrate to a larger view. It involves self-scrutiny and may even require subsequent public confession and recantation. Humility has nothing to do with obsequiousness. It does not require excessive self-doubt or self-effacement. It does involve the desire to improve, or else it is simply self-abasement. It conflicts with unilateral power, for it recognizes that one depends upon others for one's own growth. The better professor is the one who is constantly interested in intellectual growth, the one who is willing to venture beyond his or her own areas of mastery to explore, cultivate, incorporate, and then share new learning. And humility also delights in the accomplishments of others, rather than calling constant attention to one's own achievements or being jealous of others. These habits of hospitality model for students the life of engaged inquiry.

## Thoughtfulness

The second overarching virtue is thoughtfulness. Like hospitality, it is both an intellectual and ethical virtue. Mark Schwehn reminds us that thoughtfulness incorporates the two elements of judicious evaluation and sensitivity to others (Schwehn 1993, 58). The one is intellectual in thrust, the other is moral at heart. Thoughtfulness is attending to matters of importance and also to the welfare of others—being both reflective and considerate.

Being reflective involves being informed and competent—being reasonable in the positions one argues and providing support commensurate with their scope and intensity. For instance, thoughtfulness repudiates indoctrination—the use of spurious arguments and withholding of evidence to support vested interests—because it is unreasonable and violates critical reasoning. But indoctrination should also be repudiated because it is inconsiderate. One can not be thoughtful and also force others into submission through unilateral power. Indoctrination works only by violating such things as keeping promises, providing sufficient information to allow others to make informed choices, and avoiding deception. But thoughtfulness as considerateness requires respect for the autonomy of others and the conditions necessary for their exercise of that autonomy. It requires treating others fairly and justly—that is equally, not necessarily identically, with recognition and acknowledgement of their particular circumstances.

Both the moral and the intellectual senses of thoughtfulness require making clear to others the nature of the positions put forward. Adverse evidence is not hidden or ignored. Matters of dispute are identified and treated as such. Debated issues are distinguished from relatively settled ones. Levels of confidence are indicated. The intellectual and the moral senses of thoughtfulness are suggested by the one term; this conveys the ultimate connectedness of truth and goodness. They are inseparable in that one cannot be thoughtful in one sense without being thoughtful in both. Failing in one means failing in the

other as well. In the relational model, being foolish but considerate of others is
no more possible than being insightful but indifferent to others. Being thoughtful
in both senses points to the importance of fidelity—fidelity to the inquiry and
to the interests of the student or colleague. Here too one cannot be faithful to
the one without being faithful to both. One cannot keep faith with students or
colleagues at the expense of being true to the common inquiry, nor can one be
faithful to inquiry and also ignore or betray those linked in the inquiry.
Fidelity, or loyalty, is both an intellectual and a moral virtue.

Thoughtfulness is reflected in modes of expression—how we choose to
express ourselves. It involves determination to find and use the right words
and to select the best images—those that provide clarity and support to the
assertions presented and that engage others with appropriate sensitivity and
respect. Thoughtfulness is connected with courage, for it requires upholding
responsible discourse. It demands foregoing and challenging impulsive, thoughtless repartee or cheap shots, self-indulgent complaining about institutional,
colleague or student foibles, responding in kind to personal attacks, dwelling
in polarizing rhetoric, and the other forms of degraded speech too present in
the academy. Courage also means acceptance of one's vulnerability as a
teacher and scholar. One cannot control the other—efforts to do so regularly
bear bitter fruit. Courage is the recognition that mutual freedoms are enhanced, not restricted, by relationality and diversity. Accordingly, courage
means coping with one's vulnerability without resorting to displays of abusive
and controlling power, dwelling in a cynicism in which one closes oneself off
from others and the possibility of pursuing a common good, or retreating to a
despair in which one hardens oneself against hope.

There is a profoundly personal element to educating. There is risk in deeply
involving the self, but also the potential of substantial reward. Thus the
collegial ethic speaks as well to internal integration. It is insufficient simply to
announce the desirability, even the necessity, of hospitality and thoughtfulness. The virtues of learning cannot be simply commended to others without
also being professed and modeled. In fact, announcing without also embodying and displaying this ethic is in effect not to announce it at all. We teach the
virtues by exemplifying and enacting them. We cannot proclaim their importance without exemplifying them. The examined life must be modeled, for
knowledge cannot be entirely inert and external to the knower. Nor, for the
same reasons, can it remain internal without receiving collegial expression.

Writing recently of the crisis and promise of professionalism today, William
Sullivan mounts a powerful argument that our times call for an ethic of
vocation on the part of professionals—competence joined with a disinterested
public spiritedness evident in a commitment to service and to larger social

goods. The self-preoccupation, concern with self-protection, and secession from social good too evident among professionals of all kinds today are threatening the health of professions at the same time that the exigencies of our society require more from them—more competence characterized by public responsibility. "If the ethic of vocation did not exist, our society would need to invent it now" (Sullivan 1995, 195). Professional integrity, Sullivan argues, is a public good serving the public welfare. But professional integrity can be nurtured only within communities—structured to promote public good rather than only private advantage and opportunism. Commitment to this civic good is elicited and developed; it cannot be commanded by economic incentive, external regulation, or administrative fiat. Hospitality and thought-fulness are the academic elements of this ethic of vocation and are cultivated and expressed within a collegium, not an aggregation of individualists. It is collegial professionalism for which our times are calling.

The same holds for institutions. Too often, James Laney notes, the institution of higher education "perceives itself as performing an educational function rather than engaging in a moral enterprise" (Laney 1990, 51) That is, the institution fosters neither moral reflection nor moral development, nor does it examine itself and its activities as contributions in relation to the common public good. In the terms developed here, such an institution is neither hospitable nor thoughtful. This ultimate separation of education and morality is pernicious. Without commitment to ultimate goods and values, instrumental reason is directionless and unable by itself to generate an adequate ethic.

## CONCLUSION

Both models we have examined have subtle impact, for how we think of the academy and our roles within it influence our behaviors and our relationships with others. These models both derive from our environments and help to create them. Opportunities are produced or lost. The first model results in a less effective academy and deprives its members of satisfactions they might otherwise enjoy. The second model recalls a resource already embedded in our traditions.

However elusive they might be, the concepts of the collegium and of improvement are common possessions at the foundation of our calling. We need not be imprisoned in ourselves or in the outposts of narrowly understood disciplinary communities. The ideal of the better is always before us, available to help us to criticize ourselves and our communities and to search out and welcome richer and deeper insights—all to the end that we participate in, enjoy, and enrich our common good.

The collegium is a form of togetherness amidst plurality, neither an aggre-gation nor an undifferentiated totality. It takes time to create a collegium, of course. It has a past which must be understood as informing, not determining, its future. This history is communicated, shared, revised, and reinterpreted by its members, old and new. It provides continuity and stability. But the collegium requires attention to the present and future as well. A healthy collegium is a community of inquiry, marked by robust conversation about fresh questions and new ideas. The discourse honors, reinforces, and extends the connectedness already present. These shared, reaffirmed, and extended commitments constitute the agency of the whole, exercised through the parts. If the collegium is to make a difference, we must work at it—or else it falls apart.

Society grants the academy extraordinary freedom from external controls and supervision on the expectation that partial and personal interests are not equated with public interests, that temptations to self-aggrandizement and indolence are adequately conquered, and that power is not allowed to corrupt. Society looks to the academy to be both hospitable and thoughtful. The task before the academy is to cultivate and embody the collegial ethic, to articulate and improve upon it through reflection and debate, and to nourish it in others. The academy needs to honor these improvements and refinements—and it needs to confront those who ignore the virtues and violate the obligations it entails. This is a significant challenge. Insistent individualism and the sepa-rateness of academic disciplines work against a strong, sustained intellectual community. The next two chapters review some of the difficulties.

# CHAPTER 3

# Professionalism
## Academic or Collegial?

W e start with a fundamental question about the ways in which academics can credibly claim to be professionals. Then we explore the argument by Bruce Wilshire and others that some of the ways professors understand themselves to be professionals actually work against their larger academic and personal interests; professors are often victims of what he calls academic professionalism rather than liberated by what we shall call collegial professionalism. Finally, we move from theory to practice and examine a variety of problematic behaviors suggesting the influence of insistent individualism—behaviors that work against the common good and the collegial ethic and that can lead to malaise and alienation.

## THE MEANING OF PROFESSIONALISM

"Profession" resists tight definitions. In its classic sense there were only three—medicine, law, and the church. The term has undergone a complicated evolution over the centuries and in the history of this country (Kimball 1992). Today, reference to a profession is usually positive, imputing status and prestige. It denotes a desirable form of work. The adjective suggests doing a job competently, even gracefully. For these reasons, hundreds of occupational groups claim the title in their struggles for social position and approval. Yet this is not the whole story, for recently the term has also been associated with self-centeredness and withdrawal from larger social goods. Concerns are now raised about the "crisis" of professionalism, particularly a lack of adequate accountability and an accelerating loss of social consciousness and conscience. As one scholar notes, "the abuse of privileged positions by greedy professionals without effective control by their peers or public oversight has weakened the public legitimacy of professional self-regulation" (Sullivan 1995, 193). Concerns about the abuse of position also extend to higher education, in ways that recall unattractive dimensions of insistent individualism and disconnectedness from common pursuits and values.

## The Difficulty of Definitions

This chapter considers how academic (as opposed to collegial) professionalism emphasizes autonomy at the expense of the common good; but first we will reflect on the difficulty of definitions. It is difficult to construct a list of necessary and sufficient hallmarks of a profession. Instead, most students of the subject identify a range of factors. Important characteristics include possession of intellectual expertise valued by society, an extended period of training to acquire the expert knowledge, a large degree of autonomy in the practice of the expertise, protection and advancement of the interests of those served regardless of the personal convenience of the professional, a public service aspect to the practice of the expertise, and an official code of ethics together with a membership organization committed to the implementation of the code and to other elements of self-regulation (Rich 1984). Some professions have licensing requirements before members are authorized to practice. Many professions require that members periodically demonstrate continuing competence. Others require evidence of growth in competence.

The applicability of these criteria to higher education is clearly uneven. By any rigorous calculation, we in the academy have a rather tenuous claim to professional standing. For example, only some areas have licensing requirements. Expectations of continuing education are spotty. Public service dimensions are often thin, especially where *pro bono* work is concerned. Without adequate assessment measures, student interests are insufficiently protected. Most glaring, there is no national membership organization or association committed to clear standards of admission, to self-regulation, to enforcing a code of ethics, and to disciplining or even expelling those whose behaviors fall short.

These deficiencies have not prevented some in the academy from contending that there are few problems. We are told that "perhaps in no other profession is there such excruciating pressure from one's peers as in college teaching, nor...does the practice of any other profession involve such constant and critical scrutiny of the quality and quantity of one's work product" (Pettit 1990, 37). Most of us do believe deeply in the value and importance of teaching, and surely it does involve moments of considerable challenge and self-questioning. Yet we know that scrutiny by others, while often critical, is rarely sustained—in either teaching or scholarship. Even friends of higher education acknowledge that academe lacks sufficient self-regulation. Thus, it is difficult to credit the claim that "the academy is subjected to more rigorous and demanding standards than are our colleagues in politics, business, or even law and medicine" (Pettit 1990, 35). Clearly this goes too far. Parts of the evaluation of probationary faculty may be rigorous, but this rarely applies to senior, tenured faculty. What higher education does have in large amount is autonomy and individualism, not constant and exacting peer review.

Professions do require autonomy in the exercise of expertise—but autonomy needs to be counterbalanced by a clear structure of public accountability. The question before the academy is whether our structures of accountability are sufficiently clear and strong. Some problematic behaviors reviewed later in this chapter suggest not. The absence for the profession as a whole of a national association known for strong standards of membership admission and exclusion reinforces concerns. Our inability to assure the public of uniform and effective performance evaluation suggests that a key element of professionalism may indeed be missing. For professionalism means that service to a clientele and the good of that clientele is paramount, and regularly reviewed. The standing of the academy on these matters is hardly assured. The good efforts of many seem jeopardized by the self-preoccupation of some—and by inadequate associational, institutional, and colleague attention.

## An Uncertain Status

Accordingly, academics do not dwell in uncontested territory as professionals, much less on high ground. Any general argument we might advance for our professional status rests primarily on three propositions in the list above: that society attaches important value to higher education; that specialized knowledge is involved; and that there are high-order intellectual judgments and skills required in the largely independent acquisition, extension, and application of that knowledge.

The first proposition does seem solid. There is widespread public agreement that higher education is worth the effort. Most of the public accepts the economic argument that investment in earning a college degree will pay off. Likewise, there is widespread public trust that professors do advance knowledge and the intellectual lives of students. Some professors take a much greater role than others in creating new knowledge. However, all but the most alienated professors presume that the learning they advance bears in important ways on a public, common good. And the presumption is broadly accepted by society. Learning is seen as valuable. Admittedly, the academy's ability to document either knowledge or intellectual lives as advanced is uneven, but it is improving.

Support for the second proposition is somewhat more tricky. Professorial claims to specialized knowledge appear to be widely accepted. However, the particular erudition is almost always disciplinary knowledge, rarely expertise related to its communication. The public may expect professors to be skilled in teaching and applying this specialized knowledge, but the traditional academic professions usually understand the intellectual judgment and skills in question to relate primarily to the systematic acquisition and extension of knowledge. The situation is complicated in that even certification of this expert knowledge is often indirect. Institutions commonly rely initially on testimony from the instructor's graduate school as summarized in the award of a terminal degree. Thereafter some indication of continued familiarity with or addition to a knowledge base is expected.

However, faculty connections to knowledge bases vary enormously. Some professors contribute frequently and significantly; others, hardly at all. There is no widespread requirement of continuing education without which one's good standing in the profession lapses. Nor is the academy known for frequent informal discussions of teaching and how to relate intellectual inquiry to student learning needs. Unlike other professionals, much of the professoriate spends little collective time or energy reviewing ways to improve service to students. Institutional structures do not provide much help, either. Beyond certain standard points in the typical career there are few mechanisms for serious assessment of teaching, scholarship, or service. Decisions about tenure and promotion provide the best opportunities for judging professional performance. Thereafter, annual evaluations are often *pro forma* activities and rarely present significant opportunity for substantial review. Without institutionalized periodic evaluation of senior faculty performance—what is often called post-tenure review—higher education lacks adequate counterparts to the continuing education requirements of other professions. But post-tenure evaluations are not widespread nor are they endorsed by the one faculty organization with the greatest claim to national standing, the American Association of University Professors.

On these grounds, then, public skepticism about higher education as a profession may well increase. Society can ask whether higher education regulates itself effectively and contributes sufficiently to the common good. Without continuing contributions to society and effective certification of continued competence, the status of academics as professionals is hardly secure. In the long run, public confidence requires credible evidence that professions have high standards of entrance, periodic review, and willingness to rebuke or exclude those whose practice is found deficient. In these respects, higher education continues to draw upon accumulated capital and may not be adequately replenishing it.

The third proposition—regarding high-order intellectual skills needed in acquiring and sharing expert knowledge—reflects the autonomy necessary for professionals. Here too academe often displays inadequate self-regulation and risks increasing public skepticism. Skills required for the acquisition, development, and application of the special expertise claimed for academic professionals are almost always highly abstract and intellectual in nature. Standards of excellence are jealously guarded and deemed internal to the professional exercise of these skills. It is only members of the profession, not the public, who are qualified judges. This narrow base of judgment creates increasing difficulty for academe. As the practices of the insistent individualist remind us, there is often tension between the autonomous exercise of these skills and attention to the good of another. The individualist downplays connectivity with the broader social good, but the public is demanding more involvement in the form of accountability.

In contrast to insistent individualism, the model of relationality holds that the full exercise of high-order intellectual skills demands engagement with students, colleagues, and the broader public. It is only in application—in teaching and service—that intellect is completed and fulfilled, thereby also satisfying and completing the other two professional requirements of value to society and expert knowledge. Informed by the relational model, the academy is better able, and more likely, to regulate itself. The hospitality and thoughtfulness that are marks of the relational model and the collegial ethic push individual faculty toward greater openness to others and to the common good. The case for our status as professionals is much stronger when presented through the relational model.

## ACADEMIC PROFESSIONALISM

However, the relational model has rarely enjoyed the dominant influence in academic or disciplinary professionalism. Rather, it is attention inward that characterizes the deeply entrenched professionalism of traditional academic disciplines; and this has been the case for some time. Increasingly over this century professionalism in academe has defined itself as disciplinary professionalism. Each academic discipline, not higher education, constitutes a profession. One is a professor of history or chemistry, not simply a professor. And it is research, not teaching, that provides the expertise that qualifies one as a professional. By the turn of the century, most traditional academic disciplines had already created their membership associations and special learned societies, and established regional and national annual meetings as well as scholarly journals. Special canons and distinct methods of research were regularized, along with terminal degrees as apprenticeship programs for inducting new members. This apparatus identified a discipline as a profession, established hierarchies of status among members, and defined intellectual legitimacy and prestige.

Begun in the last century, academic professionalism was centrally established well before the 1920s but deepened its hold in the two decades following the second world war, so that by the end of the 1960s it enjoyed almost complete success organizing both curricula and faculty self-understanding. It was in those recent decades that "higher education enjoyed public confidence, rapid increases in enrollments, large-scale research projects funded by public and private sources, and shortages of qualified faculty" (Weaver 1991, 25). This confluence of social and economic factors enabled earlier movements toward disciplinary professionalism to be consolidated. This chapter examines how this professionalization affects faculty individualism and satisfaction. The next one looks at its impact on the institution, the curriculum, and the public.

## Some Hard-Hitting Criticism

One of the more severe internal critics of the research university, Bruce Wilshire writes of the educational "bankruptcy" of the university, holding that it "has failed to provide a matrix within which our common concerns for meaning and being, and for humane and ethical knowledge, can thrive" (Wilshire 1990, 34). He argues that it is the professionalizing of the academy together with an institutional disciplinary structure emphasizing separation that has exacted such a heavy toll, serving the interests of neither students nor faculty. We consider his argument in some detail.

Student interests are not served because academic professionalism excludes them as important and valuable. Wilshire argues that the very status and authority of the academic professional rests in an identity achieved only through excluding students and the broader public. Edifices of learning are erected to keep away outsiders—esoteric language and publications inhibit and constrain, rather than extend, communication. Academic professionalism encourages faculty to feel primary obligations less toward students and the public, and more toward protecting and advancing private interests viewed in terms of the discipline and a group of similarly preoccupied colleagues. Graduate students and even probationary faculty often have only a marginal claim. It is the professional society and its credentialed members, not the campus classroom, students, or public good that really counts. Other critics have also pressed this charge against academic professionals, arguing that academic societies are best understood as "principally self-serving professional bodies whose existence is based primarily on the coordinated exercise of power over certification and academic legitimacy" (Weaver 1991, 96). Academic disciplines bestow the recognition that creates the professional self. Students are decidedly secondary.

Yet faculty as well as students pay a heavy price in this arrangement. Academic professionalism alienates, separates, and sets apart—isolating those in the professoriate from each other, and also from themselves. Faculty are isolated because traditional disciplines are marked more by competition than by cooperation. Status and standing follow from individual rather than collaborative work, leading to careful guarding of research in progress. Many insistent individualists are like economic protectionists—harboring, sequestering, doling out knowledge in minimal amounts or units. Affirmation of others might deplete one's own capital. Between and within the disciplines, hierarchies of standing, prestige, and national rankings are established—creating invidious distinctions between higher and lower order intellectual endeavors and reducing some faculty to the status of minor academic functionaries.

## Separation of Work and Self

Academic professionalism also works against recognition and integration of the personal. It abstracts from the inward life of immediate experience and then leaves it behind. Even the fact of abstraction is overlooked. Thus, the anxiety and vulnerability of the educator as person is masked and hidden through disciplinary allegiance. Personal identity and meaning as well as the significance of work are taken for granted, neither questioned nor enriched. The professional knower is divided from the personal self. Parallel tracks are created so that work does not impinge on personal values and understandings—on oneself as a unified person or moral agent—or vice versa.

For example, the import of discovering natural processes usable in nuclear weapons or the study of the Holocaust leaves the self unshaken by the capacity of humanity for good and evil. The scholarly analysis of the fragility of ecosystems or the widespread impact of pollution is conducted without connection to one's own consumptive lifestyle. Connections with the larger community of students and the next generation are rarely encouraged. Even reason as a tool through which to ponder the deeper questions of self and the causes of anxiety as well as to identify and celebrate transcending values is put to the side. Technical or instrumental reason is celebrated, isolated from ends and ultimate purposes, leaving little possibility that the self will be transformed by its knowledge. When selves are not implicated in instructional and scholarly work, the posturing, intimidation, and score-keeping characteristic of the narrowly defined competitions of the academy increase.

Separation of work and self converts public relationships that should matter into means toward private ends. Instead of celebrating the workplace as valuable in itself, dissociation of work and self reserves this experience of intrinsic value for the isolated and private self. Inevitably, this separation favors the assessment of productivity in quantitative ways that further distance self from others. It promotes insistent individualism and the autonomous community; and it generates the pain of disconnection and the lack of fulfillment, if not also the sense of anguish, we examined earlier.

One could argue that separation of work and self is necessary, that we must stand back from our professional lives sufficiently to reflect upon their moral dimensions and therefore we need to maintain a personal and psychological distance and detachment. But this suggests that there are not moral resources already ingredient in true professionalism to provide assistance. I am not arguing for the collapse of the personal into the professional—that generates an arid one-dimensionality and a reduction of the self at odds with the richness promised by the pursuit of knowledge. Nor am I arguing for the collapse of the professional into the personal—that risks a dilettantism and egoism incompatible with the discipline required for knowledge. Instead, I am arguing for integration and balance, such that what one knows affects who one is, and who one is is exemplified in what one does. This integration requires effort, especially at the beginning, but then our past plays into and affects our present—defining our capacity for future experience. I believe C. Wright Mills was making the same point some years ago when he wrote that the most admirable scholarly thinkers "do not split their work from their lives. They seem to take both too seriously to allow such dissociation, and they want to use each for the enrichment of the other." To be a scholar, he argued, is to design a way of life, to make "a choice of how to live as well as a choice of career; whether he knows it or not, the intellectual workman forms his own self as he works toward the perfection of his craft" (Mills 1959, 195–196).

Wilshire buttresses his points about the separation of the professional and personal by arguing that the heavy investment of academic professionalism in critical, analytical consciousness occurs at the expense of "our sense of the englobing world as we directly live it" (Wilshire 1990, 45). He appeals philosophically to the primacy of immediate experience—the pre-critical, indeed pre-reflective, unity that grounds and lies beneath the separating and selecting activities of consciousness. His phenomenological description of immediate experience parallels what William James, Whitehead, and others provided as correctives to the influential and overly intellectual analysis of Descartes. The primacy of immediate experience reminds us of the priority of the whole which serves as the experiential foundation for the actuality of others, for connectivity, and for value itself. Wilshire notes that "as directly lived, the world is not experienced as divided into boxes, but as one vast, supremely great whole. Attention abstracts and selects from a moody and vague background, an immediate sense of the encompassing world and our-selves in it—lingering, habitual orientations for living inherited from archaic personal or communal pasts. This background may be vague, but if we are to feel solid and real it must be felt to be coherent" (Wilshire 1990, xix).

This primal and abiding experience, the background sense of the totality from which consciousness selects and out of which our more specialized inquiries are formed, is the essential foundation for our sense of self and other. As Wilshire contends, "despite confusion, distraction, and a strange kind of loneliness, there is a vague but fundamental level of experience in which we directly and pre-critically experience ourselves to be one self, to be in a community, or set of communities, and also, of course, in *a world* . . . . It is the deepest, if most obscure, source of authorization of self" (Wilshire 1990, 44). The heightened professional consciousness selects data for manipulation from this pre-critical, pre-linguistic experience of the encompassing world and then abandons it. Having abstracted from it, technical consciousness ignores the primary context of our existence and suppresses evidence of the communal layering and multivalence of our lives. In the typical professional conscious-ness one's sense of underlying meaning, of essential connections with others, and of personal integration is left unsupported—leading inevitably to loss of wonder and excitement.

## Primary Experience and Meaning

Precisely because this pre-reflective unity is vague and obscure, describing it is difficult and complex. One can read the phenomenologist Edmund Husserl as holding that it is in primary, immediate experience that our sense of self and meaning is rooted and the sole evidence for all scientific and cultural concepts is to be found (Husserl 1970). Accordingly, he considered the evasion of this englobing and unified world by modern science and culture to constitute a crisis of meaning. Whitehead too argued that greater fidelity to the pre-given and pre-reflective world as the matrix of our intellectual and personal con-cepts is required to avoid the misplaced abstractions that plague contemporary understandings. A key virtue of the concept of self developed in the last chapter is that it incorporates and builds upon this background experience. Who we are is grounded in our connections with others and in a variety of already existing communities. The point before us is not only to reflect on the reality of this vague experience of the boundless world, but also to be aware of how it is regularly taken for granted and forgotten. Pausing from time to time with this intent helps one regain perspective and replenish ties of common purpose and connection.

Loss of meaning inevitably occurs when individuals are systematically separated from the ground of personal and cultural significance. When the rootage of self, science, and culture in concrete personal experience is overlooked, alienation is a natural consequence. When the intimate experiences of value and of others are excluded at the outset, they can never be persuasively introduced later. Their credentials and standing will always be suspect as secondary and derivative—fact will be seen as superior to value, self to other, etc. This is the insidious burden that positivism so effectively creates and reinforces in the university. Acknowledging this constantly presupposed, primal background experience of connectivity is crucial to our ability to understand ourselves as more than isolated intellects seeking meaning in intellectual combat with other intellects. It is precisely grounding in this primitive totality that provides the experiential sense of being embodied selves within a community of many, of the contributions we make to each other, the dependencies that result, and the priority of values that sustain. In fact, these are the ultimate experiential grounds for recognizing that insistent individualism is badly flawed—that because it is not rooted in the fundamental realities of our lives, it will in the end disappoint.

Wilshire grants that the professoriate is rarely conscious of what he calls the archaic processes that limit formation of more adequate professional identity. The individual is socialized through rituals of purification that define the professional and establish his or her authority over others. Because academic professionalism promotes the separation of one's professional from one's personal self and elevates theory over practice and objective fact over subjective value, the effect is to reinforce the isolating character of the academy—what we call the insistent individualist and the insistently individualistic department. Isolation and fragmentation are compounded, because the disciplines possess their own discrete objects of inquiry and intellectual equipment, making it difficult to cross boundaries to improve tools or to acquire new ones. Indeed, boundaries are accentuated. Disciplines, enshrined in departments, separate and isolate teachers and scholars, rather than facilitate inquiry across borders. Attention is inward. In fact, the geography of academic professionalism can be mapped as a series of narrowing circles, each inwardly oriented, making for increasing isolationism and exclusivism associated with status and prestige.

According to Wilshire, the research university is constructed on a concept that works against recognition of the unity and connectedness of the self and provides little space for exploring questions relating to the person and the personal. This is reflected in the separation of the departments and disciplines as well as in the incorporation of individuals into the academic professionalism of their departments. Increasingly the research institution has served as the model for other institutions of higher education. Those faculty who are not themselves in the grip of academic professionalism are usually aware that others are. They find themselves excluded and so struggle with issues of self-worth, status, and position. They are understandably resentful that the others are not carrying their share of the departmental and institutional "load."

In contrast to academic professionalism the model of relationality promotes a collegial professionalism. Here, professionalism is converted *from* credentialism and exclusivity, protectionism, and isolation from others; and it moves *to* an emphasis upon connectivity and imaginative empathy, competence, and dedication to the learning needs of the other. Hospitality plays a large role, pointing to the values of openness rather than exclusion—of recognizing students and colleagues as fellow learners from whom insight can be gained and with whom experience should be shared. Likewise, thoughtfulness figures importantly—holding up rigor and fidelity both to the inquiry and to the other.

## PROBLEMS IN THE CONTEMPORARY ACADEMY

As Jensen, Tompkins, Wilshire, and others remind us, collegial professionalism is a significant and promising part of the academy, but only a part. We turn now to behaviors that build on the model of insistent individualism through disconnection from colleagues, students, the institution, and, on the whole, through an unfulfilling self-centeredness. What follows describes the dark side of the academy. Exploration and acknowledgement of its geography is a necessary step toward hope and planning for the future. All of us know these descriptions are not accurate renderings of the whole landscape, but they point to troubling elements that have moral and spiritual overtones. One serves the positive through naming and addressing, not ignoring, the negative. The point is not to dwell in failures but, in correcting them, to become more vibrant and less mediocre, more exciting and less routine.

### Colleagues

One can scarcely examine the contemporary academy without noting the aging of the professoriate. Older faculty remember how quickly its promise diminished—the occupation entered in youthful anticipation that it would remain a growth area, quickly became a mature industry with minimal mobility and restricted opportunities for advancement. The position taken with the expectation of staying only three or four years became instead a position lasting two decades and more. Since professional status and prestige are conveyed by the relative standing of one's institution, academic professionalism has created for many a defensiveness about their very home. Adding to these burdens, the purchasing power of paychecks remained flat over the years and public esteem slipped.

Colleagues have not always helped. Rather than remaining companions, many became distant and competing figures with time. Grim, unilateral competition can loom in the mentality of the insistent individualist. The desire to excel at the expense of the other displaces desire to pit one's best against a colleague, thereby coming collectively closer to the truth. This displacement seems particularly evident at research institutions. Writing from his experience at one, David Damrosch observes that "no doubt there are campuses on which genuine community exists, and I know of a few fields in which scholars are more concerned to work together than to upstage each other; but I believe that such campuses and such fields are the exception rather than the norm" (Damrosch 1995, 104).

### Difficult People

As the professoriate ages, insistent individualism nurtures curmudgeonliness and other antisocial behaviors. Robert Boice reports that department chairpersons identify "difficult" faculty as their biggest source of personal stress and department disruption. Two kinds are described: one is the disillusioned, inactive, and socially isolated person often known as "deadwood," and the other is the uncooperative, disruptive, intimidating, angry, even explosive, individual (Boice 1993, 132–133). The Solomons term this latter type "rotten wood" and describe him or her as the far greater danger to the academy (Solomon and Solomon 1993, 245). As might be expected, Boice's research suggests that both types appear in greater number and proportion among senior than junior faculty.

We return later to the aggressively hostile colleague who thwarts hospitality at every turn. We look now at how the academy produces other individuals who become unsupportive and indifferent faculty. Consider the common failure to support colleagues at campus presentations, symposia, or colloquia. Unwillingness to attend one's fellows at these moments seems particularly ungenerous. More than simple rudeness, this is poor citizenship and unprofessional behavior. If one knows the scholarship to be reported and discussed will be unexciting, plebeian, or substandard, the presenter should be offered help. If the work is promising, it merits thoughtful attention and comment—not the indifference and inhospitality so effectively communicated by failing to show. Not just work in progress but even finished publications can fare poorly. Exchanges in print can be vicious and nasty, marked by slashing attacks neither hospitable nor thoughtful. Even more temperate exchanges can struggle for balance, given the inability of many scholars to communicate a straightforward assessment without attaching a diminishing qualification.

Offering illustration of the disaffection and cynicism he finds so widespread in academe, faculty member Ejner Jensen observes that for every supportive comment about an individual's scholarly efforts, "there is a chorus of disapproval. Moreover, the public chorus (in reviews, citations, and other public notices) is a faint echo of private voices that minimize, discount, or denigrate the work" (Jensen 1995, 9). Often it is colleagues who provide the most acerbic criticism. Jensen concludes that underneath the veneer of cleverly qualified endorsements of others' accomplishments a fundamental mean-spiritedness toward colleagues, and even contempt for the whole academic enterprise, may lurk; and is especially evident in ill-tempered sniping and undisguised muscular attacks on the naivete of colleagues' work. Departments and schools become containers of individuals preoccupied with grievances and resentments. Old conflicts and animosities linger, secretly nourished and surfacing at surprising moments. Former dean Henry Rosovsky observes of his faculty that "a significant proportion own difficult and childish personalities .... Nice guys don't necessarily finish last, but it would be hard to argue that they are especially well represented among the frontrunners" (Rosovsky 1990, 242).

Perhaps Jensen and Rosovsky are describing worse cases. The behaviors in question conflict with the objectives of the academy; they undercut fundamental values of individual fulfillment in the context of community. But insistent individualism and academic professionalism do dull collegiality over the years. This happens when the stimulating conversations of youthful dreams only rarely materialize. Earlier successes have not been sustained. Shared memories of deeply satisfying, fortifying, or even hilarious events provide support, but the pedants next door and down the hall also take their toll. Idiosyncratic colleagues are no longer humorous, but adolescent or hopelessly limited in dealing with others. The pompous and bombastic have become transparent and annoying. A few are now curmudgeons—complaining, fulminating, inflaming, and provoking. Conversations with them have harder and sharper edges. Some of these colleagues are embarrassing. They include those who are forever disorganized, unable to return papers on time, observe timetables they themselves established, get their grades to the registrar, or their book orders to the bookstore or library; those who cancel classes regularly; those who cannot be counted on to meet appointments or make faculty meetings—in short, the self-preoccupied who give "absent-minded" a bad name and for whom the rest have grown tired of apologizing. A few have even become academic attack dogs, permitting their interactions with others to become vicious.

## Academic Traditions

Might traditions of academic freedom and confidentiality contribute to these behaviors and be the shield critics allege—protecting faculty from having to present reasons for their actions? Tenure is to support the free exercise of academic judgment without fear of intimidation by others. When tenured faculty insist upon secret ballots and are reluctant to present reasons for their votes on curriculum or personnel issues, one wonders what protection would possibly suffice. If lifetime security is not enough to warrant candor, what would be enough? Perhaps secrecy provides relief from the discouraging scenes that the Solomons describe—"it doesn't take very many conversations with academics or departmental meetings to make it obvious that politics and intrigue, professional feuds and rivalries, ideological battles over minor merit raises, and wholesale warfare over hiring and promotions utterly eclipse whatever shared life of ideas may in theory tie faculty members together" (Solomon and Solomon 1993, 49). Secret balloting may provide the academic community a veneer of civility, for things could be worse. But given the privacy of their vote, some individuals say little to educate others or contribute to an enhanced process of decision-making. The secret ballot does not protect against abuse or discrimination, either. The traditional defense that honest assessment of issues or of persons is unlikely without ironclad confidentiality appears demeaning—both to individuals and to the rational processes central to the academy. These practices of secrecy appear as unacceptable ironies and contradictions in a community given to the pursuit of truth and rational argument.

Even the peer review process can be presented publicly as considerably more objective than private academic practices support. Ken Coates reports on the practice of editors soliciting external reviews of a manuscript until a sufficient number supporting antecedent judgments has been located (Coates 1995, A40). Of greater concern to him are those who do not wish the peer review process to overturn antecedent judgments on personnel matters, and who threaten retaliation when peer assessments of merit are at variance with their own. He finds evidence of a "substantial gap between the rhetoric about peer review and the reality that rigorous and honest analysis of a person's work actually may be strongly discouraged." The academy suggests that it is above the special arrangements and personal deals that afflict the larger society. In effect, universities "tell the public that peer review protects scholars and scholarship from the vagaries of personality, spite, and bias. Unfortunately, it does nothing of the sort." Accordingly, Coates calls for an end to confidentiality in peer reviews. Eliminating it will be painful, but making peer reviews public is an excellent way to assure that errors will be corrected. And openness will help to reassure the public that academe is fully committed to standards of excellence.

### Familiar Behaviors

Other forms of disconnection from colleagues are familiar. They include the unreliable manuscript reviewer who despite repeated reminders reneges on his or her promise to provide comment, jeopardizing tenure or promotion decisions. Other scholars come to regret depending on colleagues to honor commitments to a collaborative project, as publishers are particularly aware. Often the academy excuses these behaviors by speaking of professorial inertia or procrastination, thereby bleaching out the moral issues. The Solomons are more direct in noting that "the embarrassing truth is that our profession is filled with—almost defined by—missed deadlines and broken promises" (Solomon and Solomon 1993, 219). They propose periodically publishing the names of offenders in the national academic press. Perhaps this, they speculate, may push professors into more responsible behavior!

At professional meetings, disconnection from colleagues is familiar to panelists commenting on papers they never received in advance, and may be hearing for the first time with the audience; not that they have much time for comment, given the unchecked tendency of some speakers to exceed their allotted time. Rare is the moderator with the courage or ability to hold speakers to time limits. And then there are those who rise from the audience purportedly to engage the speaker only to deliver their own mini-paper in the time devoted to questions from the floor. Of course none of these kinds of behaviors would be tolerated from the payroll office. It must provide valid checks for correct amounts on time. Yet inquiry is far more important than money.

### Trivial Writing

Academic writing presents a special case of inhospitality. Critics like Martin Anderson excoriate faculty for trivial writing, arrogantly celebrated; and there are grounds for the charge. There are insubstantial publications whose sole purpose appears to pad a resume, but we rarely celebrate them. The issue of trivial writing is better cast in terms of whether the writing serves fundamental academic objectives. Writing becomes trivial when it deals repeatedly with the same issues, dwells exclusively in minutiae, breaks no new ground, extends no new inquiries, or serves no other values. Fundamental values that writing should serve include the clarification and self-criticism of one's thinking and its clear communication to colleagues and a wider public. What may pass muster in conversation, speech, or lecture is subject to a higher standard when in print and open to potentially infinite review and assessment by others.

Patricia Nelson Limmerick raises thoughtful questions about the ability of much academic writing to meet this test of clarity. Lamenting time wasted on ideological disputes, she deplores the common failure to address the more serious problem of "horrible writing." Indeed, "for all their differences, most right-wing scholars and most left-wing scholars share a common allegiance to a cult of obscurity. Left, right and center all hide behind the idea that unintelligible prose indicates a sophisticated mind." This cult of obscurity reflects the timidity, not arrogance, of the academic author. The pedantry of academic prose provides a line of defense rather than a helping hand. "Professors are often shy, timid and even fearful people, and under those circumstances, dull, difficult prose can function as a kind of protective camouflage. When you write typical academic prose, it is nearly impossible to make a strong, clear statement" (Limmerick 1993, 3). Surely she is correct that the effect of some, if not most, academic writing is to privatize the work of the professoriate—to keep others at a distance. Such academic writing may also be trivial in the way that Anderson and other critics suggest, but if Limmerick is correct the greater challenge is first to understand it. Clearly hospitality is in short supply.

An additional issue is whether the extent of multiple authorship can signify just who is responsible for what. The academic press recently noted that a physics journal article devoted one-third of its six pages to the names of all 437 authors and their 35 institutions. A second article in the same issue listed over 403 authors (McDonald 1995, A35). Despite the appearance of awesome collaboration, the underlying facts suggest individual piecework. Even the need to record the multiplicity of authors attests to the unhealthy grip of individualism on the academy. Nor can there be accountability. Despite this pronounced individualism no locus of responsibility can be identified when there are hundreds of "authors." In these cases individualism has merged into collectivism.

### Generation Gaps

Relationships with younger colleagues also present a special case of the inhospitality of academic professionalism. The problematic behaviors described above are part of the context into which the next generation of faculty is coming—new instructors delighted at last to find an academic job but unsure how to make it work. Many junior faculty are understandably apprehensive about establishing academic futures in unfamiliar environments where determining the "real requirements" for success can be difficult. Many still leave graduate school having been educated to teach in their own graduate school, not in the new environments they are entering. Other challenges abound. Junior faculty often struggle with demands of new marriages or young children. Frequently there is inadequate mentoring by older colleagues, and newcomers fear reprisal by conservative senior faculty unsympathetic to novel teaching practices and research projects. Many older faculty are not available to younger colleagues in an open and affirming way. In his extensive study of new faculty, Robert Boice summarizes his findings: "As a rule, new faculty report feeling neglected, isolated, overworked, and deprived of vital support and feedback" (Boice 1992, 44). Almost invariably, they describe a lack of collegiality and intellectual stimulation—the very things for which the academy should be known.

Under the influence of insistent individualism, the academy reflects a form of social Darwinism. Anxious to secure approval, junior faculty experience the double bind of not knowing whether to propose collaboration with older colleagues or even to ask them for help. Asking for help risks appearing naive and uncertain about academic fundamentals—in effect, proclaiming to significant others that one is doubtful and hesitant in an environment in which special respect is reserved for those who have sufficient insight, skills, and self-reliance to make things happen on their own. People with the right stuff succeed. Asking for help risks violating the culture of insistent individualism and diminishing oneself. On the other hand, ignoring more senior colleagues risks appearing disrespectful, arrogant and, inappropriately, self-confident— hardly a prudent course of action. The dilemma can be debilitating.

Further, trying to work outside or across traditional department structures, as some junior faculty are interested in doing, can spell doom at various institutions. Of course, all of this is happening at a time when standards for retention, promotion, and tenure are demonstrably higher than they were for many now making the decisions—a situation loaded with emotional difficulty. Younger faculty may feel exploited and subjected to unfair standards. Older faculty may resent that rules under which they were hired have changed and that their contributions are no longer valued.

## Students

Every instructor knows moments when teaching seems not to work, despite heroic efforts. These are difficult, demoralizing moments. They happen even in the midst of an exhilarating run. "Teachers regularly confront failure: its regular presence is one of the factors that leads to academic snobbism, which often serves as an internal defense mechanism in dealing with failure" (Getman 1992, 41). Snobbism is not inevitable, but it is a version of academic professionalism—excluding others from the authorizing group that provides professional identity. Students are held at a distance rather than welcomed into the community of inquiry. The difference between master and tyro is magnified and common ground undercut.

## The Academic Persona

Some suggest the underlying reason for this behavior is to protect self and to seek approval. Getman notes that faculty often create artificial personalities to facilitate their goals. "Unsuccessful teachers develop personalities to protect themselves and shift responsibility for their failures to the students or the system. Many attempt to develop a role that suggests that they are too brilliant to be understood by the students they teach. The insecure merely develop a style that suggests greater success, importance, and originality than they feel entitled to" (Getman 1992, 27). Playing a role, creating a persona, impedes genuine communication—one must protect the projected self-image. Because they are artificial, these personas separate rather than integrate the professional and the personal self. Often they cease being temporary, limited stratagems to get through challenging and difficult times. They can take hold and perpetuate themselves, and uncovering them takes work and risk. Jane Tompkins relates her discovery that despite years of thinking she had been helping her students, she had actually been more focused on promoting and protecting their images of her as smart, knowledgeable, and well-prepared. Since faculty are role models, "this is what we teach our students: how to perform within an institutional academic setting so that they will be thought of highly by their colleagues and instructors" (Tompkins 1991, 30).

Faculty less bent on self-promotion and protection also need help. For many, the initial supply of hope and confidence necessary for teaching has been drawn down, and replenishment is difficult. Careful observers know that most instructors are still like students—"still looking for more or less immediate feedback, working for grades, so to speak, for praise and recognition" (Solomon and Solomon 1993, 206). Most people need and seek approval by others; faculty are no exception. But the concrete affirmations needed to sustain good teaching are unpredictable, often not there when needed, and too spare when they do come. The insistent individualist finds this especially agonizing—unilateral power should mean control, not dependence, and certainly not dependence upon an unpredictable other.

Even when affirmed, instructors can find that fear of appearing shallow, ignorant, or otherwise inadequate distorts the task at hand. "Teachers lecture longest when they are least sure of what they are doing: that is when they parse concepts without end, unwind the interminable and irrelevant 'illustration'" (Palmer 1983, 71). Discomfort with being engaged by students drives some faculty to minimize that possibility—despite the prospect that they could be affirmed and enriched by students' questions and perspectives. Better to lay low than to risk failing, being ignored, or creating resistance, anger, or scrutiny. To teach is to be vulnerable. It is to depend upon others, to risk a shift from unilateral to relational power. Students may be afraid of faculty rejection, but faculty too fear rejection by students and colleagues. "Higher education is filled with people who were great students but do not know how to deal with the uncertainties, anxieties and small rejections that are a regular part of teaching" (Getman 1992, 42).

## An Adversarial Relationship

Some faculty report that the tension between providing students rigorous grading and extending compassion and encouragement can be draining. Doubts mount over the years about how best to serve students—through stark, frank assessments of their work, or through more hopeful, optimistic assurances about a vague future. The very individuality of students compounds the problem. For some students too much bluntness too soon chokes off growth; for others, delaying it encourages misplaced self-confidence. In either case, being both coach and judge of one's own teaching success may in fact be a conflict of interest, and thus part of a larger problem.

Faculty typically have the dual role of facilitating and evaluating student learning. On one hand, the instructor is obligated to present the inquiry and evoke student interest. The task includes coaching and supporting students in their efforts to appropriate the inquiry and to master its skills and competencies. On the other hand, at most institutions the instructor is also charged with assessing the adequacy of student accomplishment. The instructor must, therefore, evaluate the success of the very process he or she has been directing. Some see an inherent conflict in this twofold responsibility; they point to the awkwardness for the instructor and the ambivalence students must feel toward the instructor. The asymmetry of power is most evident in testing and grading, but it goes beyond evaluation to "taint" other interchanges. It creates an unusual professional situation, establishing an adversarial rather than a helping relationship—"with knowledge on one side, ignorance on the other; prosecutor on one side, defendant on the other; the power on one side, the weak on the other" (Wilson 1982, 273). Being a scrupulous, fair, and objective grader of student work is one species of excellence, but giving the job to those with no vested interest in the evaluation and certification of the students is a less ambiguous model.

## Complaining about Students

Colleagues provide little help on these issues, rarely speaking in depth about their own teaching experiences, whether successes or frustrations. Ironies abound—for the commonalities of difficulty and vulnerability in teaching and scholarship should nourish the relational community, not reinforce isolationism and withdrawal. "The universality of failure should give academics a sense of being involved in a common risky and frustrating enterprise, but it often drives us apart" (Getman 1992, 59)—except when we can complain about students. In recent years, students seem to many faculty not only less able, but less interested and engaged in their own education. Today's enlarged pool of students, incorporating those from quite diverse environmental and educational settings, is seen as a liability and burden rather than a professional challenge. Complaining about them is on the upswing, and often functions as a preemptive strike. A common question is Who has the most compelling, the most egregious story of student ignorance or incompetence? Chronic complaining distances oneself from obligations to students. It sheds responsibility for advancing student learning and illustrates the academic professionalism of which Wilshire wrote. How can one be expected to teach if students are ill-prepared and not interested in improving or even owning their learning?

For some faculty the task becomes sorting and culling. The weapon of choice for the more aggressive combines direct belittling of student abilities and deliberate arousal of fear. Grading becomes an instrument of control. Derogatory comments about student abilities combined with unreasonably demanding assignments is a potent combination. The instructor may present it as a bold pedagogical tactic to force student ownership of their learning. Some students do rise to this challenge, but most rush to change sections in search of a different, more responsible, instructor—one more welcoming and helpful. However, the issue is not the empirical effectiveness of abusive strategies, but their ethical adequacy as violations of hospitality and thoughtfulness.

Fortunately, overt harassment and abusiveness are rare. More common, and more troubling, is the low-key, grinding suggestion that students today are too dumb to learn or merit the full energies of the professor. This kind of complaining is corrosive, and it creates a hostile environment that violates the students' academic freedom—their freedom to learn. Students have little opportunity to rebut these suggestions of presumptive inadequacy and inferiority. Anyone who claims the right of academic freedom has a correlative duty to colleagues and students to honor their right to conditions for learning; and this requires an atmosphere characterized by respect and civility.

Some faculty complaining is probably necessary—it provides catharsis, elicits recognition of the difficulty of teaching well, and secures validation by others. The relational community not only permits, but encourages, constructive complaining. It provides collective acknowledgement of the difficulty of teaching and enables faculty to return to the classroom refreshed and revitalized. However, complaining that converts impatience with student learning into contempt for what is identified as a lower intellectual life form is a different matter. When intellectual abilities are employed to hurt, not instruct, no amount of brilliance compensates. Treating students as means, as entities to be manipulated and dismissed, is a high-handed form of reductionism, even when disguised as high standards. It is surely reductionism when students are excluded as potential fellow inquirers, when their right to useful feedback is denied through careless or delayed grading, or when minimal or unhelpful evaluative comment is provided. In what one hopes is an overstatement, Steven Cahn asserts that "virtually any undergraduate or graduate student can relate harrowing stories about tribulations suffered at the hands of irresponsible instructors" (Cahn 1994, xiii). We trust these faculty are a minority, but the few have an impact far beyond their numbers and academe seems unable to change their behaviors.

### Inappropriate Relationships

At the other extreme are educators, one hopes also few in number, who have inappropriate interest in students. These are the promiscuous, self-indulgent faculty. We try to draw the line at their liaisons with undergraduates but often look the other way when their affairs are with older students. We often do not agree, but say nothing since they are colleagues, perhaps of many years; and who are we to judge? When challenged, offenders point to the special circumstances in which they pursue romantic entanglements or friendships with students: the relationship is by mutual consent and the instructor will, of course, be objective, respecting the educational needs of the student. Most of the public, and more than a few of the professoriate, find this extraordinarily self-serving. Peter Markie observes that we do not attribute such powers of objectivity to other professionals and we do not accept their special pleading even in the lesser cases of friendship. "We require the most respected jurists to excuse themselves from hearing cases that involve the interests of a friend, because we doubt their ability, if not their willingness, to control the strong inclination to favor a friend" (Markie 1994, 71). Why should educators think they are different? Why should we assume we have abilities for which we do not credit others? And certainly these abilities must be even stronger when the relationship is romantic.

Most agree that the best professors are friendly rather than insensitive, uncaring, withdrawn, or threatening. But should they cultivate even non-romantic friendships with their students? Careful analysis suggests caution. Friendship can create conflict in the obligation of the faculty member to be equally available to students—and here appearance is as important as reality. Of course, equally available does not mean identically available, for there may be relevant differences. Yet should friendship, much less romantic involve-ment, be one of these? Peter Markie suggests it should not, assuming that by friendship one means what is commonly understood to involve mutual sharing of otherwise private information; mutual sharing of affection and enjoyment; and mutual, personal, and special expectations and commitments having moral weight and character (Markie 1990, 136). Inevitably, friendship implies favoritism and is inconsistent with the duty to evaluate and advise fairly and avoid bias or the appearance of it. We are not talking about faculty being warm rather than cold, about being interested in student needs and concerns. We are talking about special treatment for some, and not others.

At most campuses the character of relationships with students calls for closer scrutiny. All too often the topic is not raised—perhaps from a desire not to embarrass colleagues, perhaps from the hope that people will behave rightly and a sense that it is not the business of a faculty senate to dictate what that might mean. Unfortunately, some will find a way to betray the academic trust and to rationalize betrayals. If the academy possessed more resources in codes of ethics, this problem might be reduced. In any case, the task of teaching with integrity challenges one not to interpret (or to seek) the attentions of students personally. Faculty must find ways to be transparent to the instructional inquiry while at the same time using the particular strengths of their personal-ity. The fundamental objective of the faculty member must be to advance the interests of the student.

Discussions about these matters can be difficult. Yet if we give up expecting faculty to articulate and defend before colleagues judgments about standards for teaching, grading, relations with students, and personal scholarship, then we give up the collegium and the academic institution as a center of value and settle instead for a mere collection of individuals—the aggregation we exam-ined earlier. When this is the case we should expect increased public scrutiny and criticism, and we risk having the whole condemned because of the indefensible behaviors of a few.

## The Institution

Academics have obligations to their institutions beyond those to colleagues and students. However, there are various ways of "calling in sick"—ways of disavowing duties of common citizenship. Any registrar and most department chairpersons can provide tales about faculty notorious for their indifference to a common schedule. Despite a workplace largely free of detailed reporting requirements, some faculty still cannot bring themselves to turn in grades when due, submit syllabi and library orders according to the common schedule, or write letters of recommendation in a timely fashion. These are not victimless offenses, for others suffer—often repeatedly and sometimes dramatically. Peers seem unable to address these behaviors. The essence of the relational self and community—that others are primary, not secondary, to individual human fulfillment—is then lost.

### *Polarizing Discourse*

The professoriate is not known for conscientious attendance at meetings, either. Accounts of low attendance are familiar. Some faculty rarely read their mail or attend to e-mail or phone message reminders, claiming not to have received what is known to have been sent. Others are less apologetic, expressing amazement that their attendance should be expected. Stories resound of heroic efforts to assemble a quorum—successful strategies sometimes being the redefinition of the number required. Once meetings are actually called to order, discourse can be less than exemplary. Colleagues rise to "express concerns" and to appear forthright and courageous in labeling and denouncing mischief, perhaps even appalling deceit and corruption. The fate of Western civilization is not at hand in a decision to restrict parking or reduce library hours, but sometimes appears to be. One recitation of concern triggers another, provoking still others, each calculated to appear worse than the previous one. Responsible discourse suffers, and may disappear.

Catharine R. Stimpson develops the point. Drawing on past experiences as a dean and reflecting on how to quieten raucous curricular controversies, she argues for the necessity of "a renewed ethic of professionalism" and contends that academics must forgo the pleasures of rhetorical excesses that a so-called commitment to tolerance and freedom of speech have allowed to occur. This rhetoric "sports a melodramatic, belligerent, self-serving hysteria in which a person claims...that the gravest of principles are at stake and that this heroic martyr is willing to defend them valiantly against the lowest of slimes, hypocrites, and creeps. The heroic martyr has no self-interest at stake—only morality and justice" (Stimpson 1992, 53). Along the way opponents are created and then bludgeoned.

Polarizing discourse appears in a variety of guises. At times it is shrill and belligerent in the way Stimpson's brief account suggests. Faculty meetings do lend themselves to undisciplined, slash-and-burn declamations and can be treacherous places for proposals for substantive action. Competing turf investments, the general conservative bent of scholars as custodians of the past, and a need to analyze everything in detail can combine to prevent effective discussion of constructive proposals. Julius Getman, a former national president of the AAUP, observed of his own institution that it is at faculty meetings "where the least rational aspects of academic life most frequently arise." He found meetings regularly disappointing and over time he lost earlier hopes for rational conduct. "The issues were often petty, the arguments irrational, and the exchanges marked by anger or discontent. Prolonged debates but very little productive discussion took place" (Getman 1992, 91). Insistent individualism was much in evidence.

At other times, polarizing rhetoric is not at all shrill, but disguised as a scholarly observation or concern and delivered with ample wit, double negatives, and gentle self-deprecation. In these cases, wit and charm can mask a fundamental contempt. An easy cynicism covers a deep-seated nastiness. A patina of collegiality and hospitality hides a disgruntled, alienated core. The effect is the same—to diminish, if not to dismiss, the opponent or the opposing position.

In these ways the academy gives itself permission to hold in abeyance the very standards of evidence and critical reasoning it otherwise insists upon. In essence, academics act in these ways without effective rebuke by colleagues. Whether melodramatic or delivered with a deceptive good nature, polarizing rhetoric lacks civil, patient, judicious, or balanced scrutiny of evidence to determine support for the claims presented. It repudiates critical reasoning and a sense of proportionality, creating instead separation and distance. Indulging in this rhetoric may generate momentary satisfactions, but the price is steep. When engaged in this behavior, the academy demeans itself. Failing to model its teaching role, it contradicts itself and diminishes the public trust it requires. It is in crafting measured, rather than polarizing, rhetoric that the virtues of academic training should be most evident.

## Looking the Other Way

Failure to assume a share of the "overhead" work for keeping the campus functioning is another well-known problem. Many colleges and universities find it necessary to secure affidavits from committee chairs that members have in fact attended meetings and made contributions. Similarly, truth-telling as a standard is eroded when colleagues avoid confronting the tough issues of rigorous faculty evaluation. Allowances can be made for colleagues well beyond acceptability, and then covered by talk about the difficulty of assessing instructional performance. Yet, despite our verbal facility and occasional declamations that teaching excellence cannot be measured, we know that it can be—at least sufficiently. The moment of truth arrives when we are asked whether we would advise our own child to enroll in Professor X's class and the answer is an immediate, resounding No! Understandably, the public wonders why we retain those professors from whom we shelter our family members and better students.

It is not only older faculty members who present challenges to chairs and other academic leaders; in fact, a traditional role of the chair is to mentor junior faculty. But for now the biggest challenge on most campuses *is* the older faculty—there are far more of them, given the demographics of the profession; they are more likely to experience burn-out, disciplinary obsolescence, and fatigue; and the helpfulness systematic evaluation procedures can provide is usually not available to senior faculty. Yes, these are colleagues, maybe even long-standing friends; but department chairs, other academic leaders, and colleagues have the same twofold roles as the classroom instructor—to support and evaluate. And if evaluation suggests deficiencies, then the chair or dean has the same responsibility as the instructor—to provide further support and evaluate again. When there is persistent failure to improve, more drastic action is called for. Repeatedly looking the other way, failing to bite the bullet, passing things on to one's successor or the dean diminishes the academy and its public standing. Who has an acceptable response to the graduating students or the returning alumni who ask why the college retains Professor Y when year after year they wrote letters of complaint and voted by walking out of his or her class?

No doubt it is these kinds of behaviors that led former provost Milton Greenberg to observe critically that "the way in which faculty members choose how and when to perform their academic functions most closely resembles the behaviors of *volunteers*" (Greenberg 1993, A68). Trying to conceptualize the nature of faculty work in contrast to "the rest of the world of work, where regular schedules and accounting for time are normal expectations," Greenberg finds this metaphor best conveys the flexibility faculty enjoy in choosing which work they will do and when they will do it, and the resulting difficulties colleagues and administrators experience managing the academic enterprise and explaining it to outsiders.

Apart from teaching assigned classes, most faculty work is optional and even the manner in which teaching is done is largely a matter of individual discretion. The length of the class, how it is conducted, and the papers assigned are all matters usually decided by the individual instructor—as are matters respecting what if any scholarship to pursue, consulting to conduct, meetings to attend, or service commitments to assume. Such individual discretion, Greenberg notes, is characteristic more of volunteers than professionals. Volunteers must be persuaded to carry out work necessary for the organization. Some are stalwart, but others are rarely seen. Volunteers rarely chastise other volunteers. Persuasive powers are uneven and many volunteer organizations lack sufficient structure to create an effective sense of obligation to the common good. Most importantly, volunteers are by definition unpaid. Collegiate professionalism ought to demand much more. Greenberg asks, "does not full-time employment, on full pay—frequently on tenured, lifetime contracts—call for faculty members to have responsibilities as well as rights, obligations as well as the autonomy befitting a professional group?" It is high time, he concludes, to "view our college or university as a full-time professional engagement and insist upon rigorous and thorough peer judgment of all professional *work*—be it teaching, research, or service." The question is whether the peer process of evaluation at institutions characterized by insistent individualism is capable of the rigor for which Greenberg calls.

## The Self

Focusing on aspects of one's unhappiness often seems only to deepen them. Negotiating how to remain creative and productive throughout a long tenure at the same institution is often difficult. Some faculty are extraordinarily successful in this challenge—maintaining sustained productivity and enthusiasm over long periods of time, functioning as models of collegial professionalism, and displaying persistent hospitality and thoughtfulness in all of their work. Others are far less successful and appear susceptible to the initial attractions of insistent individualism despite its long-term liabilities and disappointments. This section describes some of the causes and the consequences of insistent individualism respecting the integrated self—viewed not as a description of numbers of faculty but as a hazard or trap into which they can fall.

### Personal Vulnerabilities

For some faculty, familiarity breeds indifference to colleagues, routines entrap and flatten the landscape, recognition of immobility deflates and diminishes, and the discouraging realization that these things are happening accelerates their progress and deepens their hold. Repeatedly teaching introductory and survey courses seems to channel and restrict energies, rather than provide opportunities for fresh and exciting revision. Over the years it becomes harder to challenge intemperate colleagues who threaten the dignity and integrity of the academy. At the same time, earlier dreams of fame and accomplishment have often dimmed; the grand research project has been done by someone else; options for other projects have closed; marriages may have failed; and addictions, illnesses, and deaths have added to the burdens. Physical and intellectual energy has diminished and younger colleagues seem able now to threaten as well as revitalize. The past is as much a burden as resource. As Parker Palmer notes, with the large number of aging faculty in the contemporary academy, "lots of people are looking around and saying, 'Is this all there is?'" (Palmer 1992a, 4).

Familiar rhythms of the academic calendar repeat at an increasing rate. There are ends, and then new beginnings. Even this comfortable pattern can seem an eternal recurrence in which one is trapped. The rhythms cause pain even as they soothe. The fresh starts provide hope but the points of closure are a reminder of loss. Though there is always next term, the options for fixing things dwindle as the semester proceeds and they vanish as it ends. The failures are often palpable—course objectives not reached, material not covered, and student competencies not achieved. Responsibility for these failures is difficult to assign, and this difficulty can become an additional burden.

Julius Getman correctly observes that "widespread insecurity" among professors seems almost certain. "Able academics are inevitably seekers after discovery and enlightenment, and these goals are far more difficult to achieve than success in many other fields or success as a student, which is the experience most likely to lead people into academic life" (Getman 1992, x). Students have definite, set objectives before them, and the possibility of knowing when they have been accomplished. For faculty, however, there is always something left undone. The evidence of excellence is far more elusive, even slippery—difficult to identify and certainly difficult to achieve. It is no surprise that some academics cope by dwelling in what Getman calls "the indicia of success: how often one's work has been cited and by whom" (Getman 1992, 55). Far from a permanent solution, this method of coping usually generates still more anxiety. One can never rest.

Other faculty report that research no longer provides the satisfaction it did earlier. Even those who continue to publish may not find rewards sufficient. Belief in the larger social value of scholarly work recedes when one realizes how small the audience often is. Many feel they have already explored their best ideas, and new ones seem elusive. Continuing to write up the old ideas seems undignified and cheap. These professors have read too many trivial works, and suspected that they were frantically written to get tenure or deny the aging process. Why go through the motions and contribute to the list? Efforts to redirect matters can go wrong—developing new areas of inquiry can be subtly discouraged by one's department, as risking dilettantism or abandoning the specialty for which one was hired. Likewise, even consulting activity can pale. What initially may have been an exciting opportunity to transfer technology in both directions—between the academy and business, generating and applying new ideas—can become problematic. The chance to apply ideas outside the classroom and to bring new ones in to enrich teaching can get out of hand, creating conflicts of time and interest. For others, consulting becomes repetitive, contributing nothing new to teaching or research.

For most faculty there is a price for letting intellectual activity slip. Given the value attached to academic prominence, letting it go can seem like failing. One's standing as a professional appears to be diminished. Personal failure is difficult to acknowledge, and it is much easier to assign blame elsewhere—to colleagues, the administration, students, or the system in general. Given the expectations of insistent individualism, the result of reduced or abandoned research and other forms of lessened contributions becomes for some faculty another reason for "a cynical negativity directed at some aspect of the enterprise they serve but ultimately turning back on themselves" (Jensen 1995, 11). The importance of these broader issues of one's impact in both teaching and scholarship looms larger with age.

Yet impact is relative to the community to which one is contributing. Worth is connected with sharing—receiving and giving. Insistent individualism is a constraint that deprives us of a richer and thicker understanding of ourselves and the satisfactions available to us. As Wilshire and Whitehead remind us, individual existence has a communal ground. We must claim our communities as integral to who we are. Failures are inevitable, but they have a different face when seen in the context of a community of give and take. Insistent individualism obscures this resource and sees failures only as negativities. When collegial professionalism is converted into academic professionalism, faculty come to feel that there are few ways to succeed, but many ways to fail.

Ironically, increased vulnerability is associated with the very independence that makes the academy attractive. The quest for personal autonomy means that as failure becomes more likely, it becomes more difficult to accept and explain to others or even to oneself. In the model of insistent individualism one alone is creator of one's own destiny. The culture informed by this model works against accepting inevitable setbacks. Instead, they become nagging reminders of personal inadequacies. It is understandable that even the apparent mark of success—promotion to full professor—may seem insufficient. Some achieve this rank before turning forty, leaving the prospect of thirty years or so with little additional institutional sign of accomplishment. That is a long time to be anxious. Not many colleges or universities have steps within or beyond the rank of full professor, thus eliminating one avenue of incentive and reward.

### The Uncertain Impact of Tenure

Even the special privilege of tenure may psychologically work against the professoriate, leaving faculty subconsciously defensive. Many non-academic professionals in mid-life are now conspicuously underemployed or out of work altogether, corporations having merged and downsized—often suddenly and harshly. Other professionals have taken control of their lives, changing their careers ahead of changing economic and employment conditions. By contrast, tenure has sheltered faculty economically, but it is a commonplace that few educators have exercised in any daring way the academic freedom it was designed to protect. Verbal commitment to unfettered, untrammeled inquiry may remain steady, but not many have asked the really hard questions in teaching and research or launched creative, risk-taking initiatives. More than a few observers have concluded that instead of emboldening professors, "tenure has the opposite effect on many. The longer and more secure their period of safety, the flabbier and more faint-hearted they become, the more they fear they have to lose" (Wilshire 1990, 252).

Consequently, there are charges that tenure is corrosive or at least a degrading defense of job security. Once awarded it often requires no compelling evidence of further productivity. Apart from the constructive, supportive energies present within the healthy collegium, the choice to remain a vibrant, contributing member lies solely with the individual. There are few external incentives or pressures to continue self-renewal year after year. In a situation marked by insistent individualism there may be inadequate internal incentives as well. The rewards of contributing to a common good have faded and lost their attraction. Too often, it seems, one hears the boastful yet defensive statement, "I have tenure and they can't do anything to me."

Tenure also leaves problem individuals to fend too much for themselves. Those who develop chronically disruptive and dysfunctional traits are left without institutional structures that might attract them into more useful, productive behaviors. Autonomous individuals leave each other alone, looking the other way rather than acting to help or remove a troubled colleague. As a result, many experience the further guilt engendered by blocking excellent, non-tenured instructors' access to permanent positions. This too demoralizes and erodes community. And how is one to advise students about taking courses taught by these troubled colleagues; by saying nothing, being evasive, or simply lying?

Thus for some faculty and academic leaders, the excitement has faded. What was once a "calling" with enchantment and nobility has paled and become a job—mechanical and routine. Insistent individualism reinforces and accentuates this problem. Reassurance and reinvigoration from colleagues is insufficient to remedy the malaise. Alienation from self as an educator increases. Outside attractions—writing the academic novel, jogging or playing golf, managing real estate, or pursuing other business interests—appear and take precedence. When this happens, the point and possibility of effective collective self-regulation—guarding the guardians of knowledge—diminishes. Having withdrawn, these individuals remain at, but are no longer part of, the academy.

## CONCLUSION

We laugh, nervously, at the old line that faculty morale is *always* at an all-time low. We know it conveys a deep and troubling truth. The malaise and bitterness to which Ejner Jensen and others refer have become too pervasive. How did this happen? Have we insufficient self-confidence and self-esteem? Are we afraid to acknowledge the dark side of the academy? Have we acquiesced in our own self-diminishment? Academic professionalism contributes to the situation. It promotes disconnection among faculty as well as between faculty, students, and institutions. It encourages exclusiveness rather than relationality. It rarely facilitates internal integration. Reflecting insistent individualism, academic professionalism separates professional from personal lives. The result is the difficulty of modeling publicly to students and colleagues what the liberation associated with the pursuit of knowledge might mean.

Things can be different. The whole point of the relational model is to deny the walls that insistent individualism erects and maintains. Relationality promotes hospitality and thoughtfulness. Collegial professionalism means competence and dedication—doing the job well and even gracefully. It suggests dignity and highlights commitment to the good of the other, rather than the exclusivity and self-protection that academic professionalism fosters. It calls for and makes possible more honest and candid discourse and relationships. It discourages injudicious and insensitive speech. Excessive privacy, secret balloting, and incomplete peer review reflect the deficiencies of the academy as aggregate, not as collegium. Honesty is dangerous and corrosive when used with unilateral, not relational, power.

Collegial professionalism directs the academic outward to promotion of the larger social and civic virtues through the extension of empowering and liberating knowledge. The relational model helps one acknowledge the porousness of disciplinary and organizational boundaries and appreciate how ideas and actions can have profound multiple effects. It holds that even disciplinary distinctions can unite as well as divide. However, the very structure of knowledge institutionalized in higher education encourages the isolated self and the isolated department. As we see in the next chapter, traditional disciplinary and departmental barriers create conditions for institutional fragmentation.

# CHAPTER 4

# Institutions
## Fragmented or Connected?

Institutions of higher education also illustrate insistent individualism. They too suffer internal fragmentation, disconnectedness, and lack of integration. By dwelling in excessively private pursuits, colleges and universities also become disconnected from other institutions and from the public.

We look first at the well-known separateness of disciplines and departments. This common form of internal fragmentation almost always generates corresponding curricular disconnectedness. Some institutions also suffer from the splintering within the faculty that collective bargaining can create, heightening suspicions between faculty and administration as well. Compounding these organizational biases toward internal separation and division are traditions that define academic leadership in terms of individualistic values and mythologies. Disciplinary associations and organizations provide little assistance, because their codes of ethics are often only hortatory with no provision for enforcement.

In addition to internal fragmentation, institutions of higher education can display unattractive forms of privatism. They often take their own importance as self-evident, though much of the public is uninformed about the internal workings of higher education. Sometimes colleges and universities contribute to these misunderstandings. Making greater efforts to educate society would help, as would displaying greater candor in public statements. Accreditation is the chief instrument of institutional self-regulation, and it too needs repair and more vigorous explanation outside the academy—and even within it.

This chapter follows naturally upon the last, as institutions provide the context within which faculty and students work. Institutions are constituted by faculty and students, and influence them in return. The values of the relational model of community cannot be advanced if we ignore the environing structures within which individuals work and by which they are shaped; for the structures should support and advance the educational mission. They should be consonant with the enlargement of knowledge, with extending the capacity of students and faculty alike to grow. They too should promote hospitality and thoughtfulness.

## INTERNAL DISCONNECTION

However, the very ways institutions organize themselves and conduct their activities often promote fragmentation and stand at cross purposes to the values of the relational model. Consider the financial and educational expense of uncoordinated instructional inquiries. Even simple matters illustrate the point. Gerald Graff and Michael Berube observe how students read the same texts in different courses, almost always without collaboration by their instruc- tors. Fragmentation is not confined to selection and interpretation of texts, either. "In one typical year, a campus with which we're familiar offered no fewer than three courses on 'women, feminism, and technology,' not merely in different departments but also in different colleges. None of the instructors knew of the existence of the other courses" (Graff and Berube 1995, B1–2).

Examples could be multiplied and found on every campus. Autonomy and privatism characterize not just professors but whole curricula, as well as department and school activities. The lack of coordination extends to extra- curricular events, many with potential to enrich the classroom significantly. Campus lectures and panel discussions are rarely integrated into class activity even when eminently appropriate. Fragmentation flows naturally from the traditional boundaries that academic and organizational distinctions create. Isolation is apparently a small price to pay for customary, familiar control of discrete, rather than collaborative and complex, undertakings. Yet, as Graff and Berube observe, "there's something wrong with a system in which teachers and whole programs work in modules cut off from one another, unable to make the most of, or make anything of, their common interests or their salient disagreements."

This unhappy situation is not necessary. Broader coordination of events is one answer, though that would require a degree of advance planning that is often not characteristic of insistent individualists. There are also intriguing opportunities for collaboration and interchange among the professors who assign the texts and develop the courses that overlap. Symposia devoted to exploring common intellectual ground could be created, in which relevant

differences could also be highlighted and discussed. Greater intellectual coherence would be one outcome, as would enlarged intellectual community.

However, what Graff and Berube describe suggests a much larger problem—the fragmentation of knowledge, curriculum, and instructional activities that the very structure of the university generates. The situation is
compounded by the variety of institutional aims and purposes. Surely each
institution claims to advance learning, but other aims and purposes are often
in competition—particularly at the large research university. Every issue
cannot be pursued, and some are decided through unilateral rather than
relational power. Other choices occur by default, by the inability of the
institution openly and deliberately to embrace common aims and purposes.
Almost all institutions need to work toward more coherent intellectual inquiry. Rigid distinctions between curricular and extracurricular should be
eased. Internal barriers must be lowered to address pressing social problems
such as the environment, racism, hunger, crime, and homelessness.

The departmentalization of the academy, as it is currently structured,
creates artificial separations and boundaries. It enshrines an insistent organizational individualism, a fragmentation of the intellect. Interdisciplinary efforts are attempts to put back together what the academy had previously
separated, but often there is little opportunity for sustained reflection on
complex issues without special centers or institutes. These special places are
anomalies of structure within a fragmented university, usually established with
great difficulty and standing in awkward relationship to departments. Too
frequently efforts are "hampered," as Damrosch notes, "by the archaic
hyperindividualism of our prevailing academic ethos" (Damrosch 1995, 7).

The problem is not new. The organizational complexion of the American
university was basically fixed a century ago when the research university came
into being. Burton Bledstein explains the isolation that the department structure was able to create and maintain throughout this period: "The university
not only segregated ideas from the public, intellectual segregation occurred
with the development of each new department . . . . [that] emphasized the
unique identity of its subject, its special qualities and language, its special
distinction as an activity of research and investigation. Any outsider who
attempted to pass judgment on an academic discipline contained within a
department was acting presumptuously" (Bledstein 1976, 327–328). Although
there have been extraordinary developments in the intervening hundred
years, the basic structure of the university has not changed. The university is
much bigger now, but as Charles Anderson notes, "it would be instantly
recognizable to anyone who knew it from its founding" (Anderson 1993, 7).

The organizational structure of the university misleads by suggesting that it mirrors reality. Often we simply presume "that the organization of the university rests on some logical necessity, that the order of the disciplines, the specialized fields of study, actually *reflects* the order of nature. We do not even recognize the contrivance. Rather, we suppose there *are* sciences, social sciences, and humanities in perfect triune equilibrium" (Anderson 1993, 6). We are beguiled into thinking that study in the university is in fact the study of the universe, but of course the order of the university is constructed. Departments and courses do not reflect correspondent divisions in reality. It is not natural that departments and disciplines are viewed as self-contained. But the very structure of the university invites this conclusion and the corresponding fallacy of misplaced concreteness—accepting a limited selection from reality as adequately descriptive of it.

## Disconnected Departments

Bruce Wilshire takes these issues considerably further in his argument that the sprawling research university is burdened by deeply engrained organizational structures that, combined with academic professionalism, actually work against educational objectives. Separated as they are, the disciplinary departments of the modern university discourage full analyses of issues. These structures also tend to separate knowledge and experience, theory and application, reflection and practice, thinking and doing. They separate work and the self—one's professional and personal life. Wilshire concludes that the modern university is impoverished because it provides no place to acknowledge and reflect on the person as an intellectual and moral agent. If he is correct, the research university is not a very hospitable context for the collegium. And the research university has been a powerful model for other institutions of higher education.

Following Whitehead on the origins of the modern university, Wilshire argues that the problem with the twentieth-century research university is that its early development incorporated much of the worldview of scientific materialism. Although the principles of seventeenth-century Cartesian-Baconian-Newtonian physics were being challenged at the very time the research university was coming into being, "the revolutionary physics of our century, with its repercussions for reconceiving self and world and for integrating fields of learning, came too late to be incorporated in its structure" (Wilshire 1990, xx). Instead, the formation of the university and much of its ecology reflected the subtle influences of the reigning materialism—ultimate reality is physical, and privileged knowledge relates to the sense-bound data to which positivistic tools provide access.

## *The Positivistic Influence*

The modernistic worldview associated with this materialism has meant that the quantitative is privileged over the qualitative. The subjective is interpreted in terms of the objective. The world is an object to be studied, rearranged, and used. Cause and effect are best understood in mechanical terms, with every higher entity explainable in terms of the lower. Reason is properly utilitarian, oriented to the control and manipulation of things. In short, unilateral power is enshrined. Knowledge is a tool for domination over, rather than reception of, the other. Since they are not sense data, purpose and value are marginalized and the factors that make for personal meaning and self-respect become elusive if not inexplicable. Little room is left for the connected knower in a unified world.

Of course, common sense rebels against this positivistic and reductionistic tradition. Since meaning is primordial—prerequisite for the conduct of all intellectual activity—it must somehow be admitted, even as a stepchild. But the structure of the university replicates the Cartesian separation of thought and extension in the separation and specialization of the disciplines. The concept of knowledge reflected in this inheritance split us into minds and matter, and inquiry about matter remained cognitively privileged. To save the appearances, issues of fact and value are located in different spheres—factual inquiries in a school of sciences, value in a school of arts and humanities. On the surface, this arrangement honors both realms, but it inevitably raises questions about their comparative reality and meaning. This solution attempts to protect the integrity and wholeness of experience, but at the expense of bifurcating it. As a consequence, inquiry relating to issues of value and of meaning often finds itself in a secondary, defensive position. Wilshire describes our inheritance: "Implicit within [the university] project of the production of useful knowledge was a conception of knowledge, and of the knower, which was constricted and outmoded . . . even before it was embodied in the university. It was a conception which . . . tended to invalidate intimacy, freedom, and ethical responsibility. It isolated persons from themselves, others, and Nature" (Wilshire 1990, 33).

Although various theories have been regularly refuted, the influence of the broad positivistic epistemology and world view of scientific empiricism has endured. Other philosophical movements in the twentieth century such as pragmatism, phenomenology, existentialism, linguistic analysis, and the various forms of postmodernism have had their supporters, but these have yet to influence the structure of the university or the basic way it does business. William Sullivan speaks of the implications for the professions of the continuing ethos of positivism and the elevation of technical reason over concern for the social good. Overall, generating and applying information displaces the examination of moral and social good. Trained in the universities, members of professions emphasize technique and expert opinion over the purposes of knowledge. This broad positivisitic elevation of means over ends is also a partial cause, he thinks, for increased public concern about higher education. At the very time that it struggles to cope with increasing change and complexity, society demands of its citizens greater ability to balance multiple goals and purposes—not the narrowly analytic approach of technical reason with its reduction of value to the achievement of maximum instrumental effectiveness. Echoing Wilshire, Sullivan judges the continued seduction of the research university by positivistic technical reason to be "the source of both the narrowness of much of the academy and its nearly invincible self-righteousness" (Sullivan 1995, 171).

## Challenges to Connectivity

In any case, the disciplines continue to divide and separate departments from each other. The research university is rarely able to secure the common commitments and mutual accountability constitutive of a collegium. As commonalities recede, abilities to bridge gaps diminish and knowledge becomes fragmented and confined to departments or factions within them. The larger truths recede and partial perceptions swell. Two possibilities come to define the status quo—a state of constant unrest and conflict between disciplines or an easy, relativistic tolerance. The former is characterized by border disputes, skirmishes, and—on occasion—all-out wars. In the latter, partial perceptions dominate but are rarely pushed to resolution. As a consequence, those in the academy seem in principle unable to adjudicate fundamental disputes. Cynicism if not alienation inevitably results.

Jensen may be accurately reporting alienation and cynicism as deep-seated and endemic among faculties. However, the underlying reason may not be primarily the unevenness of a reward system, as he thinks, but rather the loss of common ground for the pursuit and adjudication of truth claims together with the loss of the self that the academic risks in a partitioned university. If Wilshire is correct, the research university pulverizes and partitions the self. Questions of personal and ultimate meaning cannot be answered. The scholarly ways of knowing are directed elsewhere and self-identity is formed in relation to professionally authorized inquiry. The utilitarian concept of reason is elevated and the grounding for values relativized. The unity of the self is lost, as well as its interdependence with others and its connectedness with communities.

Institutions other than the research university may offer better environments for learning, intellectual debate, and self-understanding. Later we will explore the promise of another model called the New American College. In any case, there are always some individuals and some parts of the research university that defy trends. There are individuals who master several disciplines. There are interdisciplinary centers and projects these individuals create, sometimes supported by external funding in order to study issues no discipline alone can address. There are new disciplines that emerge at the boundaries of the old and cultivate traditional strengths in new and more inclusive settings. And there are those whom Clifford Geertz describes as blurring the genres and boundaries of inquiry (Geertz 1980). But the blurring is not yet dominant and most institutional structures work against it.

Most institutions diminish the likelihood of identifying more general truths by continuing to associate academic inquiries with departmental structures that isolate and separate rather than synthesize and connect. Departments excel at isolating items for study, not relating studies across disciplines. The disciplinary structure of the university focuses on inquiry, but it short-changes and constricts broader concepts of reason. Many have concluded that the university as such is empty of distinctive pedagogical and cognitive commitment. It is "a holding company for the set of organized disciplines" but lacks defining educational purpose itself (Anderson 1993, 29). The university generates parts, not unities. The assessment movement challenges higher education to specify where and how the parts are to be assembled. The relevant question becomes, What does the generally educated person look like? Unfortunately, few institutional curricula provide clear answers.

## Disconnected Curricula

The difficulty institutions have answering this question led the Association of American Colleges (AAC) several years ago to review extensively the connection between the capacities associated with liberating education and the academic, discipline-based majors, where undergraduates spend much of their time and energy. Of specific concern to its task force was the tension between the isolation typical of departmental majors and the broader capacities sought as the fruit of liberal education. How can curricula be fashioned into more coherent instruments designed to address student learning needs?

### Discipline-Preoccupied Majors

Institutional curricula reflect the influence of academic departments. The major becomes the key focus of attention, and prioritizes other organizational energies and activities. Institutional research offices collect data on student choice of majors. Admissions recruitment strategies emphasize the variety and strength of majors. Budgets are structured by majors, and funds flow more rapidly to showcase departments. But little institutional attention is given to majors as integrative of different inquiries. Too much of the burden of integration is left to general education programs. In fact, most faculty look to students to integrate there what they themselves rarely do in their own departments.

Traditional majors are frequently characterized by narrowly drawn boundaries. The departments in which they are located are often self-contained— "little nation-states," Damrosch calls them, "with largely self-contained economies" (Damrosch 1995, 29). Even departmental curricula can become excessively self-referential—preoccupied with procedural and methodological issues internal to the discipline, rather than engaging the world. Ironically, this very absorption in the assumptions and norms of the field often works against adequate second-order reflection on the field itself. Outsiders wonder what the fuss is about or why it's relevant. This self-preoccupation has plagued schools of education and now threatens departments of philosophy and literature. But even the horse-trading with other departments that defines the broader construction of most disciplinary curricula often works to protect boundaries, level tariffs, and secure a favorable balance of trade. Concentration, not connection, seems to be the plan and the result.

The extensive AAC study asked whether there were ways in which academic majors could be part of the solution (AAC 1991). Among its recommendations was that majors help students develop "intellectual habits" rather than simply internalize specialized discourse and subject-matter. These habits would point toward connected learning rather than enculturation within discrete and self-enclosed disciplines. Majors should induct students into the use of specific tools, but the tools should also entail social dimensions pointing to larger realms of connectivity. Rather than abandoning the major, the AAC recommendation was that it play a much greater integrative role, functioning for students as a temporary intellectual center through which they reach out and develop broader competencies. Specialized knowledge should provide a framework for generalizing knowledge, heightening the ability to deal with complexity, change, and contingency. The AAC argument reminds one of Whitehead's thesis that in well-executed specialized study "the external connections of the subject drag thought outwards" (Whitehead 1929, 23). The major as an organizing center incorporates principles of curricular coherence, critical perspective, and connected learning. When it does not play this empowering role, the major imprisons rather than liberates—it is bound by its parochial and limiting dimensions.

A variation of the AAC recommendations is to reconstruct the concept of an academic concentration along the lines of a divisional major. Jaroslav Pelikan endorsed this concept in his study of graduate education where he noted the interdisciplinary character of good scholarly work and argued for "divisional admission to graduate school, together with its counterpart, a divisional major in the college" (Pelikan 1983, 36). Rather than being a pregraduate form of specialization, a divisional major would stand on its own as a "summation and a climax for undergraduate study" (Pelikan 1983, 34). The concept could go far in overcoming the structured fragmentation generated by traditional departments and majors. And at the graduate level it might help address the continuing, cruel oversupply of often narrowly educated doctoral students that the academy has consistently produced in recent decades—though this would also require significant restructuring, and likely "downsizing" of many graduate programs. The question remains whether the guardians of the process can be expected to change what they have worked so hard to establish and replicate.

An additional AAC recommendation was that institutional faculty as a whole review the content and objectives of each major. Often the broader faculty provides extensive review of the general education program but does nothing comparable for the programs with which students identify far more closely and in which they invest much more time and energy. The broader collegium could assume a valuable role in reviewing programs of study that lead to majors—reviews that focus on elements of connectivity and the integrity of the whole. The collective faculty is particularly well-positioned to ask how each major contributes to the overarching goals for all student learning—and through the curriculum to craft institutional statements of what the educated person can know and do.

One alternative to these recommendations is to abandon the major. This is unlikely given faculty and institutional investments, values, and identities as well as common societal expectations. A second alternative is that the academy give up the rhetoric in which breadth, generalized knowledge, and liberalizing competencies are celebrated and valued. This would be widely and correctly seen as a scandalous confession of educational deficiency. Failing either of these undesirable routes, something like the AAC and Pelikan recommendations seem to be in order. Overcoming the separations and disconnections between majors and general education then becomes a task for faculty, chairs, and deans.

### Liberating Education

Our increasingly pluralistic society presents another challenge to curricula built entirely on traditional canons. Such curricula often appear disconnected from the current realities of society and too innocent of the experience of women and of diverse ethnic and racial groups. Learning should combine critical inquiry with greater understanding of multiple communities. The basic objective is to be hospitable while also being thoughtful. Some faculty and institutions appear to consider these objectives incompatible—radical open-ness to the other cannot coexist with standards that define rational inquiry. Those on the "left" allege these very standards reflect a hierarchy of values inevitably political and in the end exclusionary and oppressive. Those on the "right" fear that openness will inevitably lead to the neglect, indeed demise, of an inherited consensus of essential concepts or structures of understanding that define truth and importance. There is usually little openness to the other side and each position expresses unilateral, not relational, power.

This multicultural challenge is part of the larger task of relating the curricula of one department to another. At most institutions, the truths in question are departmental truths and faculty rarely model the wider integra-tion of truths they might privately endorse. Complications are added when knowledge communities are declared incommensurable—that truth pursued within one department or community of inquiry is unavailable to others. Perhaps the academy has yet fully to recover from the impact of the wide-spread decline of the core curriculum in the later 1960s and beyond, for that decline reduced the need for faculty to talk with one another and to collabo-rate on common goods.

## Faculty Governance and Collective Bargaining

The organizational structure of a number of academic institutions includes faculty collective bargaining. What impact do faculty labor unions have on institutional fragmentation? At first glance, a unit formed for the purposes of collective bargaining meets the definition of a collegium. Its members are members of the institution. As union members they appear to have checked some of their dispositions toward insistent individualism. They are united in a common commitment and they may display various forms of reciprocity.

### Issues concerning Collective Bargaining

The most forceful arguments supporting faculty unions occur when they are formed—often in response to perceived violations of academic freedom or other bedrock principles and concepts of the academic enterprise. In these moments the union may appear as a helpful agent in defense of the academy, perhaps supporting its very continuance. The difficulty is that once a faculty union becomes certified, the logic of its justification shifts. At this point the unit falls outside the collegia that constitute the institution. It is now external to the academic community, because the common forms that give collective bargaining units ongoing identity and continuity are defined independently of—and separately from—those internal to the academic collegium.

The primary forms of togetherness in ongoing collective bargaining are neither educational nor intellectual. It cannot be a faculty labor union that grounds a curriculum, deliberates and determines learning objectives, judges that those objectives have been met, and awards degrees; that warrants and assesses claims to knowledge; that inducts new members into knowledge communities; or that assesses their competence and accomplishments. These are roles for the senate and other agencies of the collegium. Rather than enjoying the form of togetherness of a collegium, established collective bargaining units are aggregations of individual interests. Further, the purposes of the ongoing collective bargaining unit are external to the collegium. It seeks goods that are extrinsic to the conduct of inquiry—goods such as salary and working conditions for its members. Its purposes are utilitarian, unconnected in direct fashion to the defining mission and objectives of the institution. The cultivation of hospitality and thoughtfulness means that the collective pursuit of money and unilateral power are always secondary and external to the educational process—never primary and internal. Accordingly, it seems that the very appropriateness of ongoing faculty collective bargaining to academe is inherently debatable.

The simplest argument in support of continued faculty collective bargaining is the convenience and relative stability a contract provides for the conduct of operations. The contract becomes the first point of reference and often dissolves gritty points of dispute. These elements of tradition and convenience can be substantial values. Otherwise, ongoing faculty collective bargaining furnishes few compelling arguments that do not conflict with broader and more fundamental professional values. Indeed, the very passions that bargaining negotiations can arouse risk obscuring significant features of collegial professionalism—especially the concept that a professional works for the good of the client, not the self. During negotiations bargaining units may use the threat of unilateral power through withholding of services to secure a more favorable outcome. Administrations may be similarly belligerent. But tactics of confrontation belittle the rational debate essential to traditional academic collegia. Such maneuvers are at odds with the hospitality and thoughtfulness that must characterize the institution and its activities—in order to distinguish it from other organizations.

### Withholding Services

Additionally, withholding services conflicts with the requirement that professionals attend to the needs of their clients. This is obviously true in the outright refusal to meet classes or laboratories, but even lesser forms of protest generate the same conflict. A slowdown in student advising activity, a decision to withhold grades, or even an avoidance of committee work has bargaining punch only because it neglects students. Diverting attention from the commencement ceremony, for instance, displaces the good of the student with promotion of union interests. Only by an extraordinary argument could the good of the student be presented as requiring such acts. Even information sessions with students risk compromising educational processes and the implicit contract that the professional not use clients to promote his or her personal, economic interests. There seem to be few ways to promote union positions that do not injure the interest of the student.

The collegium may also be injured. At times of negotiation, for instance, polarizing rhetoric can flourish. Those interested in the work of the collegium, intellectual exchange, or just in simple discourse can be ostracized for colluding with the other side. The sense of community falters as do faculty self-understandings of healthy individualism and relational power. A puzzling, perhaps extreme, illustration of this phenomenon is offered by Henry Rosovsky in his reference to a private university collective bargaining agreement that prohibits faculty members from providing recommendations in cases of tenure and promotion (Rosovsky 1990, 198). Here the whole concept of peer review as central to the work of the collegium is repudiated. One hardly knows how to describe what remains and can only speculate about fear that effective peer review would be identified as faculty "management" and render the union vulnerable to decertification. To be sure, an institution may have inadequate peer review without collective bargaining; and collective bargaining need not entail this inadequacy. But it is difficult to deny significant tension between the traditional academic position that professors define and evaluate the faculty as well as manage the curriculum—and the union position that faculty are employees under the authority of others.

There are parallels between ongoing faculty collective bargaining and the academic professionalism of which Wilshire is critical. Paradoxically, the celebration of independent judgment that characterizes the insistent individualist is placed on the back burner—for instance, refusal of a faculty member to pay union or agency dues is rarely considered or permitted as exercise of academic freedom. In both academic professionalism and collective bargaining, members of the professoriate tilt their independence and individuality toward interests of the group narrowly defined—not those of the student, the institution, or the broader public. This tilt is particularly apparent in agreements with no provision beyond promotion for recognition of individual accomplishment. To hope that promotion alone provides sufficient access to this principle dilutes the acuity of discrimination academe prides itself upon in other realms. To hold that the common academic life can do no better than a salary step system in acknowledging individual faculty accomplishments stands in stark tension with its public commitment and confidence to do so thoughtfully regarding student accomplishments.

To be sure, individual campuses have different experiences with faculty collective bargaining. Some enjoy positive and hospitable arrangements that on other campuses contribute to internal fragmentation. But on the whole the analysis presented here points to what is often a problematic element in the academy. Noting that the judge, priest, and scholar represent the only three professions entitled to wear the gown, Rosovsky cites E. K. Kantorowicz: "Why is it so absurd to visualize the Supreme Court Justices picketing their court, bishops picketing their churches and professors picketing their universities? The answer is very simple: because the judges *are* the court, the ministers together with the faithful *are* the church, and the professors together with the students *are* the university" (Rosovsky 1990, 165). Such is the historical concept of the academy; it remains deeply rooted in our traditions. The task is to keep it alive and to address and ameliorate the forces that might fragment and undermine it.

## The Mythology of Academic Leadership

Given the individualism of the academy, the challenge before any academic leader is to create an appropriate unity out of an aggregation of faculty individuals and to foster institutional structures that support integration rather than separation. "Create" may suggest too much; "elicit" may be a better term. It is skills of cooperation and collaboration as well as willingness to share responsibility that leaders should foster—skills and dispositions that both precede and then express relational community, increasing the stability and attractiveness of the collegium. These traits cannot be ordered, commanded, or imposed. The powers of the chair, the dean, or the provost are quite bounded.

### Limits to Leadership

Leaders do not enjoy the aura of expertise that comes from the professional credentialism of the academy. Doctorates in educational administration do not command the cachet associated with traditional disciplinary degrees. Even traditional disciplinary degrees have limited authority or "halo effect" when it comes to academic leadership. Some leaders also struggle with narrow expectations that they resolve the different annoyances and pet peeves of various faculty. Other academic leaders may be confronted with inflated, even lofty, expectations—that the leader address and resolve fundamental financial or structural issues completely out of his or her control.

Difficulties flowing from the radical individualism of faculty and the fragmented organization of the academy are compounded by an unhelpful mythology respecting the value of administrative leadership. The academy has an elaborate set of customs respecting correct behavior and language. One should not readily acknowledge willingness, much less ambition, to become a leader; nor should one highlight prior management experience, for that usually arouses suspicion. Instead, one is advised to downplay what may privately be regarded as a great triumph. Double entendres are okay, such as acknowledging "having done time in administration." Statements by institutional administrators about their ancillary, supporting roles express sentiments that everyone expects, though rarely believes. The successful academic leader needs to honor, while also circumventing, this mythology.

This state of affairs perdures because it is not yet academically permissible to value administration on a par with full-time teaching and research. Not all of the satisfactions academic leaders acknowledge privately can be celebrated publicly. Ironically, it is the individualism of the academy that seems at root in this mythology. For if individuals see themselves as locked in competition with each other rather than enriched by collaboration, then leaders are viewed as opponents rather than colleagues. Power is understood as unilateral, not relational. Leadership is inevitably more necessary and less satisfying in situations illustrating insistent individualism than in those characterized by the relational model.

Such leadership carries its own risks. In the orbit of insistent individualism, academic leaders find themselves pushed toward overstating institutional accomplishments. Achievements are embellished; enrollment numbers and SAT or GRE averages are rounded up, as are levels of annual fund and development campaigns. The fortunes of institutions are often attached to the coattails of energetic, action-oriented leaders—those determined to employ their energy, stamina, imagination, and creativity to advance the standing of the institution, and thereby their own. Few of these individuals are interested in keeping accomplishments hidden, since favorable momentum broadly known is perhaps *the* key to further institutional success. Because leaders in other institutions know this as well, exaggerations occur for fear of risking the health of the institutions they are charged with advancing. Although this behavior is spurred by relatively good intentions, it can quickly become a slippery and dangerous slope. By contrast, leaders in the relational model are cautious about the internal and external consequences of such exaggeration. Statements of vision are distinguished from factual claims. Nuances are carefully employed, with stress on hospitality and openness.

### Administrative Rhetoric

Administrative rhetoric can also contribute to misunderstandings about leadership. Consider Henry Rosovsky's comparison of university faculty to a sports team: "Although the analogy may make some readers uncomfortable, a faculty can be compared to a baseball team—the university president as owner, the dean as manager, the faculty as players, and students, alumni, etc. as spectators" (Rosovsky 1990, 230, n. 5). The metaphor is troubling in several ways. Surely no president would care to be called an owner; trustees are the more likely candidate for this role. And few deans would acknowledge management as their calling or objective. In fact, the "dean as manager" tends to reinforce precisely the wrong concept of leadership and power.

The more problematic features relate to students and faculty. Surely the objective of higher learning is to enlist students into inquiry, to induct them into processes wherein past insights are examined in light of present experience in preparation for tomorrow's demands. To suggest that students are to be sidelined and entertained is precisely the wrong counsel about educational leadership. Likewise, the leadership challenge before department chairs and college deans is to create educational teamwork among the faculty. Teamwork is scarcely the starting point and rarely firmly in place. Rosovsky's description of the tenure award process he favors stresses technical, purely "cerebral" competence as the sole criterion. No importance is attached to professorial concern for others. Questions about whether a candidate will be a "cooperative colleague" are "pointedly omitted" (Rosovsky 1990, 201). Issues of personality and character are deemed irrelevant to the tenure decision and a contrast with Oxford's "clubbiness" is drawn. It is difficult to see how a faculty of carefully chosen and prominent individualists can be celebrated as a team if hospitality and thoughtfulness are dismissed at the outset.

Rosovsky's sports metaphor works no better than his use of the business metaphor that faculty are like shareholders. Shareholders can indeed have an enormous personal stake in a business, depending upon the percentage of their assets invested. Otherwise the metaphor suggests an element of passivity quite contrary to the engagement for which this essay is arguing. Shareholders invest assets, not themselves. For faculty, however, the key investment *is* themselves with special emphasis upon their hospitality and thoughtfulness. Leadership that does not insist upon these virtues creates structures that serve ambiguously the educational values argued for here.

A third comparison, of the faculty to a family, also seems forced. Rosovsky attributes a high degree of exclusiveness to the tenured faculty—suggestive of academic professionalism. Yet he also reaches for the "family" metaphor to describe the collegium—or at least the tenured faculty. As he sees things, "tenure carries the implication of joining an extended family; that is the social contract....The university needs its share of talented people, and professors trade life-long security and familial relationship for lesser economic rewards" (Rosovsky 1990, 184). However, there are major weaknesses in the family metaphor. Academics choose affiliations in a way family members do not;

affiliation with the academy is a voluntary association. As a consequence, faculty have different types of obligation to colleagues than to family members. Relationships in higher education pertain to very specific interests and con-texts. The collegium should be a community of shared purposes and commit-ment to reason, not of shared intimacy.

It is not clear how one is to reconcile these different metaphors. It is difficult to see how the aggressive individualists Rosovsky is prepared to tenure can be expected to function as members either of a team or a family. Yet we are told that "a good academic department should resemble a family: supportive, guiding, and nurturing" (Rosovsky 1990, 176). Rosovsky's metaphors and images illustrate the difficulty of describing positive leadership roles and activities against a background that emphasizes and celebrates the importance of the individualist and the pursuit of unilateral power.

Clearly, academic leaders can be insistent individualists and promote conditions that work against the relational community. Some enjoy flamboy-ant public displays of truly artful and creative, but effectively polarizing, rhetoric. Others find themselves pushed into conflictual situations where falling into such rhetoric is almost irresistible, even though regretted. Pres-sures to secure institutional funding and prestige can push some to practices that work against collegial consultation and other academic values. When these things happen, faculty cynicism and withdrawal are understandable coping mechanisms. To continue to be hospitable in the face of these admin-istrative behaviors can be heroic. Leaders cannot make lasting and construc-tive differences when the culture of academe they are promoting diminishes the collegial value of their efforts.

## Codes of Ethics

Rarely do those in the academy have explicit codes of ethics to govern their activities. Yet reports of ethical lapses have a long history. Clark Kerr cites Adam Smith's complaint about Oxford professors who "make a common cause to be all very indulgent to one another, and every man to consent that his neighbor may neglect his duty provided he himself is allowed to neglect his own" (Kerr 1994a, 9). The very structure of academe can lead to faculty being "very indulgent to one another." Kerr suggests that the key mechanism protecting ethical behavior in the academy has been what he calls "an inner ethic" and traditions handed down in the collegia. As traditions loosen, the issue becomes whether the inner ethic is enough. Kerr thinks not. "In this new situation," he writes, "implicit contracts governing behavior and informal means of enforcement are less effective. They may need, increasingly, to be reinforced by more formal codes of behavior and, particularly, by independent judicial tribunals" (Kerr 1994a, 10).

The codes of behavior that Kerr is calling for are not self-evidently helpful. They tend to be either terse and unexplicated, or bloated and unmanageable. If they are to be more than just compendia of platitudes, codes must provide standards that engage practices. Yet the specification of detail that a code could provide inevitably leaves out of consideration some unforeseen issue. Codes cannot cover every case, and must leave room for the exercise of judgment. Additionally, they are often imprecise because the democratic processes through which they are produced tend to generate less demanding and stringent language.

The difficulty faculty senates experience in devising codes for unprofessional romantic relationships with students illustrates the challenge. In a matter seemingly straightforward to an unsympathetic public, few faculty senates have been able to promulgate clear policies condemning these relationships, and rarely do they carry sanctions. On one hand, faculty opposed to the intrusion of others into what they consider private and personal matters see the very proposal of a code as unacceptable. On the other hand, faculty arguing for a clear public statement of unacceptable behavior can be disappointed by its imprecision and vagueness. To the public eye, matters seem altogether uncomplicated. Faculty have a position of trust, and this position involves unequal distributions of power. How, then, can a faculty member credibly assert that a romantic or sexual relationship with a student is not problematic as long as it is consensual? And what faculty members in their right minds would take advantage of their positions to inflict upon students unwelcome expressions of sexuality? What on earth does any of this have to do with academic freedom? And why, therefore, does the academy resist taking firm, unequivocal measures?

## The Absence of Adequate Guidelines

As the future of higher education becomes more challenging and uncertain, the low profile of national standards of behavior and the absence of common sanctions for flagrant violations become more glaring. Many disciplinary and functional associations have developed specialized codes for their members, but there is nothing comparable for all institutions or the entire professoriate. Even codes of disciplinary associations usually lack enforcement punch. Few associations seem interested in reviewing credentials and making membership decisions attesting to competence and integrity. Most of their codes are statements of recommended behavior but include no sanctions or implementation mechanisms. Unlike the associations of those practicing law or medicine, academic associations rarely act to ensure the integrity of members. Without enforcement mechanisms, disciplinary codes risk being hortatory artifacts—perhaps helpful in reminding members and the public of expected behaviors, but ineffective in bringing even outrageous cases to judgment. The academy as a whole appears to have little interest in anything that explicitly summarizes basic moral standards and commitments, identifies unacceptable behaviors, and contains enforcement mechanisms, reminding all educators and institutions of normative expectations.

The closest example is the infrequently referenced American Association of University Professors' Statement on Professional Ethics, a document not adopted until 1966, long after the famous AAUP Statement on Academic Freedom and Tenure was constructed in 1940. It is clear that faculty rights and prerogatives have been emphasized well ahead of faculty obligations. To be sure, in the 1940 statement faculty are enjoined to "be accurate . . . exercise appropriate restraint [and] show respect for the opinions of others" (AAUP 1995, 4). Obviously, this terse explication of ethical dimensions of the academic workplace provided little guidance for real-world situations and conveyed the disinterest of the academy in addressing issues of obligations.

The 1966 statement is more detailed and identifies five areas. The first section emphasizes the importance of individual commitment to the growth and improvement of one's scholarly competence. Other sections stress encouragement of student learning and protection of their academic freedom, obligations to colleagues that flow from membership in the community of scholars, obligations to the institution and the paramount responsibility to be an effective teacher-scholar, and the broad responsibility to society to promote conditions of free inquiry. Although a welcome improvement, the 1966 statement has been judged too short, incomplete, and lacking provisions for implementation (Rich 1984, 142). The AAUP has periodically issued other statements on various topics such as affirmative action and sexual harassment, but it seems clear that rights rather than obligations of the professoriate are its main concern.

Even recognition of the absence of codes of ethics is instructive. Usually one looks for codes when a profession is declining in coherence and vitality. A healthy and vigorous profession carries a natural understanding by participants of appropriate behaviors and does not require a code of ethics. The call for more formal codes by Clark Kerr and others is a comment not only on the academy, but also on our times. For increasingly, the efficacy of tacit self-regulation has slipped in much of society. Accordingly, codes of desirable and acceptable behavior have become hallmarks of many other professions and a profession that lacks one risks appearing self-preoccupied and less than vigorous. Codes are collective artifacts. They represent efforts of a profession to identify responsible behavior and assist individuals in ethical decision-making, to clarify appropriate rules and principles, and to protect those who follow relevant rules and principles. Professions that fail to assist members through codes seem deficient. When implicit understandings no longer work, the explicit becomes necessary.

## Setting a National Standard

A common code of ethics for the academy could play at least two beneficial functions. External to higher education, a national code would assure public stakeholders as well as potential customers that institutions, their faculty, and other employees will be expected to provide certain services and to observe high standards. This function would be directed outward—to reassure the public that its interests are served and that institutions and faculties may be trusted. A common code could also educate the public about the workings and commitments of the academy. Internal to higher education, a national code would provide institutions, faculty, and others a statement of ideals as well as standards of appropriate conduct and unacceptable behaviors. Perhaps with a national academic code, the prospect of the possible termination of a tenured professor for excessive absences from assigned classes would not merit a story in the national education press. And it might not require two years for a university to dismiss a professor who simultaneously held tenured positions at two major research institutions without telling either.

As things stand now, the AAUP code of ethics reserves decisions about faculty conduct (including rebuke and dismissal) solely to institutions, even though the AAUP insists upon its prerogative to censure any institutional decision. Likewise, codes issued by disciplinary associations may specify appropriate behaviors and proscribe the unacceptable, but they leave enforcement to the institution. These codes fail to acknowledge that authority is rooted in the disciplines, not in the institutions. Since peer review is ultimately grounded in authorized or certified expertise, as judged by those in the discipline, the college or university is dependent upon what may be reluctant judgments of others even though it is responsible to the public for the decisions it makes. The current arrangement places the first line of responsibility at the institutional level without a higher, national structure.

In sum, most academic institutions wrestle with the many challenges of disconnection generated by insistent individualism and unilateral power. The outdated, problematic world view on which the modern university was organized continues to separate and divide. Departments promote specialization and separation rather than breadth and unity of inquiry. Disciplinary distinctions are reified into curricular fragmentation. Typical institutional structures, sometimes exacerbated by faculty collective bargaining, dictate that faculty, administrators, and students define themselves against one another. Leaders are burdened by mythologies that do not serve the health of the institution. Codes of ethics stand only at the margins. Connectivity and integration are hampered by these energies toward separation and isolation. These energies also tend to push institutions away from closer engagement with the public—engagement that properly cultivated could benefit both institution and society.

## INSTITUTIONAL CONNECTIONS WITH SOCIETY

To be sure, the hoary image of the cloistered and ivoried tower suggests a disconnection from society that rarely reflects current facts. Society increasingly looks to colleges and universities to educate the work force and produce graduates with professional skills as well as civic and global awareness. However imperfect the campus response, curricula and institutional self-consciousness are far more globally oriented today than they were only a decade ago. The assessment movement has heightened institutional attention to competencies to be developed in students, many of which also relate directly to community service and civic awareness. Additionally, institutions of all kinds, not just land-grant colleges and universities, are now multipurpose, pursuing a variety of public service, research, and instructional activities simultaneously. Only a few decades ago academics would not have been regarded as news makers. Today, however, scientific discoveries, economic and political analyses, and cultural developments join with athletic accomplishments to become "news items" of interest to the surrounding communities (Shils 1984). Expert witnesses are drawn from academic ranks; professors and administrators serve on committees at all levels of government, in executive and congressional activity, and in the development, critique, and reform of public policy; research of all kinds is conducted; technology transfer is effected; and political squabbles and financial debacles within institutions receive media attention and comment. These developments convey the complexity of the academy and the many ways in which it is linked with society, not isolated from it.

### Shaping Societal Values

There is also an element of remoteness. The public often sees higher education as disconnected from common values and concerns—as reflected in the common expression that something is "only academic." Large parts of society are deeply troubled by crime, drugs, teen-age pregnancy, and other forms of anomie. Poverty, urban decay, struggling primary and secondary schools, and illiteracy abound. Environmental degradation continues and the increase in our national standard of living has not kept pace with other countries. Relief may be available in the learning and research conducted in the university. As a custodian of knowledge the university has moral responsibilities toward the well-being of society. Institutions need to model applied knowledge. The persistent divisiveness of race in our society suggests that universities and colleges also have opportunities to shape better race relations. Likewise, values institutions display in their stock portfolio selections, their speech codes, and their competition with other institutions for prestige and resources present opportunities for contributing to public awareness of social issues. The growing internationalism of our times raises questions regarding the society to which the university has obligations—given tensions between obligations to the good of our society (its citizens, economy, and defense) and that of the international community. Universities could contribute more to public discussion and education on these issues.

In addition, institutions could be better models of interinstitutional cooperation. Although no longer cloistered, they are not yet patterns of connectedness in which individual strengths are recognized and leveraged in common, extensive consortia. Most are insistent individualists at the institutional level, locked in struggles for students, funding, prestige, and other resources. Rankings in the media polls and guidebooks are followed closely while criticized as unscientific and misleading. Even campuses that are part of a system of institutions jealously guard their prerogatives and resources, seeing others as competitors as much as collaborators. It is unfortunate that, at the very time when unprecedented interdependence is upon us in global competition, communications technologies, and ecological realities, institutions of higher education seem isolated from each other and from the broader public.

## Maintaining Distance

Some boundaries between academe and society are essential. Efforts to promote connectivity must be balanced by appropriate distinctions. Institutions of higher education must thread a line between absorption by society, and excessive separation and isolation from it. Campus turmoil respecting the war in Vietnam or investment in South Africa reminds us of the cost to institutions that construe their educational mission too broadly. Becoming identified with a partisan issue impedes the ability of the college or university to maintain critical distance as well as its capacity to attract resources. On both counts, political activity can jeopardize fundamental educational missions. If it is to be a viable center of value, the college or university must remain in some ways independent of society, while connected to it.

This internal, institutional need for distance goes against the more aggressive forms of academic advocacy currently fashionable. Those who maintain that neutrality is impossible and that reason is inevitably in the service of power not only argue against themselves, but they also undermine any rationale for public support of educational institutions. It is better to recognize that though neutrality in the most strict sense may be beyond human powers, intellectual fairness is not. It is a key value that must be preserved and honored in academe. And fairness requires that academic value judgments be openly identified and support provided. It is not absence of values that establishes objectivity, but rather self-consciousness about their presence and openness to their revision.

Externally, institutional independence means resisting inappropriate intrusion into institutional operations as well as contesting expectations that contributions to regional economic development should come ahead of education. Indeed public expectations can themselves be at cross purposes—as when the request for extensive research on economic productivity clashes with the demand for more teaching.

## FACING THE CHALLENGES

The responsibility of setting a standard for society while maintaining distance and other challenges require that institutions pay considerable attention to educating the public, providing candid reports on essential institutional purposes and success in meeting them, and effecting industry-wide self-regulation.

### Educating the Public

Some skepticism about institutions of higher education seems related to uncertainty about their mission and effectiveness—uncertainty insufficiently addressed by institutional public relations initiatives, other educational activities, or by accreditation, the chief mechanism for assuring the public that educational institutions are effectively self-regulated. In taking ourselves for granted, we assume others do as well—another illustration of a comfortable self-preoccupation that plagues academe. As A. Bartlett Giamatti observed, "of all the threats to the institution, the most dangerous come from within. Not the least among them is the smugness that believes the institution's value is so self-evident that it no longer needs explication, its mission so manifest that it no longer requires definition and articulation" (Giamatti 1988, 25). It is just such privatization that needs to be addressed.

### Speaking the Languages of Business

For instance, the academy needs to become more fluent in speaking the languages of business—not only to the public, but also to the trustees, regents, and other friends who mediate interests of the academy to the public and vice versa. To insist upon speaking and using only languages of the academy conveys a palpable disrespect for those whose interest academe claims to serve. It risks misunderstanding and invites indifference and disregard. The increasing calls for assessment reflect public uncertainty about the effects and accomplishments of higher education and provide opportunity for campuses to speak of their goals and successes. The continuing resistance to assessment can be read by the public as another example of the difficulty academe has in applying to itself principles it applies to others.

Some might interpret this reluctance as evidence of philosophical positivism—that "good" or "better" is just an expression of feeling, a noncognitive statement. But such positivism is at odds with the typical insistence of the academy that cognitive judgments can and should be made—about others. Even allowing for qualifications for those working within various postmodernist movements, ambivalence about assessment is more likely a failure to carry out fully the principles and commitments the academy does possess and otherwise insists upon. Differences between educational and other activities are correctly emphasized but wrongly used to argue that educational quality cannot be adequately assessed. Efforts to keep private what ought to be public only impedes support for other efforts at excellence.

### Reversing Privatization

The public knows too little about the research and teaching activities of the academy. Reports on research activities are often addressed to a small group of fellow enthusiasts and couched in forbidding, technical languages. Insufficient energies are given review essays or other efforts to provide readable overviews and assessments of the state of a discipline—reviews within which current developments could be located and explicated. Professors need to enlarge the constituency for which they think and write to include the environing society—thereby making private research more publicly accessible and socially useful. Certainly the condemnation of clear writing as popularizing has yet to be aggressively challenged within the academy.

Likewise, teaching activities need to be more clearly presented to the public. Outsiders hear about teaching indirectly from children or from friends' children and from what the ratings and press report. Even department faculty may be unable to answer questions about what their colleagues are doing. Academe must be prepared to explain more clearly the reasons for its practices—or change them. And we should be prepared for challenge. We should present more publicly the warrants supporting our teaching practices and consider alternative possibilities—such as the successes businesses report in providing remedial and technical education. For the gatekeeping function of the academy is disappearing as others gain access to expert knowledge. In any case, authority—even intellectual authority—must be justified. Good reasons must be presented both for the curriculum and for claims made on its behalf. The academy can no longer credibly hold that its autonomy rests on knowledge, the validity of which can be assessed only by itself. This was always a circular argument and now it has even less force.

Other initiatives are also in order. Surely few would claim that tenure is well-understood by the public. It is widely seen as an academic perk that increasingly identifies the professoriate as a privileged and protected class in a country experiencing great social and economic change. As we noted, there are suspicions that psychologically it is a liability, since any sinecure can become a burden. Many see tenure as shielding the professoriate from accountability, if not, in some cases, protecting the grossly incompetent. Instead of tenure symbolizing the disconnection of faculty from the broader society and a special shelter for a select group unrelated to demonstrated need or accomplishment, it could ensure academic freedom for all. Tenured faculty could accept responsibility to make the award of tenure more a bestowal of an obligation to protect freedom for all than just a right to enjoy it individually.

## The Need for Greater Candor

Institutions also need to address more directly the issue of candor with the public. It is understandable that institutions make the most of favorable quantitative rankings and issue positive public relations reports somewhat out of proportion to supporting realities. Institutions are in competition with each other and accentuating the positive generates resources for the improvement of education. Additionally, selective reporting of internal developments is regarded as a common practice—why penalize one's own institution?

### Inaccurate Data

On the other hand, truth-telling should be a special obligation for higher education and questions should be raised when information is withheld or the accuracy of information released is in doubt. Yet for some time there have been problems with reliability of data released by institutions on recruitment, admissions, and retention policies and accomplishments. A full decade ago there were troubling journalistic reports on widespread "fudging" of SAT scores (Long 1992, 132). The issue was how campuses reported data to the media and the college-guide publications that rank institutions. One questionable practice was identified as "NIPS"—selectively withholding information on specially admitted, international, or transfer students on the grounds that it is "not in the profile" of the normal or preferred matriculating student. Misleading impressions were created, leading the public to make inaccurate comparative judgments.

Media attention a decade ago did not lead to solutions. In addition to test scores, questionable self-reported data now include class size, financial aid, budgets, and other indices. The title of a recent article is telling—"Cheat Sheets: Colleges Inflate SATs and Graduation Rates in Popular Guidebooks." The article analyzes such misleading practices as "cooking" the numbers or rounding them upwards, justified because competing institutions are perceived to engage in similar practices. "In their heated efforts to woo students, many colleges manipulate what they report to magazine surveys and guidebooks—not only on test scores but on applications, acceptances, enrollment and graduation rates" (Stecklow 1995, 1). The article points out that many institutions report different, more accurate, numbers to debt-rating agencies. In suggesting an explanation, the article notes that there are substantial federal penalties for misreporting data to debt-rating agencies, but none for misrepresenting figures to the media.

The public, as well as those in higher education, should be able to count on more accuracy in the marketing of institutional services and products. Without a controlling commitment to the truth, faculty and institutions simply become agitators for special interests. Efforts within the higher education community to address the insistent individualism of institutions have been sparse and largely ineffectual. In recent decades a series of self-regulatory efforts sponsored by the American Council on Education did appear. Attention focused on dissemination of different principles of good practice as identified by various lead agencies and supported by a rough consensus of institutional leaders. Examples include statements on appropriate principles governing tuition refund and standards for determining good academic standing. Other efforts involved extensive attention to various athletic scandals. But until recently nothing at the associational level had emerged respecting common practices for figures submitted in college ranking processes.

Rankings that reflect and incorporate subjective assessments of relative prestige (however reported) are naturally debatable. However, there ought to be agreement about more measurable items. Recently a college president proposed a common set of understandings and definitions to control the submission of data (Rothkopf 1996, B5). He also suggested a collective, industry-wide effort to audit data submitted to verify accuracy. It is gratifying to read that college presidents, campus researchers, and publishers are interested in being more accountable in the use of a common set of data forms, structured by over 100 carefully defined terms. Considerably less progress, however, has occurred in the development of a common validation process. Without an effective version of verification as well as common understandings of good and acceptable practice, there will still be opportunity and reasons to report data in creative, idiosyncratic ways—despite variances from other reports.

### Ever-Increasing Costs

In addition to public concern about the effectiveness and integrity of higher education, there is growing apprehension about its cost. Society cannot tolerate ever-increasing costs of higher education at the level of the consumer price index plus 2 percent. Some observers point to the health industry as a warning, where public concerns about ever-increasing costs were addressed quickly. In the process, physicians found their privileges reduced. Professors and institutions should take heed, some say, for the market will work its way. At a minimum the academy needs to redefine productivity in terms of increased learning rather than increases in the number of students taught, though this will require greater attention to assessment. The public and the media should be helped to see reasons for the higher educational price index. Institutions can also be more candid in acknowledging that a low percentage of applicants awarded admission can be a judgment on the inefficiency of an institutional recruitment process as much as a statement of high quality. And the codes of ethics that, to their credit, some of the specialized functional associations—such as the membership organizations of institutional advancement officers and fund-raisers—have developed should be given more attention and force.

The academy should also work harder at promoting the values of diversity. Additional effort could be expended both internally and externally. Internally, resistance to effective affirmative action continues and dialogue is often difficult. Greater hospitality to the values of diversity needs to be cultivated. Externally, the academy needs to address the skepticism of legislators and other public figures that value to the commonwealth is created through various programs of equal opportunity and affirmative action in higher education.

## Accreditation

Accreditation presents a distinct opportunity not only for more effective self-regulation within higher education, but also for greater communication with the public. For the public does not know much about the processes or meaning of accreditation—whether institutional or programmatic—as a key self-regulatory mechanism. Neither the extent of self-regulation nor the extraordinary amount of time and energy committed to it by peer volunteers and representatives of the public is understood. Both institutions and accreditation associations have been too quiet about what they do and how they function. Indeed, accreditation processes taken for granted by department chairpersons and deans may not be understood even by other faculty. Aggressive educational and public affairs campaigns are in order, together with clearer and more accessible statements about what accreditation does and does not mean.

### Self-Study and the Site Visit

Institutional accreditation is the chief self-regulatory instrument for maintaining institutional excellence and autonomy while also providing accountability to the public. Accreditation occurs at two levels—the institution as a whole and specific programs within the institution. There are regional accrediting bodies and specialized accrediting agencies. Common to accreditation activities are the preparation of a self-study and a subsequent site visit by a team of peers focusing on such matters as the adequacy of resources, processes, governance, mission, and so forth. Accrediting commissions that include public members receive the self-study and the report of the visiting team and judge whether to grant or extend accreditation, to deny or withdraw it, or to place the institution or program on probation.

Preparation of the self-study provides members of the program or institution an opportunity to assess whether hospitality and thoughtfulness are sufficiently prominent educational goals and to determine the degree to which they are achieved. The point of the external review and site visit is to judge compliance with agency standards, identify deficiencies and stipulate their remediation, and offer suggestions for improvement. Inherent in this accreditation mechanism is tension between the two objectives of encouraging institution and program improvement, and providing public assurances that appropriate levels of quality are in place. Each objective represents an important set of values, but they may not easily coexist. Additionally, agency review usually focuses on the clarity of an institution's statement of mission and the adequacy of organizational structure, faculty, and other resources to support and implement the mission. A variety of different conceptions of the educated person easily follows from different missions. The public, however, may take accredited status to assure the adequacy of a widespread, popular concept of education that may not even be sought, much less achieved, by the institution. Thus, accreditation can raise issues of consistency as well as quality.

### National Standards

It is noteworthy how infrequently accreditation is mentioned in recent critiques of the academy. Its role as either problem or solution goes without comment. Even among the knowledgeable, there can be fatigue at having worked hard at accreditation yet not having achieved a certain standard. Perhaps more consideration should be paid to the value of different accrediting configurations, such as transforming regional associations into national, sector-specific agencies, thereby clarifying for the public the special character and mission of various types of higher education institutions. As it is now, geography alone serves as the reason why an institution is located within a regional agency. By contrast, national institutional accreditation by sector could highlight more publicly the special characteristics particular to a type of institution, the standards by which it is to be judged, and the special excellence to which it aspires. Together with selective release of accreditation findings, this change might go some distance in helping to educate the public and reduce reliance on misleading journalistic rankings.

Support for national standards for membership eligibility in accrediting associations is grounded in part in the public perception that regional differences may mask differences in quality—precisely at a time when regional location and traditions are receding in importance. Three factors seem to be at work. First, the very existence of program-specific accrediting agencies suggests a national emphasis already well advanced. Emphasis upon national standards does risk diminished diversity and increased homogenization but the risks could probably be contained, much as they are now within regional practices. Second, international programs themselves already encompass transregional issues and concerns, and the increasing use of telecommunications technology suggests that geographical boundaries may become irrelevant to delivery of some types of education. Third, several students of higher education hold that multiple accreditations for institutions will increase with the globalization of the marketplace (Lenn 1996). Professional education is likely to lead the way in crafting transnational and, eventually, global educational standards, licensure, and certification. Propelled by regional and global trade agreements, such developments will lead to increasingly blurred national borders. It seems inevitable that regional accreditation will be antiquated— perhaps sooner rather than later.

### Increasing Public Understanding

In any case, there is value in making public more detailed, selective information about accreditation findings—about the quality of programs and institutions as reflected in self-studies and as judged by peer review. For instance, special emphasis might be placed upon the extent and adequacy of the internal structures institutions create to monitor, support, and enhance their academic excellence. Making more information public will be difficult to effect; it goes against longstanding practices of confidentiality enshrined both in institutions and in accrediting agencies. Traditional preoccupations with privacy and the obvious tension with competitive pressures support the status quo. Understandably, no institution wants to place itself at a competitive disadvantage in attracting students and resources. Expecting institutions voluntarily to release detailed plans that address self-identified deficiencies is unrealistic, and only areas commonly understood to relate directly to quality should be considered. Those institutions sufficiently sure of themselves will need to take the lead, thereby encouraging others to follow. But without more openness, the essence of the educational mission is obscured and the loss of public support risked. Unless the public learns more about the meaning of accreditation as well as some of its outcomes, people can hardly be expected to view it as a reliable and effective mechanism of self-regulation.

Increasing public understanding may also address some of its flaws. For accreditation presents opportunities for unilateral as well as relational power. The former occurs when individual agencies become more concerned about guild or program interests narrowly defined than about the context in which education is provided. Recent events in the accreditation of law schools by the American Bar Association illustrate. Only as an outcome of the settlement by the ABA of a Justice Department investigation in June, 1995, did the public learn that law school faculty and administration salaries had been viewed by the ABA accrediting process as important surrogates for educational quality. Of course, individual salaries are at best only very indirect indices of quality, and quality education is hardly inherently correlated with a median salary. Indeed, salaries often reflect a variety of individual circumstances quite unconnected with program or institutional integrity. Yet in the ABA collection of individual salary data, no apparent allowance was made for level or quality of prior service or experience, for length of service at the present institution, or—most importantly—for the quality of objectives and accomplishments in the period in question. These were obvious reasons for not relying upon ABA surveys to supply meaningful data about either the appropriateness of the salaries themselves or the quality of education provided.

In at least 42 states individuals can sit for the bar examination only if they are graduates of ABA-accredited law schools. The necessity of maintaining or exceeding ABA-provided means and mediums respecting salaries gave law faculties and schools important potential leverage over their parent institutions. Further insight into the collection of salary information is available in one of the official interpretations of Standard 405a—the ABA Standard that approved law schools shall have salaries sufficient to attract and retain competent faculty. Interpretation 2 of this Standard indicated that a faculty salary structure that ranks at the bottom of ABA-approved law schools is "presumptively in non-compliance with the Standards." It takes but a moment's reflection to realize that logically only one salary ranking is ultimately in compliance! In fact, only as a condition of the settlement with the Justice Department did the ABA agree to stop collecting and using this salary information in considering and judging compliance with standards of accreditation. While concession to external pressure may be viewed as harming the industry seal of approval that accreditation ought to symbolize, in the long run it should be healthy in redirecting attention to the quality of programs, not the narrow financial interests of a guild. At least in this case, making public what had been private is likely to promote the common good.

## CONCLUSION

We have examined a number of issues that contribute to institutional fragmentation and separation. The tendency of the academy to institutionalize disciplinary divisions works against enriching interchange and effective curricula. These institutional structures impede contributions of one department or school to another, and they reinforce individuals in their isolation and disconnection. Collective bargaining and codes of ethics often work against rather than assist collegial professionalism. Hampered by unhelpful mythologies and insistent individualists, academic leaders can be part of the problem. Rather than educating the public or promoting greater institutional candor and more effective accreditation, leaders often express and reinforce organizational insistent individualism.

The tools of the academy should be used to study and open itself to correction and improvement. None of us is a stranger to moral insufficiency. Observing correctly that others fall short of their ideals should not spare educators or their institutions from similar scrutiny. None is immune to contradiction or to corruptions. And enlightened self-interest must note that growing public criticism spells trouble. So on moral, professional, and prudential grounds, it is in the self-interest of the academy to examine critically some of what it treats as intellectual sanctuary. Careful, patient, yet creative examination that yields change is in order. Endless collection of data will be correctly perceived as stonewalling and special pleading. The academy needs reflective, but far more energetic, self-regulation. We need to resist the attractions of insistent individualism and celebrate the virtues of the relational community. The next two chapters focus on resources the relational model provides.

# CHAPTER 5

# Relationality in Teaching and Scholarship

Most academics treasure their freedom to structure and direct their work, to be guided by their own best lights, and to put a distinctive stamp upon their teaching and scholarship. This freedom is rare and, in contrast to many in other professions, we in the academy are indeed fortunate. But the private individualist moments are not enough. The ethos of independent work is diminished if commonalities are not acknowledged and collegiality cultivated. We have recognized that the solitary dimension of the professor's life presumes and depends upon collective dimensions. As Loomer reminds us, "we are at once communal and solitary individuals. But the solitariness of individuality is lived out only in the midst of constitutive relationships" (Loomer 1976, 20). Some academic behaviors suggest otherwise, but in truth we are deeply dependent upon one another. Failing adequately to acknowledge this dependence, we retard our intellectual and professional interests as well as those of colleagues, students, and the community; and we experience less personal satisfaction and fulfillment. We have suggested that insistent individualism accounts for some of the malaise and alienation that Jensen, Tompkins, and Lovett report.

We turn now to teaching and scholarship and argue that they are far more communal than the individualistic model suggests. Celebrated as moments of potentially intense personal and individual creativity, private moments of teaching and scholarship always presuppose a public moment defined by work of others. For completion they must then turn into another public moment wherein the fruits of privacy are available to be tested by others and to enrich others. Insistent individualism focuses only on the middle stage, emphasizing private self-initiative, and downplaying both roots and outcomes. No inquiry starts in a void and there is always some public outcome: presentation to others through formal reports, examinations, publications, symposia, lectures, performances, works of art, or informally through conversations or e-mail communications. In the relational model one is aware of the constant move-ment from public to public by way of private. Some form of community precedes and follows the individual act. These public dimensions may be neglected, but are never absent.

## TEACHING AND LEARNING

However private and solitary a professor's teaching appears, it never occurs apart from some context of community. Faculty prefer it to appear private. Few welcome colleagues or other visitors to the classroom. Visitations for purposes of evaluation are scheduled for the better classes, not ones where colleagues could provide suggestions about trying students and difficult topics. Many faculty still resist the notion that students can evaluate authoritatively aspects of teaching about which they are obvious experts—such as the instructor's clarity, punctuality, and availability. And it is the rare individual who discloses even to confidantes the moments of agony that teaching can involve.

Yet teaching presupposes community and has a necessary public character. It is not simply that others are also in the room or that they may be more effective agents of instruction to each other than is the professor. The point is also that any course is part of a larger project. Good teaching begins with colleagues discussing the specific purposes and objectives of individual courses. Central organizational questions, rules of evidence and interpretation, design of assignments, and methods of examination are discussed. At some point the conversation moves outside the department—into the school or the college, where broader competencies are to be nourished. These conversations address evidence that the competencies can be accomplished, given the students who enroll and their different learning styles and degrees of preparation. Col-leagues may argue for alternative assignments and texts. Hospitality means willingness to review preconceptions and revise even longstanding canons.

Subsequently, there should be periodic, collective efforts to determine whether objectives and competencies are accomplished. Members of strongly collegial departments discuss curricular issues, examine student evaluation techniques, and report to each other on individual grading practices. These discussions of department pedagogy are rigorous and intentional. They paral-lel department discussions about candidates for appointment and promotion. Far from the individual course being private property and a discrete, unconnected entity, it is from beginning to end part of a communal and collaborative project. It is in that sense community property, "owned" in common by department colleagues. It is public in its roots and its outcomes. The question may be whether an individual practice honors this communal context—it should not be whether the context is appropriate.

## Meeting the Objectives of Teaching

Faculty who teach essentially the same materials in different courses (in effect, the same course under different titles) are not exercising academic freedom. They are violating the contract the institution has with students and the understandings of faculty colleagues. Those who teach a different course from what the catalogue promises and who fail to address the materials and course objectives that others are expecting, provide a disservice to students, colleagues, and the curriculum itself—as do those who provide an advanced curriculum in an elementary class, or vice versa, or who evaluate only once in an introductory course. These are obvious failings, scarcely worth noting but for their frequency. They reflect the separatism of the individualist faculty member or department and suggest that each course is self-contained, having no connection to other inquiries. They also suggest that others need not be faithful to representations made in public documents. However common, these practices violate the collegial ethic and display neither hospitality nor thoughtfulness.

Teaching is deficient when it is a solitary act. It should not be likened to "downloading" inert data to passive learners. Downloading is simply the latest deplorable metaphor for the nature of instruction. Earlier metaphors included "filling" and "stocking"—presumably empty minds. These images are too passive and individualistic. The passivity may reflect student desire to escape responsibility for their learning, but it may also reveal faculty preference for familiar, controlling pedagogies. The individualism downplays the corporate character of learning—ways in which we help one another learn. Without genuine engagement and interaction, teaching probably *is* like the transmission of fluids, cartons, or data into separate receptacles; but this is a degraded concept of teaching. As Whitehead noted, "so far as the mere imparting of information is concerned, no university has had any justification for existence since the popularization of printing in the fifteenth century" (Whitehead 1929, 93).

Teaching as mere transmission requires no commitment to the process of inquiry. The pace of change in knowledge, the range of its application, and the rate of global connections is increasing so rapidly, that lasting education is rooted in grasping the process of inquiry rather than its product. Transmission stands back from issues of epistemology, of what we can properly be said to know and why. It bypasses discussions that make for advances in knowledge. It overlooks the relationship of what is known to the knower. Surely the overarching objective of teaching is not primarily to transmit information. It is to initiate and support the process of inquiry; and inquiry is always teleological—guided by some purpose or end. The point of teaching is to initiate particular individuals into new processes of inquiry and discovery—to think about the text or the practice and to think with it; to facilitate acquisition and use of the new language, concepts, and rules, to be able to do something with them; to elicit the desire to improve upon prevailing practice, desire fueled by the felt gap between current practice and a governing ideal; and to raise questions about the personal meaning of this new inquiry.

## Education as Opposed to Instruction

The distinction between the Latin roots of "instruction" and "education" is often noted. Instruction comes from *instruere*—it means to build in, suggestive of teaching as transmission. The instructor is the active one, the student the recipient. The object is to provide exposure to a field, to give coverage, and to instill. By contrast, education comes from *educare*—to draw students out of themselves as private selves so that they initiate their own learning, take responsibility for it, and ultimately confront and establish their identity as learners. In both cases, the authentic faculty member is faithful to the good of the student. But education cannot be forced, only invited.

The notion of learning as rooted in impersonal, objective neutrality leaves it unexplained. There is no internal engine to push or pull learning; but learning as an expression of an internal desire or drive is a different matter altogether. Cultivating curiosity as the wellspring of learning is fundamentally important. The classic American pragmatists emphasized resolution of problems, perplexities, or doubts as the key factor energizing experiential learning. Whitehead's stress upon interest or wonder—what he called the stage of romance—addresses much the same point, though without the potentially troubling element of control or manipulation that pragmatism can introduce. For inquiry to catch fire and continue, there must be the romance that skillful teachers know how to spark and engage.

Wonder is different from skepticism. Inducing skepticism at the outset is rarely a good way to initiate inquiry. Skepticism suggests certainty as an appropriate standard; but certainty is rarely attained even in the best of cases, and seeking it at the outset can result in understandably alienated students. Far better to arouse interest and wonder first and then later introduce the destabilizing but productive turmoil that skepticism can generate. Some teachers elicit interest by publicly sharing parts of their own ongoing discoveries in the relevant texts and topics, applying them to the issues at hand, and enticing others to do likewise. This is a form of teaching by example and requires that the instructor model intellectual excellence in both ownership and conduct of the inquiry. For we teach by example as well as by word, by action as well as by lecture. Good teaching cannot be divorced from good scholarship.

## Process, Logic, and Particular Students

Understood this way, teaching focuses on the process of the inquiry and its logic—the reasoning by which insight is gained, a theory derived, or a hypothesis supported. The point is to see and follow the inquiry from inside—to understand the questions asked, presuppositions involved, and conceptual consequences and linkages with other inquiries. Student inertia and resistance to new ideas and viewpoints must be overcome. Good teachers resist students' desire to locate authority within the instructor and thus to be passive. Authority ingredient in the inquiry is to be emphasized, not the authority of the professor or his or her membership in a disciplinary guild. The good of the students to be served includes cultivating their desire and ability to seek that good themselves. The better the teaching, the better the public representation of the process of discovery—selected as relevant to the particular students one has, and designed to initiate and extend their own participation. Announcing "I will be your teacher" to a class is a pledge of significant responsibility, even though frequent repetition may obscure its significance. It is a pledge and the offer of a covenant that in principle can alter the world of those to whom it is provided. Even the world of its provider can be transformed.

The obligation to tailor inquiry to the talents and preparation of particular students is implied in the mission to advance knowledge. Faculty are agents of the institution and knowledge is not advanced if learning is not facilitated. This is part of both hospitality and thoughtfulness. Hospitality acknowledges the circumstances of the individual as inherent in facilitating his or her learning. And thoughtfulness requires that inquiry be both considered and considerate. Learning objectives are to be demanding but accessible, geared in part to the preparation and abilities of students; for students rise or fall to the expectations of the instructor. Then students must make public the differences learning makes to them—their ability to carry the inquiry forward on their own and in concert with others. Ultimately, good teaching enables students to be teachers to others—able to explain with insight and to be aware of the adequacy of the interpretations they are providing a new audience.

Teaching is done better in smaller groups where the circumstances of individual students can be more easily determined and incorporated into the instructor's work as well as facilitated in student-to-student conversation.

Student circumstances are never irrelevant and some set is always presumed, though (as in large classes) they may be highly generalized. Students are no more generic problems to be fixed than they are empty receptacles to be filled. They are unique individuals from whom, given hospitality, something can always be learned—and then returned with validation, correction, and enhancement. It is the professor who establishes the terms and conditions of the contact allowed students. As already noted, the objective is not to be "friends" with students, for friendship tends to compromise other relationships, but to be "interested" in students—friendly and hospitable toward them and genuinely interested in advancing their educational interests. Collegial professionalism reminds us of this truth, for to be a professional means that one advances the good of the client—not one's own good. This requires us to be more attentive to the manner in which we support that good, including how we evaluate and certify its achievement. Traditional measures of seat-time and grades are often wooden and unimaginative ways of determining that learning objectives have been achieved, and the public is reporting its loss of confidence that these measures are adequate.

## A Potential Collegium

The classroom presents its own version of a potential collegium. The increasing diversity of students in age, economic, and ethnic background is well-known. So their coming together in a class presents another potential form of connectivity. The job before the instructor is to attend not only to the content and the logic of the inquiry but, in the process, to create collective engagement. A class can itself become a community—such that no member's learning is independent of a context within which individual differences are a source of richness, not deficit. This kind of value is also available in genuine team teaching. Even multidisciplinary, cross-disciplinary, or sequential inquiry presents practical value beyond that represented by one instructor, no matter how learned he or she might be. Interdisciplinary inquiry offers the possibility of even greater hospitality and thoughtfulness, assuming the instructors are prepared to engage one another in this manner, because insistent individualism can plague even team teaching if faculty are too concerned with their status and standing. The best teachers model relational power and illustrate the making of connections, rather than displacing this responsibility onto students. The latter rarely works.

Good teaching thus involves making connections of many kinds—among and between teachers and students, methodologies and subject matters, theories and applications, and histories and the present. Ideally, classroom teaching involves transforming an audience of individuals into an interactive community. Most faculty know the delight when students of different ages draw upon their different experiences to instruct one another. The classroom can be a source of educational value itself, a commons or public space for discourse and interactivity, providing its own ecology of mutual engagement by diverse participants. In, through, and beyond their classroom students develop their pedagogy and improve their learning—by requiring accountability of each other. Consequently, students are thereby empowered to become better citizens, able to apply knowledge, raise critical questions, and present and defend positions.

## Two Metaphors for Teaching and Learning

Two of the many educational metaphors have particular merit. Teaching and learning can be seen as a kind of conceptual construction. One can also elucidate the process of education through the metaphor of the dance.

### The Construction Metaphor

Teaching and learning involve helping students to assemble, remodel, and become at home in their foundational, conceptual dwellings. These are the elaborate constructions woven out of theories, facts, values, skills, and sensibilities that all of us create and carry with us. They were begun in early life, developed in primary and secondary school, and enhanced in college and graduate school. We both possess and inhabit our conceptual dwellings. They give us identity, location, perspective, and tools for engaging each other and the world. The sturdier and better-textured our dwellings, the more satisfying our lives. Every dwelling needs regular maintenance and refurbishment. Some are in disrepair and require substantial renovation. Floors may need to be leveled, roofs fixed, and windows replaced.

The metaphor calls attention to the bearing of one part of a dwelling upon others. Things are not unconnected. Walls support ceilings while also providing rooms—some with intimacy, others designed for gracious entertainment. Doors both open and shut, creating spaces for interaction and for privacy. Color schemes relate to room size and furnishings. The educational lesson of this connectivity is that no academic discipline is independent of others or of a larger whole. Yet academe regularly packages courses and degrees as though they were separable. General education lacks integration with the major. The major is pursued independently of related subjects. Classrooms are isolated from each other, from extracurricular activities, and from the world off-campus.

The point of attending to the conceptual dwelling is not only to improve it, but also to enable the individual to feel more comfortable in it—to own and possess it, rather than see it as a rented structure. The point is to make it a home, not a temporary address, much less a suitcase out of which one lives. And as a home, it is in need of constant upkeep. The professor is best understood as consultant, not general contractor—only the student can play that role. But professors need to be in regular consultation with other professors to assure that mutual strengths are employed and that students are not given erroneous advice. Extracurricular activities should be identified as resources and made available, as should potential resources off-campus. Technology can provide significant assistance, since information can be accessed and various skills developed through computing and telecommunications media. Often it is fellow students who are subcontractors—who help with the tools of statistics, show how to develop the marketing or management plan, or exemplify and provide the personal riches of humanistic study and insight. That is why the various images of teaching as filling empty vessels are so unsatisfactory. They present the student learner as passive, marginalized, and isolated from other learners.

This construction metaphor draws attention to the collective roughing out of structures with finishing touches left to the occupant, the importance of large windows and ample doors and pathways to other dwellings, and, overall, the undesirability of tract housing or uniformly prefabricated structures. Building codes, punch lists, and inspectors have their place. Few today would argue for tightly essentialist platonic forms of excellence, but few would deny that structures should be serviceable and able to endure. Changes in the disciplines, in societal needs, and individual student abilities play significant roles. Students bring their own individuality to their learning and each dwelling should be distinct, bearing its own marks of construction.

### The Metaphor of the Dance

Teaching and learning are rich and complex activities. Multiple metaphors describe them. Mortimer Kadish puts forward the provocative metaphor of "dancing" to capture interactions between faculty and students that are characteristic of good teaching and learning (Kadish 1991). He risks dating himself, for in many contemporary dances partners appear superfluous! However, it is the dignity and gracefulness of earlier dance forms that he has in mind, particularly the choreographed dance of ballet. Three elements of this metaphor can be highlighted—like dancing, teaching and learning are social, risky, and self-implicating activities.

In teaching and learning as in dancing there must be reciprocal engagement with others who decline to be used as mere instruments. Like the dance floor, the classroom is an active and collective enterprise: a place where students are not passive observers, where there is awareness of other individuals and the need to coordinate at least minimally with them, and where the professor is not a disconnected authority. Respect for other participants extends even to those not there—voices from the past must be allowed to speak for themselves and not be distorted. Kadish suggests that as in dance, movement is converted into gesture; so too in teaching, talk is converted into dialogue. In both there is a telos, an end purpose, and—preeminently—there is interaction. By definition no good teacher or student can be a wallflower. The more graceful the dance, the more one can presume hours of preparation and practice; the same is true of teaching and learning. They too require patience, poise, self-knowledge, and preparation by both instructor and student.

Kadish's metaphor also highlights the fragile and unpredictable character of teaching and learning. Gracefulness will not always be evident; toes will be stepped on. Some students will be reading different music and others will be unaware that the dance has even begun. The instructor does not get to choose the dancers. Their names show up on the dance card (the class roster) and some simply will not join in, remaining rooted to the floor, glued to the wall, or cowering in the wings. Even when students do participate, the movements cannot be fully choreographed in advance. There is substantial risk that the activity will fail. The instructor must work out the theme for the course and plan how the parts might fit together. But things inevitably change; nothing is completely predictable. The dancers must find their own steps, likely stumbling as they go—perhaps creating new movements. Faculty must be attentive and resourceful, guided by knowledge both of the subject area and the talents and deficits of their students. Yet even disharmonies and differences bind partners together as they struggle in common to overcome them—thereby creating new forms of relatedness.

Further, the dancers must be helped to develop their own styles—working out what is particularly appropriate to them as individuals, incorporating their creativity and gifts into something distinctively their own. Style is not understood in contrast to substance, and certainly not instead of substance. It is rather the subjective form of the holding or possessing of the substance—the knowledge or skill in question. Personal style is developed and achieved in the reciprocities of the ballet. The value of relational power should be particularly evident. The objective is that students incorporate the richness of the new dance into themselves—not simply as an instrumental technique, but something also valuable in itself. Not everything is just a problem to be solved or controlled. There can be delight and wonder in the activity itself, and students can make the activity particularly and genuinely their own.

## Learning as Self-Implicating

Two things must happen. Students must learn the techniques, rules, and guidelines of the different inquiries; different dances call for different skills. And they must learn about themselves and what it means to be part of different dances. They must attend not only to the knowledge and skills of chemistry or management, law or history, but also to themselves as future chemists and managers, attorneys and historians—they must address what it means to have these competencies as part of who they are. Pursuit of knowledge is always related to formation of the self and self-understanding. It is always sensible to ask, Why am I doing this? or What will doing this mean for who I am? This formation of personal identity and character is not an additive—not something accomplished in addition to, or on top of, the inquiry, but achieved *through* it. These are not separate and discrete activities. The formation of intellect and character go together, as the virtue of thoughtfulness suggests.

The instructor also helps students help themselves by being open to their initiatives. For the dance to work, students push and probe the instructor, just as the instructor pushes them. Each challenges the other. Faculty and students "form combinations and oppositions; they shift sides; they cooperate and oppose" (Kadish 1991, 64). Socratic dialogue means that learning goes in both directions. The master teacher is not only thoughtful in both senses identified earlier, but he or she is also hospitable—open to teaching and to learning from the most unlikely partner. Perhaps part of the ennui and alienation that afflicts the contemporary academy reflects diminished interest in being educated by students. In any case, the instructor has the opportunity to model his or her learning, and what it means personally—how it affects character and behavior, how we are different and better people precisely because we have studied chemistry or management, law or history. For in the last analysis it is who one is, not a grab bag of tricks, that makes a great teacher. As Kadish notes, instructors bring "not a 'method,' however well-intentioned, of educating others; they bring themselves." And in the ballet they experience the "reformation" not only of others, but of themselves as well (Kadish 1991, 48). Reformation can be painful, as comfortable self-concepts and routines are challenged. Nonetheless, it can also be exhilarating, returning one to earlier visions and expectations of teaching and learning.

Seeing the dance of higher education as bearing upon questions of personal identity as well as intellectual competence recalls Bruce Wilshire's lament that the research university approaches bankruptcy when it is not a place where these questions are asked and answered. Wilshire's judgment seems to focus on the size, organization, and character of the large university. Even in an indifferent—sometimes seemingly hostile—setting, the dance of teaching and learning can occur, given sufficient determination by teacher and student. However, the ballet occurs best, and most frequently, in environments of collegial, not academic, professionalism. Collegial environments are characterized by structures that promote individual hospitality, not just civility—and thoughtfulness, not just rigor. For one can be civil without also expressing openness to the other, just as one can be rigorous, without also being considerate. Civility and rigor by themselves are deficient educational habits. The dance of education requires both moral and intellectual virtues.

## Extending the Dance

Moreover, the dance of teaching and learning need not be confined to the classroom or campus. Each dance should relate to dances in other classes and should incorporate the opportunities that extracurricular activities present. The ballet can "open out" into the community as well, Kadish notes, engaging students in such activities as the arts, politics, service, and business. Not only can outsiders be invited in, but the dancers can move out beyond institutional walls into the broader community through study abroad as well as internships and practica, emphasizing participation rather than observation. In each case what is to be learned relates to personal practice, not just technical understanding. Practice generates its own mode of understanding—both of technique and of self, what Donald Schoen calls "reflection-in-action" (Schoen 1983). This is the knowing that inheres in thoughtful action, the knowing that is formed through acting rather than prior theoretical knowing that is applied to experience. In practice and action, students learn about their own identity, and make public for each other what would otherwise remain private.

The metaphor extends to professional as well as collegial education—to specialized and general education alike. Clearly, graduate as well as undergraduate education requires both theory and experience—each in relationship to the other. Without connection to experience, theory is arid. Without illumination by theory, experience is chaotic and overwhelming. And with respect to both theory and experience the self is involved and implicated. Accordingly, boundaries between disciplines, and between campus and world, need to be permeable and fuzzy, not rigid and sharp-edged. Relationship, not isolation, is the beginning and end of knowledge. In the process both faculty and students are enriched. Far from being private activities, teaching and learning are in complex and inescapable ways public in character.

As Kadish sees things, the dance of teaching and learning is active, risky, and often quite time-consuming. It requires considerable self-knowledge and self-possession. An additional merit of the metaphor is that dance as performance highlights the public element of knowledge—it is there to be seen and it can have an impact on the common good. It is not recondite, recessive, or something one only hopes is occurring. Nor is a good dance an ego trip—a show or a game; it is not simply a theatrical act, but a public offering of self.

## Improving the Dance

Kadish's metaphor is rich and provocative. It employs the power of the relational model to highlight the multiple values and excitement of teaching that brought many into the professoriate and that can still be reclaimed and restored. But Kadish's treatment may not give adequate emphasis to the collective character of the dance. More than individual good is at stake. Teaching and learning occur trilaterally—among and between students, as well as between individual students and the professor. Students have obligations to contribute to each other and to the whole class, evident in the impact of their attendance and the degree of their preparation. The successful instructor is one who is able to effect collaboration among students—to lead them to grant authority to each other in teaching and learning. And the dancers can profitably be connected in other dances as well. Recent research in learning communities and other forms of collaboration suggests that students are likely to learn more and persist as learners if they take other classes together, especially ones linked by common themes (Gablenick 1990). Such arrangements promote both shared and connected learning.

Kadish's metaphor should extend more clearly to collaboration among instructors. The best form of faculty collaboration would seem to be another version of the ballet with the reciprocity of give-and-take for which the metaphor calls. We explore this challenge for academic leaders in the next chapter. But if faculty are reluctant to engage in their own professorial dance, they should at least conduct common, periodic critiques of particular dances with students. They need to determine the degree to which desired intellectual skills and information as well as style and self-insight are achieved by students. The contribution of technology in helping students master skills and technique and develop personal styles should be explored; and what only the instructor can provide should be distinguished from contributions of technology and student peers. The outcomes of these critiques should then be used to adjust the themes and tempo of future dances.

Each of these two metaphors—the conceptual dwelling and the dance—is a device by which we image the tasks of teaching and learning. The construction metaphor emphasizes connections, but also stability. Education builds upon previous education and relates to that which follows. College presupposes secondary education, just as professional education builds upon general education. Although weakened by insistent individualism, patterns of connectivity endure and are embedded in the dwelling. The dance metaphor emphasizes activity, but also risk and change. Education, like dance, requires active personal engagement and reciprocity. Without interaction teaching and learning are inadequate. The successful dancer acquires enhanced skills and learns new competencies for creating connections. Whether imaged as sturdy conceptual dwellings or as graceful dances, good teaching and learning embody hospitality and thoughtfulness.

## Teaching and Learning as Intergenerational

Increased complaining by faculty about student abilities is profoundly troubling. Although complaining can play a constructive therapeutic function, restoring and energizing the instructor, it can also become a self-fulfilling destructive phenomenon, helping to create the very situation being deplored. As Parker Palmer notes, "nothing is easier than to slip into a low opinion of students, and that opinion creates teaching practices guaranteed to induce vegetative states even in students who arrive for class alive and well" (Palmer 1993, 11). This kind of destructive complaining often mirrors a larger malaise. Palmer suggests that neglect of teaching may not reflect greater faculty interest in research so much as broader disinterest in, and devaluation of, the young.

Palmer identifies generational rifts and divisions in our society as the root of the "pain of disconnection"—a common feeling in academe. Typical today is the institution in which "the young and their mentors gather on a daily basis, and everyone is feeling the pain that comes when the relations of the generations deteriorate. For the young, it is the pain of being neglected. For their mentors, it is the pain we feel when our own adult lives are disconnected from the ancient and renewing power of choosing to help the young grow" (Palmer 1992a, 4). This inability to affirm with joy and hope the sharing of accumulated wisdom with those seeking learning provides poignant comment on current disconnectedness and relational inadequacies. It is encouraging that Palmer sees this pain as a hopeful sign—a potentially energizing factor in what otherwise may be a dark, even harsh, time. For the pain of disconnection, of what we have been calling excessively privatized academic lives, may finally awaken a sufficient resolve for change—a resolve seen as a spiritual necessity, not simply as an economic need. It is spiritual because the key requirement is renewed honesty about the human condition—we are connected to each other and therefore vulnerable in the most positive sense of the term.

In their best form, teaching and learning attend to our common humanness. Professors and students have the common trajectories of birth and death, they experience joy and sadness, success and defeat, and everyone needs to find personal meaning. When we neglect the task of receiving, absorbing, and passing on to others achieved modes of being human, we weaken intergenerational connectedness and possibilities for regeneration. We are left unfulfilled, unfaithful to others, and also to ourselves. In fact, Bruce Wilshire suggests that neglect of teaching is really a signal of a weakening of the will to live. Parallels to a society that neglects and abuses its children present themselves. "For if we do not nurture our young and identify with them, we forfeit any hope in the regeneration and continuation of the species; we are walled up defensively within the confines of our egos and our momentary gratifications" (Wilshire 1990, 255). When we keep our students rigidly at a distance, when we refuse to let them have an impact on us, we suggest that perhaps they should not pay attention to us or our teaching either. The same applies to colleagues of all ages. Everyone remains strangers, and the result is isolation and detachment instead of community and enrichment.

In the collegium, skillful teaching and learning as well as individual strength of character are reinforced or diminished by colleagues. It is colleagues who generate what Shils terms the "self-closing circle of reciprocal influences" (Shils 1984, 48). In their interactions, members of the collegium establish its intellectual and emotional tone. Accordingly, one mechanism for overcoming intergenerational and other forms of disconnection in teaching is honest and open discussion with colleagues. Some conversations should occur with older faculty who are unwilling to acknowledge their own declining contributions or to make room for enthusiastic and energetic junior faculty. Other conversations should focus on instructional triumphs, failures, and fears. The next chapter reviews roles of the department chairperson and other academic leaders in promoting and sustaining these conversations. Such conversations recognize, exploit, and extend underlying facts and realities of relatedness—that we learn from each other and that this learning can be enriching and even exhilarating. We do learn from experience, and shared experience is even more fertile. The traditional concept of the classroom as *sanctum sanctorum* is probably the most obvious and egregious form of academic privatization.

## SCHOLARSHIP

As with teaching, scholarship demands public moments. Both teachers and scholars start from existing communities. Following intervening moments of creation, they return to the forum or agora to offer up to others the fruits of their private labor for comment, validation, and correction. Obligated to promote learning, educators have a duty to make these fruits available to others—who have a right to this learning. Like the artistic performance, this return to the larger community takes courage; it entails vulnerability. A good performance is cast in terms that are informed as well as helpful and respectful, but audiences can be uninformed and critics merciless and unfair. However, only through this return to the public does the scholar advance knowledge and community and, at the same time, fulfill self.

## Scholarship as Community Property

Scholarship starts from the public, with community property. This property includes received theories and insights embedded in the traditions, as well as neglected or even forgotten materials. Scholarship involves multiple threads of discourse and diverse lines of inquiry. Some scholars look at the old afresh, throwing it into new combinations, searching out novelty, articulating over-looked relationships, and proposing new applications as well as implications for teaching. As Ernest Boyer reminded us, this is scholarship as integration or application of learning (Boyer 1990). Other scholars seek the brand new discovery, but it too must be related to the past for more complete understanding. Validation, extension, or even radical revision of past practices, theories, or canons can result. This in turn provokes new efforts at integration, application, and teaching. Scholarship is never completed.

Scholarship in its many forms is ultimately inseparable from teaching, because it embodies learning. And learning, we have seen, has its public dimension and requires being shared with others. The hospitable and thoughtful professor is both a scholar and a teacher. Though distinguishable, teaching and scholarship cannot be divorced. They are inherently connected, though conflicts of presentation and time can occur. That is, scholarship can be pursued and reported in ways that diminish rather than facilitate learning. It can be cast in terms that only a small group of like-minded can understand. It can also be presented in forbidding and even inaccessible terms—but it is then marginal scholarship as well as teaching. Likewise, teaching disengaged from scholarship makes for poor learning—always less than what it could have been. The products of inquiry—some of its skills and part of its content—are presented, rather than the inquiry itself. This is marginal teaching, for content and even skills are often quickly obsolete and the learner left disenfranchised.

There can also be conflict in one's allocation of time and effort between scholarship and teaching. The hour spent in the library or at the computer is obviously not also available for the classroom. Henry Crimmel argues the inevitability of this conflict and writes of teacher-scholars as at best "part-time teachers and part-time scholars" (Crimmel 1984, 183). Concerned about the teaching appropriate to an ideal liberal arts college, he argues *against* scholarship and *for* "the full-time, uncompromised teacher" (Crimmel 1984, 194). But a truly "uncompromised teacher" is a contradiction in terms. There can be no teaching without making public the activity wherein insight is secured, and securing insight is achieved only through scholarship—indeed, it *is* scholarship. The relationship between teaching and scholarship is better understood as one of focus and concentration of effort. Although one cannot be in the library and classroom at the same time, one can bring the library into the classroom. Genuine teaching requires taking classroom concerns into the library in the first place to develop plans for the conceptual dwelling and themes for the dance of teaching and learning. Far from mutually exclusive, teaching and scholarship require each other for completion.

Crimmel's concern is probably better put in terms of the greater relevance to the classroom of scholarship that bears on the integration, application, and teaching of different fields of learning than scholarship or research designed to discover brand new knowledge. The teacher devoid of scholarship is compromised. As William Green reminds us, "only by knowing something very well can we convey to students its force and appeal. We cannot represent the power of the varied realms of inquiry and disclosure we want students to encounter unless we are deeply engaged with these realms ourselves." The expectation that faculty should regularly confront questions in their fields and present their findings to others parallels the expectation that students demonstrate publicly the difference their learning makes to them. "We cannot show them how knowledge is discovered, invented, constructed and evaluated without laboring at it ourselves" (Green 1993, 106). Few scholars actually extend the range of things known, but grappling with new questions keeps their learning honed. The disciplined reflection involved in constructing and presenting an argument publicly models for students what active learning means and that it is worth time and energy. The teacher-scholar practices what he or she teaches.

## Scholarship as Publication

One can distinguish between the activity of scholarship and its product, understanding the latter as typically a publication of some type. Obviously the publication is more permanent. It is an artifact, in principle forever available and retrievable, however dated. By contrast, the dance of teaching and learning is always transitory. We hope its effects persist, but its direct presence is both fresh and immediately over—it is "perpetually perishing," to use language Whitehead applies to all moments of actuality. Publication is an expression and evidence of scholarship—it is the latter that is the immediate act. As both act and product, scholarship is a form of teaching. And teaching and scholarship are honored only by being brought forward in new expressions. The publication must be read and discussed for learning to occur, and teaching is ongoing, never completed.

As Ejner Jensen reminded us, almost all faculty struggle with the issue of impact and grounds for confidence that their teaching and scholarly work have effect. What measure is the academic to use in judging his or her success and, thereby, worth? Certainly the measure absorbed in graduate school is for most faculty far too narrow. There one is socialized not only for isolation, but often for diminished satisfaction as well. In graduate school teaching is presented as a presumed, but secondary, value—and the requirements of subsequent work often do not provide conditions for easily accomplishing the primary value, which is prestigious scholarship. Perhaps part of the resistance to assessment is uncertainty or anxiety about the effect of one's teaching and scholarship. Good teaching may piously be said to "affect eternity" and the same can be held for scholarship as activity. Hoping that one's publications will have a similar impact usually seems foolish, unless they too are seen as a form of teaching—that is, as another pedagogical tool.

For most faculty, the primary value of scholarship is as a form of teaching rather than as discovery of new knowledge. The larger number are not in a position to discover the radically new and resent a definition of professorial success that by definition excludes them at the outset. They can scarcely be expected to recognize themselves in descriptions that apply, if at all, to only a small number of colleagues. Nonetheless, without a public dimension, scholarship of whatever kind will by definition have no impact on others. It is for this reason that research of a proprietary character has always had such a difficult reception in higher education. Its inaccessibility to peer review renders it mute as evidence of activity and useless as contributing to collective excitement and understanding. The marketplace of ideas requires active participation—it needs both sellers and buyers. Wares must be presented as enticing, and they must be available for assessment by others. Only in this way is a common good advanced.

## Making Scholarship Accessible

However, this common good must be distinguished from the phenomenon of extensive multiple authorship noted earlier. The ability of groups and teams to incorporate individual contributions will vary by field and by team. Granted that the complexity of knowledge is increasing, past some point the contributions of named individuals are surely negligible. Listing hundreds of co-authors for an article strains credulity, insults responsible efforts to recognize contributions and attribute ownership, exposes the practice of recognizing multiple authorship to public ridicule, and probably crosses over into dishonesty. Parody of "honorary authorship" is appropriately sharp. Jack Schuster posits what he calls the Law of Contemporary Academic Life—"the space required to list authors is increasing relative to the length of the material published at such a rapid rate that by the year 2018, authorship credits will be longer than the accompanying article in 34 percent of all published articles" (Schuster 1990, 21).

Deeply embedded within academic traditions is a high valuation placed upon style in scholarship as well as teaching. The common good of academe is advanced not just by fresh insight but also by how insight is presented. The manner, or subjective form, of expressing ideas is no less important than their content. Wit and charm are common values, as is clarity and economy of presentation. The graceful argument is bolstered by a disciplined use of supporting materials—not an unbalanced and overburdened assemblage. Patricia Limmerick reminds us that insecurity and fear may lead faculty to honor this value more in the breach than in observance. The virtues of hospitality and thoughtfulness can be ignored, even violated, in scholarship as well as teaching. Overly documented, inaccessible, impenetrable, or opaque writing and talking obscure the public moment that both scholarship and teaching demand. Wilshire's academic professional comes to mind, for the public interest cannot be served by private knowledge intentionally left private. This knowledge cannot rebound to the public good or contribute to the work of colleagues, nor can it assist the student in the development of his or her intellectual life. Knowledge must be shared—it must be made public in ways that allow others to possess it.

The others for whom faculty are writing and talking must at some point include the broader public. This is key to making private research more publicly accessible and socially useful. It is a central step in overcoming the privatization of the academy. Redefining the broader collegium in this way could help change what Derek Bok observes—"that rarely have members of the academy succeeded in discovering emerging issues and bringing them vividly to the attention of the public" (Bok 1990, 105). Higher education cannot flourish if it neglects needs of the community beyond the campus. Writing and speaking directed to this readership is essential to serve the broader society, secure its continued support, and promote the future growth of knowledge by interesting potential scholars. Otherwise, knowledge is not in fact shared—there is only pretense, and sharp-tongued critics are correct about the hubris of academics. Writing and speaking only for a small number of peers illustrates the isolationism and separatism of insistent individualism.

Surely it is excessive academic passion for the private that fuels prejudice against "popular" writing. In the professional mythos, a popularizer risks being known as a dilettante. One of the choicer condemnations of an individual's scholarship is to label it popular, thereby charging the author with diluting its rigor. One suspects, though, that what in fact may be diluted is the purity associated with exclusivity. Wilshire may be correct in his criticism of academic professionalism. Sharing knowledge outside the exclusive boundaries of an academic elite may be tacitly deplored on the unspoken grounds that it cheapens or even vulgarizes knowledge. Popularizing violates the implicit position that knowledge is most valuable when most scarce. Of course, the broader point is that popularizing makes scholarship available to a wider audience, an act that itself contributes to the advancement of knowledge. Ironically, the very popularizing that is condemned is often the more difficult to produce. It requires sophisticated ability to express learning in more accessible terms than the arcane and exclusive jargon of highly specialized journals.

## Repudiating Pedagogical Insistent Individualism

The relational model repudiates three common forms of pedagogical insistent individualism, each converting useful distinctions into contradictory alternatives. As we have seen, one of these forms is the opposition presented between teaching and scholarship. Sensible differences are presented as mutually exclusive, as though there were no connection between what are two forms of learning. But there can be no effective teaching divorced from the disciplined inquiry called scholarship any more than there can be scholarship without the sharing with others usually known as teaching, though some persist in speaking loudly of the gulf between them. Perhaps it is the comforts of established routines, the discomfort of challenge, or the distortions of an unbalanced reward system that create the alleged incompatibilities.

Another self-imposed problem is conflict between the purity and utility of inquiry. To study something for its own sake supposedly requires relinquishing other, "lesser" objectives, but how can any learning *not* have some application? To promote learning solely for its own sake, indifferent to its uses, is to render learning into mere connoisseurship and to create islands of refined consumption. The idea that uselessness is a more desirable end implies that contributing to human flourishing is somehow secondary, inferior, or even wrong. A good inquiry must pursue both objectives—acquiring insight and skill to be used in addressing the complexities of life, in making sense of it, and pursuing its immense opportunities; and using insight and skill, which carries its own delight. One suspects that the important issues may not be incompatibilities of educational purpose, but rather those of territory and status—for under insistent individualism the academy is known for persistent hierarchies of prestige in which theory is elevated over application.

And, as we have seen, some insist upon the impersonalness of the educational process—as though it were unethical to recognize the individuality of the learner or, for that matter, the instructor. Fairness and objectivity, they seem to argue, require strict neutrality respecting individuals—a requirement best met by creating and maintaining an abstract personal distance. Faculty are defined hierarchically and impersonally over other faculty, the professoriate over students, and students over each other. But it is real and diverse individuals, not ciphers, who are involved in learning and who teach each other. Students are increasingly diverse in age, gender, degree of preparation and experience, and racial or ethnic background. The circumstances and personal identity of these individuals are never utterly irrelevant. Perhaps it may be the need for exclusiveness that promotes some of the neutrality and distance insisted upon.

Ultimately, from the standpoint of the relational model the inquiries in which we participate are always public projects, at their beginning and (following our private moments) at their end. The autonomous model emphasizes only the middle stage of this process. Yet the very structures of our academic being demand that interiority be shared. Only through this second public moment does one complete his or her own work. Only then does private activity become an accomplishment. That is why educational community is so important, and why the model of the autonomous scholar is so inadequate. In his recent reflection on Newman's classic text on the idea of the university, Jaroslav Pelikan makes a similar point. Adopting as basic to education the motto of the Dominican order—"*contemplata aliis tradere*," to communicate to others the fruits of one's own contemplation—Pelikan argues that "publish or perish" applies in both teaching and scholarship, and that in both cases the phrase is not

> an arbitrary rule invented by the network of established scholars to keep upstarts out of the university's faculty . . . . [but] a fundamental psychological, indeed almost physiological, imperative that is rooted in the metabolism of scholarship as a sacred vocation (Pelikan 1992, 123–124).

The privatized teacher or scholar is ultimately a contradiction in terms.

## ACKNOWLEDGING AND CELEBRATING THE COLLEGIUM

Every teacher-scholar is a citizen of a collegium. He or she may choose to become a resident alien, but no one starts out like that. The paradox of the development of the teacher-scholar is that even the very context that encourages increased isolation presupposes and illustrates its own form of community. Every faculty member has been formed and shaped by others. Everyone dwells in a conceptual house to which others have contributed. Everyone has participated in the dance of teaching and learning. Without continuing to attend to these enterprises, insistent individualists are living off accumulated capital. It is very much in the broader interests of the individual teacher and scholar to continue to enjoy the power that comes from openness to the influence and gifts of others—colleagues and students alike.

The structure of the authentic collegium encourages mutual enrichment and accountability as well as appreciation of context and connection. It secures its strength from practices of relational power, of openness and hospitality to the other. Relational power is multivalent and embodies a variety of goods. Some goods relate to learning narrowly defined—for instance, colleagues help with teaching transcendental arguments or the finer points of zoning laws. Broader goods point to connections with other collegia and inquiries at first only dimly glimpsed—intellectual historians suggest to economists the importance of theism for the development of western science and technology. Still other goods of relational power come from the implications for self-understanding and self-identity that follow from debate on the meaning of such possibilities as genetic engineering. In these various ways collegia liberate academics from self-preoccupation and the captivity of disciplinary guilds—from the academic professionalism that prescinds from larger issues of context, relatedness, and connection and that treats inquiries separately from the practical, human, and social concerns that constitute the context of worth and significance.

## Forms of Engagement

The healthy collegium provides far more than instrumental significance for its members. The relationships involved enable individuals to see others in their originality and integrity. The more we allow others to contribute to our own internal life and experience—the more we are genuinely open to diversity of all kinds—the richer and wiser we become, and the more we are able to offer in return. This is often difficult because the autonomous self is not prepared to extend hospitality or receive the other. Defense mechanisms, lack of respect for others, and resentment of their successes get in the way. But ultimately the broader good for self is achieved only through disciplining and even sacrificing the narrower interests of the self. This discipline is not simple passive absorption of the ideas and values of others. It requires talking with, rather than past, one another—it involves disagreeing without becoming disagreeable. It requires active and critical engagement. The engagement may require combat with negative forces to convert into positive value, neutralize, or dismiss the negativities of polarizing rhetoric, calling in sick, and other evasions of hospitality and thoughtfulness. And thoughtfulness often means that one gains deeper insight into the other and into self only through the practice of charity—presuming honorable intentions and making allowances for the occasional gaff, rather than shoving others into facile stereotypes or carica-tures.

The collegium is only as good as the interactions of its members. It is derivative from the interrelations of individuals but it is more than the sum of its parts. Its members create it just as it in turn creates them. Thus, if the common coin is *quid pro quo* understandings or other forms of uncritical conformism, vitality is lost. It is in everyone's interest to ensure that healthy department and school collegia are properly nourished, so that they can nourish their members. Sometimes a collegium becomes too big to secure these values. Alternatively, an earlier healthy collegiality may have eroded as the collegium aged and familiarity turned into fatigue, indifference, or outright hostility. At other times we need to create new collegia to replace older ones flawed by racism or sexism. Indeed, the very term "collegium" suggests to some an "old boys" network. Sometimes, though, the source of trouble may be the creation of destabilizing novelty precisely by altering gender, ideological, or ethnic ratios.

Attending to commonalities as well as differences is essential to successfully addressing the pluralism of teachers and learners today. To argue that only a woman can teach women's studies or that only an African American can direct inquiry in black literature presumes an insufficiency of shared common experience. And this assumption goes against the telos of inquiry—to enrich and to be enriched. It slights the importance and the power of hospitality, the fruits of genuine openness to the other, even the stranger. Doubtless the greater personal experience and insight that comes from being a woman or an African American can only enrich one's teaching in those areas. But to hold it as a prerequisite is to hold that there are areas of learning that are in principle forever inaccessible to others and can never be learned. It is to hobble the power of education and to deprive people of hope.

We are not without ability to understand others, learn from them, and contribute to their learning. Hospitality—genuine interest in others and patient inquiry—is vital. The major obstacle to addressing and incorporating diversity may be unwillingness to attend to others, perhaps bolstered by ideological dogmatism, a presumption of absolutism, or the alleged incommen-surability of different cultures. However controlling they may become, these positions need not prevail; but one must work at attending to others. Unfortu-nately, even in our own communities we often speak about collegiality and incorporation of the new and different more than we practice it. In her study,

Mary Deane Sorcinelli discovered that "new faculty reported lack of collegial relations as the most surprising and disappointing aspect of their first year. Some expected ongoing conversations with colleagues about scholarship, teaching, and other work-related matters. Others hoped for such assistance as reading a manuscript or grant proposal or even visiting a classroom" (Sorcinelli 1989, 3). Certainly the early probationary period should be known for something other than loneliness and lack of intellectual stimulation.

## The Meaning of Collegiality

Likewise, collegiality must mean more than logrolling, agreeing mutually to be permissive or indifferent to colleagues, students, or the institution. The collegium can easily become a comfortable guild—a club with unwritten but commonly accepted customs of easy tolerance. There is no *a priori* reason to think that backscratching will not take root in the academy. These practices may find more ready acceptance there, given insistent individualism and the shelter tenure provides. Collegiality does not mean ignoring differences or striving for superficial consensus instead of challenging and engaging each other about knowledge claims. It does not mean conformity, except in that minimal sense of acceptance of the principle of intellectual reciprocity, for conformity is uninteresting and in the long run creates poor scholarship and citizenship. Nor, on the other hand, does it mean continued questioning to the point of querulousness or pedantry. The one who rises constantly to make a point of principle often weakens, rather than contributes to, community.

Collegiality does mean recognizing serious academic obligations to each other and participation in the academic life of the institution. It means working with colleagues to develop appropriate expectations: expectations that each person attend to the work of others (their teaching, scholarship, and service) and judge that work by criteria used for one's own work, and vice versa. Collegiality requires intellectual reciprocity with colleagues. Rarely is the goal agreement on controversial issues, but members of a healthy learning community do commit themselves to common ultimate ends—or at least to a common process for evaluating these ends when there is disagreement about them. Collegiality means that intellectual support is sought in reason broadly understood and in appeals to the experienced nature of things, not just in individual or collective wants. We have the capacity to recognize the need for improvement, a capacity that centers in the virtue of hope and reminds us of the ideal of betterment implicit in the collegium.

Finally, collegial professionalism calls for openness beyond the collegium. The collegial ethic has special implications for members of a profession with custodianship of the means of securing advanced, validated knowledge. Since knowledge is not self-sustaining, the primary obligation is to conserve, transmit, and extend it through engaging, respecting, and caring for the rules whereby knowledge is achieved and validated. Personal preference, convenience, comfort, practicality, or political objectives are secondary. Instead, academic obligations relate to such matters as the hospitable presentation of the best understandings of evidence, critically assessed, according to criteria of reliability and validity. All of this is in the service of distinguishing the true from the false, the better from the lesser supported claims—activities that themselves must be repeated ever again to assure that the closest approximation to truth is at hand.

Hospitality means stewardship, not exclusive possession, of these means of knowledge. It is the very mission of the academy to extend to students and the public various means of securing knowledge, not to hoard or sequester them. Part of what that requires, as we have seen, is that the institution and its members attend better to the education of the public as well as display more candor and openness in public statements about admissions, development, and accreditation activities.

## BRIDGING COMMUNITIES OF INTERPRETATION

Both teaching and scholarship reflect, facilitate, and deepen participation in different interpretive communities. Embedded in the discourse and activities of these collegia are the social justifications for the knowledge claims they establish and advance. These include the special and specializing concepts, rhetorical structures, rules, and organizational conventions that collectively characterize a community and provide the means and mechanisms by which it assesses and warrants claims. Thoughtfulness is essential, for every interpretive or knowledge community faces the danger that congeniality becomes a greater bonding agent than intellectual judgments about merit. When this happens, issues of personal fit and homogeneity become the criteria. Exclusion of others—the different and the difficult—becomes a mechanism for achieving and maintaining identity. Academic professionalism looms.

### A Community of Collegia

The relationship of each individual collegium to others can also become problematic, for specialized discourse fragments rather than connects. When this is the case, there is little to be said for intellectual commonality. Each individual has only a partial grasp on things and needs the broader resources of the group. Each group needs other groups for the same reason. The point is not that communities establish truth, but rather that reality and truth about it are best detected collectively. When each community claims to be composed of and by its own set of internally justified beliefs, one is hard-put to identify a larger set of common compelling virtues. This is a celebration of parochialism, not liberation from narrowness. Without doorways out of one community into another, there is the lure and risk of implicit solipsism—of sliding into the comfortable position that one's community is the sole arbiter of knowledge, that it defines reality. Yet with doorways, there is the challenge of relativism, the question of the comparative value and truth of claims in the different communities.

When pressed on the veracity of claims within a collegium, most members are uncomfortable appealing to the majority, the powerful, or the current fashion. More than a comfortable consensus seems necessary. In fact, it seems essential to work toward broader commonalities and shared understandings, values, and allegiances that allow and underwrite comparative evaluation of competing claims across communities. If knowledge claims are wholly self-contained within individual interpretive communities, there is no higher ground for adjudication. Without the ability to reference a common external-ity, each community is the sole arbiter of reality and truth. The academy is left with only power and its manipulation, and inquiry and authority are reduced to the politics of knowledge. And the academy's members are bereft of intellectual grounds for claiming knowledge rather than opinion, for respect-ing the stranger, or for seeking special privileges.

Malaise is natural if the academy is only a gigantic aggregation of narrowly defined and constituted collegia. The estrangement and alienation that Jensen, Tompkins, and Lovett report have foundation here. Broader community is certainly not advanced by arguments that it is in principle impossible to achieve knowledge beyond what individual communities stipulate. Collegial solipsism, if not nihilism, is ultimately the outcome. And however much the insistent individualist in all of us may desire such freedom, it is ultimately a specious and terrifying freedom. It may be a comfort not to be challenged by others, not to have pet theories shaken or skewered; but the price of this comfort is that we alone become the ultimate authority. Few of us in our hearts think that our credentials are up to this task. Confidence in inquiry as representing more than the routines of a community is indispensable. Other-wise, the credentials we do have, our tools for interacting with each other, are radically devalued, reduced to trading interesting stories or insults.

## Transcending the Boundaries

If we search for Cartesian certainty or completely objective knowledge, we will be disappointed. If our aims are more modest, though, there are ample grounds for confidence. We are all possessed of the ability to detect the need for improvement. For instance, we all can use even a vague concept of the collegium to assess and to criticize—to identify and clarify ways in which a particular collegium falls short. The actual contains, however implicitly, the notion of its ideal. Similarly, every inquiry presupposes and exhibits some degree of sensibleness, even if the object of that inquiry is to examine the degree of its own sensibleness—and one cannot dispense with the very tools of that inquiry. In this sense, reason is not an optional choice for the academy. It is standard and required equipment. It can be abused and employed for inhospitable purposes, but it cannot be eliminated. It is our one common, indispensable tool. It is presupposed even in the identification and correction of its abuses. As Benjamin Barber notes, "reason can be a smoke screen for interest, but the argument that it is a smoke screen itself depends on reasons— or we are caught up in an endless regression in which each argument exposing the dependency of someone else's argument on arbitrariness and self-interest is in turn shown to be self-interested and arbitrary" (Barber 1992, 109).

Educators must work first to enculturate and then to transcend enculturation. Since learning is acquiring facility in a new mode of discourse, the instructor is a guide to those acquiring the new language and grammar. As Kenneth Bruffee reminds us, the instructor leads students and colleagues from the knowledge communities of which they are presently members into membership in the new community (Bruffee 1993). This is another way of understanding what we earlier described as building conceptual dwellings and engaging in the dance of learning. The best instructors are conversant in various forms of discourse and adept in fashioning symbolic structures and transitional metaphors that can function as mediators—they are translators of framing concepts and dance techniques. This is a collegium composed of students and faculty engaged in common enterprises and united by the objective of achieving certain shared competencies, values, insights, and perspectives.

When disciplines and departments are not transcended, they confine rather than liberate. Disciplines and departments confine when they are discrete and unconnected, with exclusionary norms and language—when their norms and warrants are only internal, not themselves scrutinized for assurance of adequacy and directions for improvement, or linked with the norms and warrants of other collegia. The ability to function as translator and guide between different languages and communities necessarily points toward some more general vision and language. We are led ineluctably to the conclusion that there are overarching responsibilities that faculty have regardless of the standards embedded in their particular communities of discourse. These are the virtues of hospitality and thoughtfulness—the continued commitment to the dialectic of discourse across boundaries, to the search for commonalities, and to openness to the new.

We have the general tool we need to transcend disciplines and other interpretive communities in our ability to reason. Our ability to criticize our own performance and to wonder about that of others indicates that we always in some sense transcend the boundaries of our knowledge communities—we criticize what we do in terms of the standards that define these groups, but we are able in addition to ask whether we have the right standards. Here is where others—colleagues and students—can instruct us by raising and pushing issues of consistency and coherence. What is familiar can become too familiar, mesmerizing and lulling one into forgetting how strange it initially seemed. Sometimes it is precisely sharp questions of the colleague or the brash questions of the novice that remind one of the need to examine assumptions periodically in order to secure greater clarity and fidelity to experience.

The corrigibility of knowledge leads one from within a knowledge community to its margins and to its borders with others—and thereby to transcendence—not to an absolute, but to an other, a different, and potentially a "more." The tentative gets refined, though it still remains tentative, provisional, and contingent upon future corrections. It also points beyond itself, for successful incorporation of diversity of experience within a knowledge community requires a common reality, some shared territory or public sphere. This commonality must be rooted in reality—it must be somehow in the nature of things, and not simply a hope or a projection. Otherwise we are dealing not with truth but with fantasy. This requires reasoned commitment that there is a reality independent of our own desires, one that can resist and challenge our imputations and projections, one that has the power and authority to present itself as a reality beyond us as well as a reality in which we participate.

## CONCLUSION

The relational model reminds us that teaching, scholarship, and learning are all intertwined. None can perdure in the absence of the others or apart from a larger context of community. The metaphors of the conceptual dwelling and the dances of teaching and learning provide images of these connected and shared activities of the academy. Necessary in the character and constitution of the collegium is the ethic of hospitality and thoughtfulness. Those in a healthy collegium receive and share the contributions of others—illustrating the virtue of hospitality. The collegium also calls for critical and considerate analysis—thereby pointing beyond hospitality toward thoughtfulness and humility as well. Both hospitality and thoughtfulness are forms of engagement.

The grounds for assuming the certainty of a knowledge claim can always be expanded and challenged, but this provides no warrant for relativism. Reasons

are always provided for positions presented and these reasons assessed rigor-
ously. Further, the warrants used in assessment can never be solely local in
nature, as they open out toward other collegia which may well have a critical
contribution to make. The following chapter applies the relational model to
the organizational structure of the academy and explores the roles of academic
leaders in promoting and nourishing the collegium.

# CHAPTER 6

# Creating and Nourishing Communities of Hope

Successful academic leaders facilitate the growth of communities of hope. These are relational structures within which individuals experience the satisfactions that come from substantive contributions to the common good—achieved by the sharing and receiving that are the marks of disciplined commitment to intellectual reciprocity. Formal or titled academic leaders include department and divisional chairpersons or heads as well as school and college deans. Academic leaders also include the larger number of those having no formal title to whom others look for support and assurance.

This chapter explores the work of academic leadership. Fashioning and nourishing communities of hope means addressing a variety of elements in the academy. We look in particular at two broad challenges for academic leaders—incorporating diverse ideas and individuals into the collegium, and contesting tendencies to permissiveness and self-indulgence. Important strategies for chairs and deans are identified and examined. Throughout, suggestions are offered on promoting and sustaining communities of hope.

## SHARING THE WORK OF ACADEMIC LEADERSHIP

To overcome disconnections between and among work, others, and the self, the academy must renew its communities. Fear and fatigue drive us to seek security and to insulate ourselves; and disenchantment, isolation, and the flight elsewhere for professional satisfaction result. We hide from ourselves our desire for community and our need to belong. To create more rewarding and less individualistic communities, we need to recover the relational model. To help in this, we need leadership.

After describing the disaffection and cynicism he finds among university faculties, Ejner Jensen points to the need for solutions. Simple appeals for community are difficult to honor or sustain. A crisis is usually required, an external threat that is clearly nameable, such as, budget cuts, unfriendly legislative initiatives on workload or assessment, and enrollment shortages. Without a crisis, ongoing problems internal to the work of the institution are more difficult to address. "Community seems more compelling . . . when the question for faculty is 'How are we being treated?' rather than 'What ought we to do?'" (Jensen 1995, 11). But most crises are short-lived. Leaders must find ways to make institutional progress between, as well as within, the periodic crises that constitute corporate life in higher education.

Campus presidents play a key role in facilitating progress toward community. Others look to their president to display appropriate personal values and to establish and reinforce institutional direction. Presidents must articulate a plausible, reassuring, and even exciting vision for the future. They must support the values of the collegium and resist the use of unilateral power to advance institutional goals; and they must lead in restoring greater institutional candor with the public. In pursuit of this future, other academic leaders employ the strengths and talents of different individuals within the institution. As noted, leaders often describe the task before them like herding cats— inviting insistent individuals to move in roughly the same direction.

Earlier we used the metaphors of the conceptual dwelling and the dance to suggest important features of teaching and learning. There are also multiple metaphors describing leadership. Here, we use two. The leader as "stacker" sees the job of the department chair, school dean, or other academic leader as one of positioning people. In the background is the notion of the autonomous and isolated self, essentially unrelated to others and independent of them. The leader rearranges these unconnected people. Unilateral power is a key resource, rooted in hierarchical structures. Nothing really new is created. By contrast, the leader as "weaver" assumes that individuals are inherently connected—that relationality is key to healthy individuality. The leader works at the loom, inviting people into better relationships with more harmony. Relational power is a vital resource for academic leadership, and the result can be the creation of a genuinely new community.

Titled leaders depend on the larger number of untitled leaders—the good citizens of the community, the wise ones to whom others look and listen. Leaders without title work diligently—sometimes quietly, at other times like revolutionaries—to promote the health of the whole and to remind others of its claims upon them. They model the extension of hospitality and thoughtfulness to the broader community. They recognize receptionists, secretaries, custodians, and others influential in establishing an attractive and welcoming campus as individuals; their work is neither ignored nor taken for granted. Untitled leaders also help transform an aggregation of faculty individuals into an appropriate unity, achieved through a shared vision—informed by the past, incorporating present realities, and directed toward a future in which the collective good incorporates and expresses relevant individual satisfactions. Little can be done without a sufficiency of these citizen leaders.

Other leadership resources for promoting collegial professionalism, connectivity, and integration include department or division chairpersons and school or college deans. Chairs must convert an aggregation of autonomous individuals into a functioning unit. Deans need to assist the units in working together. Both chairs and deans work to cultivate the collective responsibility of faculty—their sense of obligation and concern for each other, for students, and for the institution. The challenges before chair and dean are parallel—how to overcome insistent individualism and how to promote connections. Chairs must work with those who have insufficient identification with the department or division. Deans must address those who may have too much identification with the department and lack broader institutional connections.

In their weavings, chairs and deans ideally convert individual faculty and staff talents and strengths from oppositional into harmonious factors—from destructive conflicts with each other into distinctive complements to one another. These goals are accomplished only by working through others and by making the department and the college real and vibrant learning environments, not just organizational units. The job of chairs and deans is to create a new culture of professionalism—the collegial professional. Vibrant learning environments usually require that faculty increase their skills of cooperation and their willingness to share responsibility—skills and dispositions that precede and express relational community. However, these skills and dispositions cannot be ordered or commanded, nor can they be imposed; they must be elicited. Without a supportive environment, individual integrity and attention to each other tend to deteriorate and to be replaced by opportunism. But within a favorable context, each individual act is influenced by and influences shared practices and dispositions. Loomer's vision of the expanded self that includes significant influence from others is relevant here. The more influence is absorbed and critically evaluated, the greater the substance of the individual and the wider the identification of his or her interests with those of the community. The confines of the autonomous self are transcended.

# CHAIRPERSONS

Most faculty find chairing an academic department or division challenging. New chairs are faced with at least three substantial transitions in self-understanding and in work to be done. First, one must quickly shift from being a specialist to becoming a generalist—for the chair has to represent a broader range of inquiries than does the individual faculty member. He or she must be an advocate for different subdisciplines and areas that earlier may have been taken for granted. Second, the new chair must move from being simply one individual to looking at the whole departmental operation. The span of responsibility is considerably expanded. Various habits of the insistent individualist must be surrendered—for instance, enlarging the number of those who will assume ownership of new ideas is quite difficult if one also continues to claim pride of authorship for them. Both transitions mean that the authority and credentials one earlier enjoyed as derived from disciplinary professionalism are inadequate. One's standing as chair is insufficiently supported by subject matter expertise, and alternative resources for leadership must be identified and cultivated. The third transition compounds the uncertainty and challenge generated by the first two—the new chair must find ways to supplement faculty loyalties to colleagues, the discipline, and the department with loyalty to the broader campus enterprise.

## The Challenges Chairpersons Face

These transitions also have implications for the broader collegium. They illustrate values and responsibilities in the larger communal setting within which individuals and departments work. Far more than most faculty, the chair experiences directly the force of these broader issues—the need to know about other inquiries, departments, and schools; to be aware of the multiple contributions and activities of the institution; and to situate the department within this larger context. He or she may have to address boards of trustees and regents, answer the questions of media representatives, respond to the findings of accreditation agencies, and explain to parents why faculty members are not present. Accordingly, there is significant value in rotating the position of department chairperson among faculty. Firsthand experience of these broader collegial dimensions nurtures hospitality and thoughtfulness. On the other hand, leadership abilities are unevenly distributed and there are individuals who by common agreement would be disastrous as chairs. And those who are capable chairs often need more than a turn or two to become fully effective.

Many chairs labor under the burden of role ambiguity. Usually long-standing faculty members who understand their identity in those terms, chairs now have special supervisory responsibilities over peers and colleagues. These new responsibilities can jeopardize long-standing friendships and generate destabilizing inner turmoil. Frequently chairpersons also report being presented with unrealistic and conflicting expectations—typically those of faculty colleagues and upper-level administrators. The former expect advocacy and other forms of special treatment; the latter look for allegiance to broader institutional goals and help in increasing productivity. These conflicts and ambiguity can be difficult, but hopeful and successful chairs approach them as potentially positive things, perhaps creating opportunities to foster excellence.

As a group, chairpersons make a substantial impact on the intellectual tone of an institution. Whether elected or appointed, in collective bargaining units or not, they are the academic leaders closest in the institution to the delivery of instructional services and can easily make a concrete difference. Depending on the manner of their selection and on circumstances of institutional governance, chairpersons may use somewhat different tactics, but their overall tasks and possibilities are the same. It is chairpersons who advance diversity of ideas and people, initiate program review and development, clarify or recast unit missions, and support new and old faculty in order to facilitate the incorporation of the one and the continued vitality of the other. It is chairpersons who reduce conflict and assure that the curriculum has integrity, fitting the institutional mission as well as changing faculty skills and abilities, student needs, institutional resources, disciplinary, and societal developments. It is they who take the lead in applying a rapidly changing computer technology to the delivery of instruction and the task of education. It is chairs who establish the department as a pedagogical as well as an intellectual and organizational unit.

In short, it is chairpersons who are the "custodians of academic standards" and to whom others look for assurance of the adequacy of teaching, research, and service. Running through these multiple responsibilities is the opportunity to display, reinforce, and deepen hospitality and thoughtfulness. It is only in actions—not in policy manuals—that standards of excellence have effect. The concrete life of the department displays and teaches its values far better than abstract statements. Patterns of hospitality and thoughtfulness are illustrated in practical settings, not in formal codes. In promoting and teaching values, effective chairs affirm, recognize, and celebrate individual and departmental excellence. They are equally bold in naming individual and collective behaviors that work against the collegium. Forthright descriptions of polarizing rhetoric, calling in sick, candor when convenient, and complaining about students communicate to colleagues that these behaviors do not advance fundamental departmental interests. Effective chairs heighten colleague awareness that acts have consequences that may be quite different for the department or the institution than for the individual. Faculty are agents of the institution—not just disciplinary experts with limited connections to their sponsoring institution. From the perspective of parents, trustees or regents, and other members of the public, as well as from a legal perspective, professors do represent the institution. Their actions can bind the institution, making it responsible and accountable for them. Successful chairs seek ways to augment faculty recognition of these realities.

## Chairpersons and Faculty

Chairpersons report considerable variation in the industriousness of their faculty—from those who remain extraordinarily undaunted by continuing challenges, to others who reflect insistent individualism and the afflictions that may come with long tenure. As Kenneth Eble noted, faculty "vary widely in competence, goals, energy, and general crankiness" (Eble 1990a, 100). Getting this assortment of individuals to work together and to embody the collegial ethic can be a job indeed. The increasing use of adjunct or part-time faculty adds to the task. How can these often talented individuals be brought from the margin or periphery closer to the daily constructive interaction of members that constitutes the collegium at its best? The greater the reliance of the department on adjuncts in the delivery of instruction, the greater the importance of cooperation, collaboration, and mutual respect and reciprocity. These values take time to cultivate. Adding to the difficulty are full-time faculty who regard adjuncts as skilled only in practice, lacking credentials that constitute full membership in the disciplinary profession—another version of academic professionalism.

Many chairs struggle to align faculty work more directly to collegium needs than to individual preferences. The fortunes of the collegium are advanced through those of the individual member, and vice versa. Hoping to advance the collegium independent of advancing its members is unrealistic. This views the collegium too much like a collective. However, some individual desires are incompatible with the common good and encouraging them leads to insistent individualism and the community as aggregation. Promoting a concept of teamwork is essential for the collegium—and by definition teamwork involves recognizing, utilizing, and promoting individual interests. Consequently, the task before the chair is to identify the mix of individual interests that if pursued and achieved will contribute to the desired balance of the department as a whole.

Having uniform expectations for faculty is almost certain to thwart this goal. Typical departments address a variety of tasks—ranging from the central one of delivering instruction and facilitating education, to recruiting and advising students, developing new curricula and pedagogies, and promoting common interests with other groups. Identifying and melding relevant and compatible individual interests so that shared goals can be achieved is essential. A natural diversity of faculty interests should be exploited. But things rarely stay in place for long. Accordingly, chairs should anticipate that faculty interests will change over time—and perhaps some changes should be encouraged. Then methods must be devised to evaluate individual contributions as they bear on the common good. The collegium is not a committee or task force. These can share information and perhaps even generate recommendations. Yet neither of these groups displays the key defining element of mutual interaction and mutual accountability that characterizes the collegium.

## STRATEGIES FOR CHAIRPERSONS

We turn now to strategies for developing and accentuating commonalities—strategies leading to effective enrichment of one another and to the mutual interaction and empowerment known as collegiality. Effective chairs cultivate the virtues of hospitality and thoughtfulness, and their application to self, students, colleagues, and the department and institution. Chairs promote openness to the new and the different, willingness to review the received and the familiar, and commitment to reason, civility, and sensitivity. These are key virtues in the collegial ethic and ones for which academe should be known. The strategies discussed below are practices that facilitate the development of these virtues.

In examining these strategies, we look for answers to the question of the authority of the academy and a response to Charles Anderson's troubling observation that faculties do not take responsibility for the curriculum. The public understanding of the academy is that the faculty as a whole is the guardian of the curriculum. Anderson suggests that in reality this guardianship is less than wholehearted. "Except in the most egregious cases, it is clearly understood that no one asks impertinent questions about whether what others are teaching is sound, or worthwhile. If each leaves the other alone, then we can all do as we please. Further, it is generally assumed that there are no standards of truth, pertinence, or worth that apply across fields." Anderson's disturbing conclusion is that too often "faculty may have collegial responsibilities, but they do not constitute a *collegium*" (Anderson 1993, 147).

## Recruitment, Orientation, and Mentoring

After years marked by few new faculty hires, institutions are now experiencing turnover and change. Investing time, energy, and care in hiring and nurturing newcomers is the best and easiest avenue for fashioning and sustaining a vital and vigorous department. Promoting the collegium requires the right match between persons hired and positions filled, between individual talents and departmental needs. Equal effort must be spent in integrating new faculty into the department and institution. In pursuing these tasks, a properly organized and energetic relational community has enormous advantages over passive autonomous "communities."

### *Recruitment*

Successful hiring requires first that departments and institutions know who they want to be. Department needs and future possibilities must be carefully studied and plans developed. Planning activities can themselves be lengthy and difficult, demanding skill by chairpersons in keeping goals clearly before faculty. Programs with specialized accreditation have an advantage. However burdensome other aspects of self-studies and site visits may be, they promote excellence by demanding periodic accountability to a set of external norms. Those without the benefit of an external catalyst—for instance, most liberal arts programs—need to initiate regular planning and evaluation on their own.

Assuming sufficient planning, networks should be tapped to elicit the interest of desirable and diverse candidates. Proactive and aggressive efforts to attract these individuals require energy and creativity. Even in a buyers' market, the department and institution must sell themselves. Unfortunately, the sad story of too many searches involves inhospitable or thoughtless communication with candidates. The search is a passive one, the key strategy being simply the placement of an advertisement. Questions of those interviewed reveal failure to have studied their materials. After the search is concluded, communications with applicants are terse and mechanical—creating or reinforcing negative impressions of the institution.

Alert search committees avoid these blunders. They spend considerable time studying the personal and professional goals of top candidates. Genuine interest by the new person in working with others in a relational community is as important as his or her subject matter expertise and teaching abilities and interests. Discussions with candidates cover these matters and determined efforts are made to verify their interest and ability to conduct teaching and research in a relational community. Promoting relational values starts early and continues throughout the search and screening stages.

Clear communication with candidates about present collegium realities and future hopes is essential. In addition to providing a full array of statistical information about the department and the institution, sharing significant narratives about the past, present, and desired future communicates to candidates the flavor of the situation and its opportunities. These narratives also help the socialization process and convey the virtues for which the department or division seeks to be known. Candor and honesty about tenure and promotion requirements as well as expected contributions to the collegium set the tone for future behaviors. Hiding dirty linen, negative departmental or institutional personalities, or anticipated funding difficulties provides little short-term value. Most candidates of quality can see through these strategems. Those who are misled come with false understandings and expectations, creating problems down the road.

## *Orientation*

Then new colleagues must be welcomed and included. Like Sorcinelli, Robert Boice finds that despite the younger finalists' initial optimism and obvious relief at finding a job, "what overshadows the experience of many newcomers is the despair of isolation, insecurity, and busyness" (Boice 1992, 2). Reflecting on his troubling findings respecting the initial inhospitableness of campuses to new faculty, Boice observes that becoming an integral part of a new community can take years. He adds that "even at campuses where socialization and support occur more rapidly, the process seems maddeningly inefficient and inhuman to new hires" (Boice 1992, 44). What we are calling insistent individualism rather than relational warmth predominates. Many campuses are simply not hospitable to new faculty. In fact, Boice concludes, faculty "recruitment and orientation have commonly been conducted in deplorable fashion" (Boice 1992, 229). The price is steep—first impressions linger and initial missteps have long-term impact.

Once identified, new faculty should not be expected simply to show up for work. Many institutions show their most inhospitable features at this point—once the offer has been accepted, committee members return to their preoccupations. They forget their good intentions, and their own memories of the rigors of moving to a new area have faded. This neglect quickly undoes earlier good work, creating the impression of the individualistic rather than the relational community. The new colleague should be assigned an enthusiastic contact person to provide help during the relocation process. Then, thoughtful orientation programs for new people—both faculty and staff—are in order. Careful assignments within the department and school should meet the needs of newcomers to adjust to and identify with the new environment.

Boice's extensive research findings highlight other problems for new, inexperienced faculty. His studies suggest that their ability quickly to achieve balance among teaching, research, and networking is important to successful integration into the community. New faculty's "performance and satisfaction in any one area, such as teaching, depends on progress in related domains, such as collegiality and scholarship" (Boice 1992, xii). There is no reason to think that the progress of experienced faculty is any different. Despite what new faculty may initially report, their attention to better task management rather than merely additional released time is often what is most important. Without the former, the latter is wasted. Although new faculty usually express intentions to do research and writing, overpreparation for teaching combined with procrastination and a kind of perpetual busyness plague many of them.

### *Mentoring*

Obviously, good mentoring can be invaluable for collaboration in teaching, research, and grant proposal preparation (Boice 1992, 125). Equally important, though, creative mentoring of junior faculty can facilitate better task management and allocation of time and energy. It may be, Boice suggests, that the academy simply assumes these tacit skills in new faculty. We have seen that many faculty appear to have similar assumptions regarding students. The skills are left untaught because they are taken for granted. In the implicit social Darwinism of insistent individualism, those with the "right stuff" take care of these matters by themselves. A review of department and institutional policies and practices that work against effective mentoring can pay dividends. Good mentoring is a mark of the relational community, indicating at a minimum that someone cares. Topics of regular meetings include developing a research agenda, refining teaching and examination strategies, and discussing the local characters and lore. Since new faculty are often passive about seeking collegial support, good mentors can be crucially important—these are experienced colleagues who provide social support and help to counteract the isolation that many new faculty report, especially women and minority faculty members.

Mentoring can also address different needs of other faculty at particular points in their careers. For instance, mentoring can provide growth possibilities for senior faculty, allowing them to make contributions based upon their years of experience rather than upon subject-matter expertise. For their part, younger faculty may be able to assist older professors with technology in teaching and research. The use of multiple mentors, some of them from outside the department, also advances the relational community. The mentoring experience can establish and extend trust and lead all parties to renewed and deepened reflection upon the collegium and its future.

## The Complainers, Evaluation, and the Disaffected

### The Complainers

Faculty complaining is normal and natural. It offers a way to protect jeopardized stability, and it provides catharsis. It validates the difficulty of the job, and it secures companionship with others. Hence, to hear *no* complaining ought to give concern. But sometimes complainers must be confronted, reality checks imposed, and limits to self-indulgence established. Despite what their rhetoric may suggest, faculty have large personal and professional interests in the success of their colleagues and the viability of their institutions. Their hearts may be captive to disciplinary professionalism, but faculty status and paychecks are tied to the campus. It can be easy and entertaining to lambast the administration, the governor, and various legislators or trustees for their mischief and insensitivity. Student capabilities are always an easy target. But sooner or later chairs must help these faculty attend to the fortunes of the campus and the threats before it, and to become engaged accordingly.

For instance, faculty may be seriously out of touch with developments in secondary education, and they need to be engaged in the recruitment of students to obtain accurate insight. Protecting their time for scholarship does faculty no favors if it insulates them from the realities of competition for students. Chairs can invite admissions representatives to explore recruitment realities with the department. Certainly faculty are the best ones to convey to potential students the advantages of studying in their areas of inquiry, to make them feel welcome and to generate excitement about the institution. Surely it is in faculty self-interest to assist with developing and updating recruitment literature, contacting admitted students, and securing internships and clinical placements for them. And any complaining about high school graduates ought first to acknowledge the responsibility of the university to teach high school teachers.

### Evaluation

Evaluation activities offer chairs significant opportunities to review with individual faculty how their interests relate to department goals and objectives. These activities provide occasions to recognize faculty for contributions to the common good that might otherwise go unnoted, identify changing interests of faculty as well as explore possibilities to advance them, and reinforce the obligations and strengths of faculty that are particularly important to the department and the institution.

Instituting periodic evaluations of senior faculty members has special potential to enhance both individual and institutional behavior. They are an excellent mechanism for counteracting insistent individualism and the tendency with age to withdraw from institutional involvements. Some argue that no special mechanisms are needed. For instance, the Solomons observe the need for faculty (not chairs or deans) to take the initiative in upholding institutional and professorial quality. "Inadequate teachers must be reprimanded . . . . and the faculty would be well advised to do this for themselves." This does not require administrative mandates, the Solomons suggest: "It simply takes professors who have an interest in the students, who pay attention to what their colleagues are doing and make it a matter of personal obligation to see to it that all—not just their own courses—are taught well" (Solomon and Solomon 1993, 212–213). However obvious and appropriate this sentiment, few faculty ever act on it. Reflecting the legacy of insistent individualism, peer review—acknowledging excellence, providing the helping hand, conveying concern or even rebuke—rarely takes place apart from institutionalized structures and time frames.

At most institutions, the bulk of evaluation activity is focused on the probationary period. Despite the confident and apodictic AAUP statement noted earlier, once one has achieved tenure and full professorship, there may be no formal, significant peer review for years. In fact, decades may go by before a comprehensive assessment occurs. Where they are in place, annual evaluations are often *pro forma*, rushed affairs. Only an application for sabbatical might trigger the need to articulate and defend before colleagues one's intellectual agenda. Even that occasion can be limited to discussion of the proposed project, rather than also one's larger scholarly and teaching efforts and accomplishments—or, equally important, the needs of the department and institution and how one's efforts can be directed to meet those needs.

What is often lacking is an institutionalized process through which colleagues review on a regular basis the whole complex of matters that constitute the collegial professionalism of the faculty member. Through this format colleagues can discuss with the insistent, unconnected individualist issues of citizenship. A formal structure provides incentive for more direct, honest, and searching peer review and discussion with all senior members of the collegium. It also provides additional opportunity for faculty to direct and renew their own careers within the context of the collegium. This is especially important for long-term faculty members and those with academic projects requiring long-term time frames that cannot be accommodated by annual review processes. In addition, a schedule of periodic evaluation of senior faculty provides more equity in a system that can focus almost exclusively on junior faculty. Likewise, someone needs to attend to the continuing development needs of mid-career faculty members. The easy assumption that the standard career is uniform is usually misplaced. Most faculty careers have various phases; they need institutional room for change. Many faculty need others to support and encourage (authorize, as it were) plans for self-renewal.

In periodic evaluation sessions, faculty present for colleague reaction, critique, and assistance, developments in their teaching philosophy as well as in scholarly interests and energies. Contributions regularly made to the collegium are identified, examined, and celebrated; the possibility of new ones is explored. The power of the peer group is harnessed. Yet since the faculty member has the opportunity to identify and plan future career steps, he or she retains a key element of control. The structure of periodic evaluation often includes the development of an informal "growth" or "performance" contract wherein the individual lays out his or her proposals for the future with timetables and mechanisms for evaluation.

Some institutions provide faculty a range of choices within which to emphasize teaching more than scholarship or vice versa, over an agreed-upon time period. Service is often a constant, though it too can be negotiated. This version of a dual track accommodates changing individual preferences within a collegial context of needs. The interval between periodic evaluations varies at institutions where it is practiced, usually ranging from three to seven years. Staffing the review committee with some faculty from other departments and schools enhances opportunities for mutual education across disciplinary boundaries and may result in new teaching and research projects, thereby revitalizing the individual, extending the collegium, enriching institutional offerings and competencies, and practicing hospitality all at the same time.

What otherwise would remain private is thus made public in an appropriate forum—with promise to extend the collegium as well as to assure continued individual growth. An institutionally sanctioned and formalized schedule of evaluations can foster the collegium and assure faculty and the public that appropriate relational procedures and values are in place—that faculty development activities are occurring, faculty are not left to swim on their own (and perhaps to flounder) without attention from others, and tenure is not a shield from accountability as some suspect. In the process, problems of fragmentation are addressed, connectivity encouraged, and the prospects for continued individual and collegial vitality promoted.

### The Disaffected

Surely such procedures are the best antidote for stagnation or indifference. Often, though, they were not available to those who needed them most. However, healthy collegia do not give up prematurely on the disaffected. Some of the alienated are "dozing wood" rather than "dead wood." The former may be awakened to fresh activity and contributions. Colleagues, department chairs, and deans all have a role to play in the recovery of hope. Complaining or isolated faculty may seem to enjoy indulging themselves, but on another level the opposite is more likely true. For reasons that are complex and elusive, any of us can become trapped in unattractive behaviors. We may want desperately to change but cannot because we have lost touch with the resources that could empower us to do so.

Bruce Wilshire describes the pathos of such persons: "The special authority of the university educator is a humiliating burden for persons who will not or cannot accept responsibility for their own fixations and terrors as persons, failures of self-knowledge and self-control. The temptation to drop the burden is great, to simply forgo some small status as special pedagogical authorities, and to be released in return from the responsibility of facing students and themselves as persons needing to be educated" (Wilshire 1990, 200). In these cases other faculty, chairs, and deans need imaginatively and creatively to reach out to colleagues who threaten to drag down the whole enterprise with their indifference or negativity.

Sometimes the fatigued or isolated individual can be reenergized by reestablishing connections with others through new activities—perhaps special ad hoc involvements, tailored to areas of earlier or current interest. Maybe a "buddy system" could be established with a sympathetic but productive and collegially oriented colleague. Discrete inquiry is in order to determine this possibility. The isolated individuals must be assured of their continuing worth to the institution. Defense mechanisms may need to be identified and bypassed. Discussions should emphasize specific behaviors to be strengthened or changed, not generalized judgments of disapproval. Successful initiatives start with what someone can do, not with who he or she has become.

At some point, though, it becomes clear that individuals who repeatedly refuse help cannot be helped. After limits to inappropriate behaviors have been set and time tables for implementing change have come and gone, chairs should offer these truly dead wood a way out. Mandatory retirement is no longer a solution; few institutions have the financial capacity to carry them. Flush days are gone and everyone needs to pull their weight. It is also a moral issue; who has an answer to the returning alumni asking why *that* professor is still here—when they did their best to avoid him or her decades ago. Continuing to list his or her courses as taught by "staff" in order to induce enrollments is hardly courageous. Retirement is overdue.

Even stronger counsel applies to what the Solomons call rotten wood. These are the truly disaffected individuals on a campaign to ruin not only their own happiness in the academy but others' as well. Dead wood are relatively harmless and provide little danger to the enterprise. By comparison, rotten wood faculty are pernicious. "One such professor can destroy an entire department and, with sufficient ingenuity or personal power, can keep it in ruins for decades . . . . like an infected tree in the middle of a once-flourishing woods the rotten-wood professor kills everything around him or her" (Solomon and Solomon 1993, 245). Unfortunately, faculty can agree on who the rotten wood are and yet be unwilling to confront them or initiate processes to remove them. Without sufficient colleague support, few chairs feel able to move forward. There is no national association with energetic standards of membership and exclusion to look to for help; a courageous dean usually has to initiate termination. The academy seems at its most feckless in these cases that model neither hospitality nor thoughtfulness—only the unwillingness of colleagues to confront the rotten wood in a firm and honest way. This failure of the professoriate often exacts a substantial toll.

## Promoting Communication by All Means Possible

As a form of self-regulation within the department, collegiality requires commitment to public discussion of ideas. The different disciplines provide ways of asking questions and making connections in a dynamic, changing world. Establishing connections does not mean group thinking. Appropriate balance between the individual and the collegium is the goal—the mean between an aggregation of individualists and the loss of individuality to collectivity. In the latter case the whole seems to be less than the sum of its parts. The collegium, however, is more than the sum of its parts. With the leadership of the chair and the help of good citizens, it becomes a place where individuals exercise hospitality and thoughtfulness.

Ken Eble wrote of the importance and satisfaction of good communication. He termed it a central requirement and defining characteristic of leadership— "for chairpersons, as for the faculty and students they serve, joys are greater for being shared joys, individual achievements greater for their part in the shared achievements of others" (Eble 1990b, 25). This is not without its risks. Every communication can be misunderstood, ignored, or resented by someone. Add the influence of insistent individualism and one can end up with an aversion to communication. Few chairs, Eble notes, have been scolded for cancelling department meetings. The attractions of the closed classroom and the private research project are obvious. But eventually, Eble also observes, "the oddity of people being together but not talking or gathering sooner or later affects a department . . . . [Someone] will want to break the silence" (Eble 1990b, 24– 25). Communicating is integral to being human. We are relational beings, and in the broadest sense, communicating is relating to others and allowing them to influence us. Communicating is a form of relational power. For the chairperson, as for others, relating "can be showing up for some faculty or student activity out of both honest interest and a sensed need to lend support. It can be pats on the back and kicks in the ass and the picking up of people who have stumbled" (Eble 1990b, 26).

## Providing Opportunities for Exchange

Successful academic leaders create as many opportunities as possible to strengthen the collegium by promoting discourse and exchange. One responsibility of the chair is to facilitate the flow of organizational information—to and from faculty and administrators. Providing equal access to information seems an essential part of thoughtfulness—together with appropriate consultation, discussion and agreement on operational matters. Effective chairs use these discussions to support the department as an intellectual and pedagogical unit. As Shils noted, "it is not easy, in a period when many senior academics have allowed, or even aided, the disaggregation of their universities, for the new generation of teachers to develop a sense of the university as a corporate body collectively engaged in intellectual work" (Shils 1984, 57). Yet without collective review in the public forum of the collegium, there is only the isolated and untested idea. It is in the collegium that critique, innovation, and diversity should be most highly valued. It is here that disagreeing with prevailing views should generate larger and more penetrating insights. It is here especially that disagreement should function in positive and provocative ways, and not be mere carping.

The academy is currently struggling to accommodate diversity in the curriculum and among colleagues and students. The centrifugal forces of insistent individualism are reinforced by dislike of change and difference; but we are poorer when our collegia incorporate no diversity in experience, learning, or background. Without a variety of ideas and persons to provide contrast, collegia become bland and monotonous. Of course, too much diversity introduces discord. Increased tendencies toward isolationism and separatism occur, provoking polarizing rhetoric. Destructive conflict ensues, increasing distance and diminishing connectivity. Common commitment to the importance of diversity and disagreement—the virtue of accommodating dissent with civility—is tested and strained. These situations require an even greater commitment to communication and to developing the skills it requires. Discourse is therefore a key resource for successful chairpersons. Selves are created in and through their connections to others and discourse provides the means of mutual recognition and enrichment, prerequisites for a common vision. Attention to the language with which the collegium is promoted is necessary. In cases where faculty, particularly women and minorities, have found discourse about the collegium functioning as code words for exclusion, terms such as colleagueship or intellectual community might be more effective—unless these terms are also used to exclude.

In any case, the successful leader creates opportunities for forums, symposia, brownbags, and joint projects, and makes sure that individuals are not only invited but engaged. Topics include matters of pedagogy, research interests, disciplinary and societal developments, changing student abilities and how to address them, department and institutional mission and direction, and other matters reminding faculty why they entered the academy. One of the most productive and valuable exchanges is sharing fundamental personal objectives that bear on teaching and scholarship. This requires that faculty become truly available to each other, divesting themselves of armor and conceits. Collegial review of writing is also a resource. Some colleagues restrict themselves to simple notations of typographical or grammatical errors, but others provide helpful bibliographical suggestions or even a full-scale commentary on structure and content. Sharing writing in draft form with colleagues not only enhances the eventual product, but colleagues are more likely to respond to something where they feel they can make a difference. Thus, many feel complimented by a sincere request for feedback.

### Healthy Interactions

Members of a healthy and hospitable collegium are willing to seek the judgment of others on new ideas and directions—willing to articulate and defend judgments about academic standards before colleagues and to place similar demands on others. Likewise, members of a healthy collegium credit new colleagues with a share of its power and authority, a share commensurate with the share each claims for himself or herself. The creativity of a collegium and those in it is a function of this receptiveness to novelty. A good idea is rarely sustainable unless it is part of a larger environment of coordinated ideas—sustained by a community because of its attractiveness and usefulness. When this happens, possibilities for knowledge are "in the air." In Whitehead's technical terms, propositions become available for appropriation and for functioning as lures within the collegium.

Civility and hospitality are essential. It is only through conversations of respect that genuine accommodations of intellectual differences can be reached and participants become more sensitive to the limitations in their own particular perspectives. These must be more than political accommodations, private arrangements of mutual benefit—perhaps devised to ignore troublesome people or issues. They are intellectual accommodations wherein one's own position is strengthened by taking account of opposing considerations. The Marxist economist confronts the advocate of free markets and vice versa. They do not ignore one another and call such indifference toleration; nor do they label mere custom the product of intellectual principle or conviction.

Once vigorous and respectful discourse is a habit, it is easier for faculty to acknowledge that the collegium is created, expressed, and extended through activities wherein participants engage each other and seek common ground on language, knowledge, values, and mores. Departmental direction is better determined after open discussions where individual hidden agendas and fears are uncovered, identified, and negotiated. Once surfaced, disagreements become opportunities for creative resolution and initiatives. Likewise, acknowledging fear of failure creates the possibility for enlarged community and the support from others establishes freedom. Sometimes even complaining is a disguised request for recognition and affirmation. It can be a curious, indirect way of making one's private self public, so that one might be acknowledged in the end.

At other times, though, complaining seems to be chronic self-indulgence. Since the collegium is defined by its discourse, consistent negative complaining is ultimately corrosive and must be checked. When complainers carry the day, the community loses its will or energy to change and, in the process, its ability to hope. Complainers settle for the unattractive alternatives of cynicism and despair. Newer faculty become discouraged as well, retreat to their own classrooms, and give up on the possibility of contributing to colleague renewal.

## Public Celebration of Teaching and Scholarship

Chairs can tap two other mechanisms for building communities of hope. One is the adroit use of opportunities to recognize and celebrate individual accomplishments and to relate them to the unifying values and themes that inform the common good. A second resource is provided by the further use of peer review—an implicit repudiation of individualism and cynicism.

### Internal Acknowledgement

Special recognition should be provided faculty who are consistently creative in their approaches to student learning. As argued here, teaching and learning cannot remain private transactions, but must become public acts. Successful departments find ways to share teaching and research successes, as well as explore frustrations and disappointments. Since teaching remains the private reserve of some faculty, it is important that chairs develop ways for colleagues to speak of their instructional work and the establishment and achievement of learning objectives. For teachers not to teach each other is an ultimate irony.

Celebrating the importance of reciprocal teaching and learning is the first step toward overcoming privatization. It is also a poignant comment on a collegium when a faculty member is better known regionally than locally for his or her scholarly and research achievements. Research and scholarship are also acts of teaching, so the department is poorer when it overlooks these accomplishments. And this faculty member can easily become lost to the collegium, for one naturally attends more to those who provide recognition and affirmation. It falls to the chair, with the help of informed colleagues, to prevent this from happening.

The best way to celebrate teaching and scholarship publicly is for the chair to play cheerleader for the department and its members. Faculty vary widely in their degrees of modesty. Some delight in bringing to the attention of others their accomplishments, few of which may actually be significant. Other faculty keep to themselves genuine achievements for fear of tooting their own horn. Chairs can relieve the discomfort of the latter by publicizing their accomplishments, perhaps thereby also quietening the former. Effective chairs recognize individual accomplishments *and* relate them to the common good, perhaps using traditional ceremonies to do so. Rituals magnify and amplify the values celebrated—in larger gatherings academic garb reminds us of our continuity with the past. Among their multiple values, these rituals help the collegium recognize and apply to itself the same standards of practice and accomplishment members expect of others. Relational community is reinforced, for celebrations acknowledge interdependence and the need to nurture intellectual reciprocity.

We are reminded that the critical and constructive scrutiny that peers can provide is an essential part of collegial professionalism. The only alternatives are stagnation or external regulation. Far from an exercise in partisanship or conviviality, peer review demands critical distance as an essential part of the presentation and defense of scholarly claims. It repudiates both objectivist knowledge that has no impact on the self and subjectivist knowledge that is completely private and devoid of compelling authority. Peer review is associated with the recognition that the scholarly community is always more than what one brings to it, that issues of meaning and truth are not exhaustively reducible to the particularities of one's situation, and that there is an intersubjectively available reality that makes demands upon us.

### External Recognition

In principle there is always a place for external peer comment in tenure and promotion decisions. If no letters of evaluation are ever sought, the impression is given that the department, school, or college has sufficient data to make decisions. The implication is that each community has sufficiently in view appropriate standards and evidence of excellence, and that it is disinterested in broader, external public canons of reason and assessment. By contrast, seeking external comment reaffirms connectedness with other communities and commitment to broader concepts of authority. The practical issue then becomes the identification of peers and the areas on which they are to comment and the standards to be used. Unfortunately, recent years have brought increased concerns and lawsuits respecting the reliability of external comment, so careful direction as well as protection against liability must be provided these peers.

In the end, honest peer review returns to the local collegia the final responsibility for judgments on faculty accomplishments. Some institutions depend entirely too much on assessments by outsiders. For instance, collegia may place too high a premium on refereed publications. Articles placed in journals with a high rejection rate are deemed better than others. The worth of a book manuscript is correlated with the standing of the press that publishes it. Rather than directly judging the importance of an individual's scholarly work by reading and discussing it, collegia use these external proxies—often as a first, rather than a last, resort. They then displace onto others what is their responsibility, at the same time that they miss an opportunity for mutual education and closer collegial communication.

External factors will accelerate the return of some of these judgments to the campus. The costs of printing and marketing highly specialized scholarly monographs and books are rising rapidly, diminishing publishing opportunities. Similarly, research institutions that define the appropriate peer community in national and international terms are experiencing reduced funding from external sources. They need to shift from relying heavily on successful grants activity as a key criterion of excellence to considering local assessments of scholarship, teaching, and other campus contributions. It seems unfair and unproductive to have institutional expectations for particular forms of faculty productivity that external agencies are no longer supporting in accustomed quantity. In any case, assessments of excellence ought to rely significantly on informed internal judgments of quality.

## Governance Considerations

Chairpersons also must assure that sufficient mechanisms are in place to check logrolling and political opportunism. Without national codes of ethics and good practice, the academy can fall into arrangements of convenience it rightly condemns in others. These include the tacit understandings that each can do his or her thing, unchecked by rigorous review—understandings that overlook how easily pursuit of knowledge in academe can be transmuted into pursuit of unilateral power. Accordingly, the collegium needs to attend carefully to its own governance processes. As we saw, many collegia use secret ballots on controversial matters of curriculum revision or faculty appointment and promotion. Proponents of confidentiality cite the need of members to work together over the long haul—a condition presumably made more difficult by having colleagues know one's vote on an issue of potential controversy. But surely the practice can also be seen as a failure of nerve, and another case in which the academy dwells in excessive privacy. The best mechanism for assuring academic honesty is to require that one present reasons for one's position. Then there is a community of the known as well as the knowers. A policy of confidentiality and privacy would be desirable only as a last, not a first, resort.

In sum, the department is the context for reciprocity among its constituent members, as the school or college is the wider context for departments. The chair has a leadership role to play in advancing the reciprocity that creates a vital department. As the department collegium is continually recreated and membership renegotiated, the conversations should be broadened so that allied departments are referenced and eventually included. Collegia will come to overlap, and to encompass smaller units, helping to create and support the broader common good of academe. However, without sustained, vigorous activity that effective leadership evokes, the collegium disappears, weakening other communities of learning to which it is related. Without intellectual reciprocity the academy loses moral and intellectual authority. It jeopardizes its ability to contribute to the commonwealth and to make legitimate claims upon the public purse. The stakes are high.

## SCHOOL AND COLLEGE DEANS

Chairs and academic deans are themselves natural, indeed indispensable, allies. Both dean and chair must work through others to create and maintain collegia—to enhance connectivity and counteract fragmentation. To this end, deans depend upon chairs just as chairs depend upon department faculty. In turn, faculty look to chairs for support and help just as chairs count on the dean. So there are relationships of dependence in both directions, as there should be in the relational model. Obviously, for chairs and deans to succeed as leaders there must be collaboration. They must attend to each other.

Effective deans help chairs welcome new faculty into the institution. Together, dean and chair plan how to use to advantage the innovative and constructive understandings of academic standards, scholarly authority, and styles of teaching that new faculty bring. They seek to empower newcomers and incorporate them into the collegium. Dean and chair also puzzle over how to work with new faculty who bring inappropriate, unhelpful understandings and practices. Similarly, good deans assist chairs in constructing opportunities to support and reinvigorate mid-level and senior faculty as well as to identify rotten wood and devise strategies for relief. What chairs and deans attend and notice is noticed by others. Priorities are communicated by where one spends time.

Academic deans often find that some chairs work in isolation—paralleling the insistent individualist faculty member. Sometimes chairs prefer isolation, perhaps for the same reasons that motivate faculty. Other chairs do not, and yet may not know how to cross the barriers. In both cases the dean needs to be alert to opportunities to provide help. One possibility is creating communities of support and learning for chairpersons—for instance, an institution-wide council of chairs with a small budget for regular meetings. Chairs in quite different departments frequently face many of the same problems and can be resources to one another. Certainly new chairs may need mentoring. Deans and other chairs are the best candidates to provide guidance and support.

Chairs often have different attitudes toward the tasks at hand. Some bring considerable seriousness of purpose to their positions and are hopeful about their ability to make a difference. Others give in to cynicism or anger, perhaps after initial optimism is dulled by too many failed initiatives. The cynical chair usually seeks the path of least resistance, opting to preserve the status quo rather than make waves. The angry chair may diminish the common good by aggressively working against larger initiatives. Deans need to help cynical and angry chairs renew themselves so that they can again offer leadership to the department. Provosts and chairs need to help the cynical or angry dean. Hopeful chairs and deans feel little need for the apologetic, defensive rhetoric about leadership that is all too prevalent in academe—rhetoric that academic leadership is an unfortunate necessity, not something to be celebrated. This historic devaluation of leadership has served the academy poorly.

## The Power of the Budget

Other tools at the dean's disposal include the budget and the power to interpret institutional events. However limited, budgets and financial rewards are important. Even small financial perquisites and salary increases provide recognition and incentive; and the overall impact of decanal financial power can be marshaled to significant effect. For instance, there is considerable evidence that annual salary increases awarded by chairs and dean have contributed to the increased emphasis upon individual research defined in contrast or even opposition to teaching—despite what they may have intended. "Regardless of institutional type or mission and irrespective of program area, faculty who spend more time on research and who publish the most are paid more than their teaching-oriented colleagues" (Fairweather 1996, 67).

Incentives can also be used to foster the collegium. Goals established for a department as a whole provide an incentive for members to work cooperatively—perhaps even collaboratively, thereby creating a culture of shared responsibility. The road is uphill, however, for almost everywhere department performance is judged by limited criteria. Faculty as individuals may have prominent research records and distinguished teaching reputations or both. But a department composed of these individuals can be altogether undistinguished in its work as a department. Its students can display low graduation rates, perform poorly in GRE examinations, or fail in other measures of accomplishment or satisfaction. If departments are to encourage and nurture collaborative activity, some rewards need to be collective ones. Traditional practices provide little reason for colleagues to have stakes in each other's teaching, for instance, when rewards reflect only individual accomplishments. Deans can help chairs by establishing compensation policies that actually reward teamwork as well as individual performance.

For instance, deans can recognize, commend, and reward budgetarily departments whose members commit themselves to a common purpose and set of performance goals and make progress in meeting those goals—departments that function as teams, that work as collegia rather than just as aggregations. This is fairly common respecting extramurally funded research. As Richard Chait observes, departments often receive collective support for research in the form of a return of a percentage of indirect costs. "Such an approach creates precisely the proper incentive: the more sponsored research department members conduct, the more the department benefits. Everyone has a vested interest not only in doing research, but also in encouraging others to do so" (Chait 1988, 23). Group rewards for collective teaching accomplishments, though still unusual, would provide similar incentives. Providing formal recognition and reward for departmental teaching accomplishment would not be difficult. Student evaluations are commonly administered. Other assessment instruments can be created and data aggregated to identify departmental effectiveness.

Focusing on collective performance might encourage contributing members to call "alien residents" to account for their failure to contribute to the common effort. When the collegium agrees to pursue specific goals and measurable outcomes, individual members have greater reason to demand peer accountability. As a result, the arguments of insistent individualists diminish in force and persuasiveness. Precedents for such agreements abound in the crafting of common syllabi, text assignments, and evaluation activities in different sections of a course. Few departments have gone the extra step and agreed to pursue common student performance outcomes. To be sure, such an agreement requires considerable trust among participating faculty and the recognition that quite uneven results between classes can be expected from time to time. The trust that participating faculty will not undercut one another or abandon the goal is created only by first presupposing trust and regularly discussing progress toward achieving the goal.

Moreover, departmental efforts to achieve other institutionally desirable goals such as affirmative action can be stimulated and supported by appropriate incentive structures administered by the dean. A number of institutions do provide such incentives, sometimes awarding extra positions for those departments or divisions meeting diversity objectives in hiring—or authorizing positions only if diversity candidates are identified. An even more radical approach is to make other departmental perquisites such as increased travel funds contingent upon recruitment success. Such policies should not be contemplated without also considering potential complaints of injustice from departments facing small pools of minority candidates. And those in state-supported institutions will need legal counsel before proceeding. These would all be examples of aligning institutional rewards with the promotion of greater collegiality, teamwork, and hospitality.

## The Power of Interpretation

The academic dean also has the obligation to interpret and reinforce the college and institutional mission. Interpretation is the power to locate various developments within an overall context of meaning. Good news can be announced and celebrated—its impact upon the institution identified, its significance assessed, and its import for the future communicated. Setbacks can be acknowledged, enabling others to talk more freely about present losses and impending difficulties. This role is rarely one of making elegant speeches. Some occasions do require that the dean speak resolutely, even eloquently. But more often the requirement is that he or she look for opportunities to hint, to nudge, and to reinforce. Interpretation is often the best means for the dean to address the phenomenon of implicit organizational relativism—the tacit sense that despite institutional priorities, each department is as worthy as the other. Discernment goes hand in hand with budget. All departments are important, but rarely are they equally important. Some are obvious candidates for expansion as changing student interests, societal needs, or disciplinary or technological developments suggest. Others may be in stasis or decline for the same reasons. Interpretation is a form of empowerment—liberating others to accept the truth and to respond with insight and courage rather than denial or despair.

## Exercising Influence

Deans must work against insistent organizational individualism. The natural academic tendency is centrifugal—each department, however unified, tends to follow its own pursuits independent of other departments. Highlighting the undesirable messages about institutional values conveyed by this tendency is the first step toward addressing it. The next step is working closely with faculty and department chairs to define workload and citizenship expectations. Additionally, the curriculum can be just as effective as faculty stars or resident aliens in promoting organizational individualism and fragmentation. Although faculty rightly view curricula as their "territory," there are areas where deans can exercise influence. For instance, deans can help mediate wars over the curriculum in ways that promote rather than retard the growth and extension of collegia. Usually one side argues that the canon has been constructed at great expense and should not be tinkered with because it has worked over long periods. Those on the other side regard the canon inadequate to the realities and rapid developments of the contemporary world because it sanctions limited, dated, or even discriminatory perspectives. Some even argue that the very concept of a canon should be abandoned because of its privileging of oppressive, hegemonic, and exclusionary positions, ideas, and values.

George Allan recently analyzed this challenge before deans in terms of the melioristic role advocated by William James—the role of mediating between competing positions respecting the objective hierarchy of values (Allan 1991). A canon is by definition hierarchical, for it asserts that some texts, theories, and methods are more important and worthy of study than others. Advocates of the canon argue that reality, likewise, is to be understood as ordered into more and less essential elements. The more essential are more worthy of study and the job of a canon is to insist upon that distinction and to present authoritative materials. The noncanonists point instead to the nonhierarchical plurality of conflicting truths, practices, and beliefs of our increasingly diverse age. Reality is to be understood as a pluralism of individualities rather than essences. The issue is far from incidental, as it raises the very point and meaning of learning—and hence of the academy, which is charged with facilitating and transmitting learning. If all is relative to the learner, there is no authoritative role for the academy.

## Building Bridges

James rejected the position that knowledge is a matter of objectively mirroring reality in our minds with no involvement of the knower. Instead, he held that there is always a human factor in knowing. As he put matters, "the trail of the human serpent is...over everything" (James 1991, 31). Because of this human involvement, all claims are fallible and contestable; all contain an admixture of the human and the real. "Does the river make its banks, or do the banks make the river? Does a man walk with his right leg or with his left leg more essentially? Just as impossible may it be to separate the real from the human factors in the growth of our cognitive experience" (James 1991, 110). Building on James' position, Allan argues that the educational canon is to be understood as a framework of texts, methods, and other materials that has proved effective in making sense of things, in living within and understanding a culture. Canons are not arbitrary—texts are not equally valuable or insightful. Yet no canon is inviolate; each bears the marks of its origins, indications of the circumstances of its human construction. Each canon is partial, and new texts and insights are needed to supplement it—perhaps even to replace it. Every canon both frames experience and is itself an object for investigation and potential correction. Canons give coherence and purpose to human existence, but communities change and novelties emerge. To be adequate, canons too must change—complementing, correcting, absorbing, and adjusting the new to the old, rather than simply piling it alongside. The new must be married to the old. Bridges must be built and crossed.

Allan argues that the dean's job is to assure that absolutists of neither right nor left win. The canon is neither sacrosanct nor arbitrary. The goal is to secure a collectively owned responsibility for the good of students—to disown curricula that enshrine disconnections between general education and majors, between liberal and professional, between campus and the world. We can add that the dean needs to teach that debates about the content of the canon can obscure how the quality of reading is as important as the text. The questions asked release or restrict the power of the text. To recall another metaphor, the act of dancing is as important as the dance.

## Marrying the New to the Old

Marrying the new to the old is a rich metaphor. We can apply it not only to the curriculum but to other department and college work. It characterizes the need to relate new hires to established, perhaps even entrenched, faculty. It describes the periodic work of program review and development. And it describes the continuing challenge of examining department, college, and institution missions as student populations, societal needs, and disciplinary directions change. These leadership roles of marrying the new to the old are best effected through relational power, through receiving influence as much as providing it, through weaving rather than stacking or imposing. Stacking suggests simple coexistence. However, weaving leads to supplementing, correcting, perhaps even fundamental restructuring.

Effective academic leaders make judicious use of committees to promote and secure these larger institutional values and perspectives. Making careful appointments and giving thoughtful charges provide benefits to both personnel and curricular committees. In neither case must all committee members have subject-matter expertise. Instead, their role is to judge more broadly—to assess the credibility of the reports of subject-matter experts and to ensure adherence to institution-wide standards. In personnel matters, college or institution-wide committees should promote fairness in the application of standards and in the assessment of faculty accomplishments. And in curricular matters, the task is to incorporate new realities without jettisoning traditional values.

Overall, the task of the dean is to get chairs and faculty to develop genuine questions and dialogue across departments—to cultivate the expectation that one will learn something from the other, that reciprocity is worth the effort. For a college to have integrity, the hard, impermeable edges of its departments must be softened. Passage back and forth must be possible and encouraged; and then joint projects must be created. More than the brave or the foolhardy must cross the boundaries to start to talk and work with one another. The cooperation of chairs is critical to frequent passage. In periodic consultations with the dean, chairs can identify their efforts to promote and develop their departments as well as to overcome barriers to broader cooperation and collaboration. Deans can then appraise these efforts. Appeal by a chair to conceptual incommensurability with other departments can be discussed at length, the dean's expectations clarified, and strategies explored. Fuzzy boundaries between departments are infinitely preferable to sharp edges or rigid barriers.

## THE INSTITUTION

The organization of the college and university into academic groupings corresponding to distinct and discrete ways of knowing has generated a profound increase of knowledge in this century. The yield has been so impressive that the academy can lose sight of important correlative principles—knowledge flows from cross-disciplinary work and from engagement in concrete practice as well. Tools and insights from one discipline can have suggestive power for others; anything is potentially helpful that counteracts the bias that divisions between disciplines mirror divisions in reality. Likewise, the boundary between thought and action, theory and practice, is crossed in both directions. Concepts inform and induce action, but action generates and evokes concepts as well. In interaction, each renews the other. Thus the incorporation of professional schools *into* the university rather than just their location *at* the university provides bridges between otherwise narrowly defined communities. Professional schools mediate the intellectualness of the university and the practical concerns of society to each other.

## The Authority of the Institution

The point is broader than the value of conceptual and practical cross-fertilization between schools or colleges. The college or university is an intellectual institution, necessarily more than a convenient context for the pursuit of individual, departmental, or school interests. It has its own integrity. The university stands for something. Presenting a curriculum of studies, it privileges certain inquiries over others and assures the public of its confidence in a solid core of knowledge and of procedures whereby the true and the reliable can be isolated from the false and the misleading. As an institution, it asserts that the curricula it sanctions are appropriate and defensible. The college or university does make room for the eccentric and the odd—not to indulge some expensive, antiquarian hobby, but because it has learned that truth can come from these quarters as well. This, after all, is the message of hospitality and thoughtfulness.

Institutional leaders rely on what Shils calls the "invisible senate"—those whose loyalty is to more than just their own department or school. Their loyalty is to the institution—not as a composite of obligations to individuals, but as loyalty to the context of interactions that constitute both it and them. It is not an abstract loyalty—nor is the object of loyalty abstract. Their loyalty is a concrete commitment to a concrete common good. Together, these individuals constitute "a stiffening spine which, outside the formal and official committees and boards, spreads its concern for the university beyond the boundaries of departments and up to the boundaries of the university" (Shils 1984, 58). The effectiveness of the college or university rests on the loyalty and energy of its "invisible senate" members, making it "an environment of high standards of intellectual exertion and achievement . . . . a constant reminder of the urgency of searching, studying, criticizing, re-examining old texts and data, seeking new data and putting them together with the old data" (Shils 1984, 70). Beyond its effectiveness, though hardly divorced from it, the ultimate authority of the institution requires the unqualified commitment of its faculty for the center to hold. Seeing the institution as simply the source of a paycheck reduces it to a legal entity or epiphenomenon. But the institution as a whole has a stake in the values and practices of the subcommunities it encompasses. In an extended sense, it too is what we have been calling a collegium—an entity created by its members, which has agency through them, and which is owed allegiance because it too sustains its members. They are both recipient and contributor, effect and cause.

To be sure, this collegial integrity has degrees and there is good reason to evaluate the claim of the multiversity to allegiance as significantly weaker than the claim of smaller, more integrated institutions. But in both cases, faculty receive their academic appointments from the institution, not the department. Rank and tenure may be departmentally recommended and located, but it is the institution that reviews faculty for promotion and grants tenure. It is the institution that applies its stamp of approval on overall standards and criteria in personnel decisions. And the institution then uses these criteria in support of the corporate assurance it provides the public that its faculty members are professionals. Sometimes it provides this assurance by using corroborating material and evidence received from a specialized membership body or from peers external to itself; however it often provides assurance on the basis of evidence provided internally by peers, chairs, and deans. If the assurances are misplaced or questioned, then it is the institution that must answer in court. It is the institution as broad collegium that then awards students degrees and so attests to the adequacy of the various curricula. Consequently, this is how one might respond to Charles Anderson's lament that "faculty may have collegial responsibilities, but they do not constitute a *collegium*." (Anderson 1993, 147). He is right that as the coherence and integrity of this broad collegium is perceived to weaken, so does its authority.

## Consortia among Institutions

Beyond the individual institution, the next step in thinking of extended community in higher education involves consortia among institutions. Competition for students, faculty, prestige, and funds has characterized much of the recent past and present—not interinstitutional cooperation and collaboration. As a consequence, consortial arrangements are fairly modest. But increasing financial pressures alone will almost certainly ensure searches for greater efficiencies, and working with contiguous institutions offers promise for enhancing collegial as well as fiscal realities. Connectedness between and among educational institutions will parallel the connectivity within institutions for which we have been arguing. In both cases there is better modeling of relational behavior and self-understanding.

Cross registration of students and joint purchasing agreements as well as sharing of buildings, student services, libraries, and athletic fields are already underway and will surely increase. Sharing of faculty and joint appointments is likely to be more common as will formal agreements to place selected academic programs on only one campus rather than several. Partnerships with like-minded non-collegiate institutions to achieve mutual objectives such as student counseling and other health functions are likely to replace more traditional arrangements. New forms of collegiality will develop and familiar ones erode.

Healthy connectedness can only be modeled and invited—not commanded. Freedom for the kind of self-formation that works against community cannot be eliminated. Controversy and dispute is what fuels the academy and the search for truth—even where one party to the debate may deny the terms that define the very possibility of the debate. To prohibit that possibility is to legislate against the freedom that defines the greater community. There is no community or institution worth the name that does not contain within it potential seeds of its own decay and eventual destruction. It seems inevitable that some of these seeds will sprout. There will always be some form of the insistent individualist. The academy needs to identify this fruit as bitter. Some selves in higher education are not enlarged, confident, and generous selves— but bounded, flat, and unimaginative. Some have limited perspective or tunnel vision regarding the good of the other. Some are not very honest and many do not work well together. But everyone in the academy, and particularly the titled and untitled academic leaders, can make a difference by addressing the fragmentation, academic professionalism, and lack of personal integration that the structure of the academy can foster. Everyone can celebrate forms of togetherness in which mutual enhancement is the rule rather than the exception.

## CONCLUSION

Certainly we have ample emphasis upon individual rights today. Creativity but also loneliness, intensity but also separateness, are the result. The organizational structure of higher education reinforces these tendencies. Departments and schools focus but isolate inquiry and those engaged in it. Fragmentation promotes unilateral power even as it is expressed by it. The academy is often deficient in the responsibilities and the virtues that push us to attend to one another.

The calling of each of us in academe is to create, nurture, and extend the collegium, thereby affecting the academic department, college or school, and university. We are all responsible for promoting habits and traditions of cooperation with colleagues, appropriate and civil respect for their contributions, and willingness to explore with each other scholarly ideas and work as well as teaching triumphs and frustrations. Department chairpersons and deans have special opportunities to encourage collegiality through hiring, evaluating, mentoring, celebrating, budgeting, and interpreting. Genuine and respectful discourse needs to be nourished and separate conversations need to be connected. The task before us is to create, elicit, and evoke (perhaps provoke) shared understandings, values, and practices sufficient in number that our communities are known for them.

The institution will be what we make of it; and that in turn is a function of what we make of ourselves and of each other. The invitation before us is to grow and develop by allowing others to influence us and by pursuing the good that embraces their good as well. In this enlarged fashion we enlarge ourselves. When we discipline ourselves in these ways and provide a more inviting environment in which to work, the number of unproductive scholar-teacher colleagues is reduced, polarizing rhetoric and calling in sick are minimized, and we no longer graduate so many poorly prepared students.

# EPILOGUE

## THE CURRENT SITUATION

### Seeking to Understand Academic Malaise

The academy is now a mature industry with heightened competition and lessened mobility. The professoriate is aging and not all members report the degree of personal satisfaction that the freedoms of the academy should provide. Nor do the behaviors of the academy always display the hospitality and thoughtfulness that the nature of inquiry calls for. In seeking to understand why a privileged environment does not provide more satisfying and appropriate forms of togetherness we have analyzed two models of self and community, as well as their respective concepts of power.

First, we explored a number of ways in which academe images the rugged individual that has relations and experiences, rather than the self that is and becomes through its relations and experiences. The former images are reinforced by the model of insistent individualism, pushing members of the academy toward isolation, exclusion, and fragmentation. The autonomy of the self is purchased at the expense of isolation from others. The academic professional is defined as above the uncertified others—particularly students. Even colleagues are held at arm's length. Personal strengths are forged and displayed in competition with others and modes of achieving excellence accentuate elements of social Darwinism. Unilateral power is abundantly evident and often prevails. In these circumstances the best defense is often a good offense, though most faculty tire of constant readiness for battle. Insistent individualism assigns hard edges to persons, things, and processes. Sharp elbows and hard words repel invasions and intrusions, leaving the self un-tainted but also unchallenged by the other. In order to help the defense effort, internal barriers are often erected between the professional and personal self, generating further fragmentation.

Academe's organizational structures often provide only marginal relief. Most faculty are sorted and placed by discipline and department. Even departmental faculty are often disconnected from one another and boundaries separating departments work against broader connections. Overall, organiza-tional structures lean toward aggregations of individualists rather than vibrant intellectual communities. And aggregations do not provide contexts in which most faculty gifts and talents can be developed, shown to advantage, or provide personal satisfaction. Nor do aggregations provide the most produc-tive context for advancing learning. Teaching and learning are activities that occur best in community—eventually broadening out and pointing to connec-tions with other interpretive communities. Apart from a relational context, academe reflects self-preoccupation and self-protection. It excuses itself from critical inquiry about individual and collective activities. It dawdles on estab-lishing assessment measures as well as mechanisms that promote professional development and growth. It celebrates modes of accomplishment that are often unconnected to the teaching and learning for which collegial profession-als are charged. Malaise and alienation result. Outside the academy suspicions increase about the quality of our professionalism.

The collegial model engenders hope because it opens individuals to re-sources beyond themselves. Self-identity is relational, not independent of others. The collegium provides for self-determination and differentiation *within* a community and promises the satisfactions that come from forms of togetherness marked by mutual reciprocity. A community of hope does not deny its fragmentation and isolation, but is energized by the very ideal it uses to judge it—an ideal that draws members beyond atomistic competition and toward mutual openness and co-creativity. This healthy and hopeful col-legium is composed of distinct individuals, each honored for his or her unique gifts and talents. Instead of a one-dimensional view of faculty success, these collegia celebrate the wonderful complexity and diversity of faculty lives. It is not insistent individualism that is cultivated, but forms of togetherness where it is in the interest of each to promote the good of the other—since the other in turn contributes to the self. Individuals are not self-enclosed and in a win-lose battle with others. Rather, each has the possibility of contributing to the good of the collegium (and thereby of the other) and of enjoying that good as derived in part from oneself. In fact, we should attend to others at least in part because only in this way are we faithful to ourselves.

Mutual relationships with this level of openness and energy are rare, reflecting the mixed character of the human condition and the inveterate tendency to unduly favor self. And some tasks simply do not permit relational power. Yet the rarity also reflects our own deficiencies, our habits of calling in sick and of indulging in polarizing rhetoric, of being candid only when convenient, and of complaining about others. It reflects the communities in which we participate and to which we contribute—communities that often do not provide the conditions for the development of the relational and liberated self.

## The Need for Better Institutional Models

We need more models of institutional excellence than the two dominant national models: the major research university and the selective liberal arts institution. The research institution reflects the German university tradition with its emphasis upon graduate students, disciplines, and the production of new knowledge. The research university is vast, an assemblage of diverse activities and inquiries with few explicit internal connections. It is complex, its pursuits diverse, and its people often remote from each other. By contrast, the selective liberal arts college is small, concentrating on undergraduates and liberal education. It reflects the colonial college tradition with its emphasis upon students and community. The development of mind and character are key objectives, with minimal attention to the application of knowledge or its professional dimensions.

The majority of institutions today fit neither of the national models. Most institutions are either smaller comprehensive institutions or community colleges; they should stop trying to emulate what they are not. Some of these institutions illustrate evolving organizational paradigms that might foster greater cooperation and healthier competition respecting teaching and learning—if the institutions can see their differences from the national models as opportunities rather than liabilities. I have particularly in mind the smaller entrepreneurial institutions that enjoy a greater ability to adjust academic structures to societal and student learning needs as well as to disciplinary developments. The boundaries between their departments are more permeable and their smaller size means that faculty are more likely to find themselves explaining to colleagues in other disciplines and departments what they are doing—thereby creating conditions for greater hospitality and mutual understanding as well as more individual growth. Likewise, there is greater possibility that students can find and educate each other.

The nascent New American College movement is one effort to identify a distinctive model and concept of institutional mission along these lines—

sharing strengths of each of the two reigning national models, but possessed of its own distinctive competencies (Wong 1994). The New American College model aims for student-centered education with faculty whose primary commitment is to teaching. However, these faculty inform their teaching with diverse scholarship oriented toward application and connection. Curricula emphasize competency but also conscience. The New American College model stresses the importance of connectivity between theory and application, abstract and concrete, undergraduate and graduate, curriculum in and out of class, campus and community, knowledge and service. Liberal and professional education are seen as related, rather than separate and distinct.

The concept of scholarship illustrates the point. Rather than holding up knowledge for its own sake or discovery of new knowledge as the model of excellence and expectation for faculty, this model emphasizes integration of spheres of knowledge, application of knowledge to new areas, and study of how knowledge is acquired and possessed. Hierarchies of status that plague other institutions are more easily bridged. In short, the New American College model provides an organizational structure congenial to the exercise of relational power. Perhaps somewhat bold, the use of "American" seems appropriate when one thinks of the value of the pragmatic and practical in our history.

Variations of this developing model occur in other movements today. The metropolitan universities and the public liberal arts universities are examples. So too, with appropriate changes, are developments in some community colleges. However, even in these smaller, more flexible institutions, community is never fully at hand. Challenges to the collegium are compounded today by the rapidly unfolding telecommunications revolution. The ability to communicate directly, easily, and inexpensively with colleagues elsewhere may promote more disciplinary and interdisciplinary inquiry. It may also blunt vital connections between an individual and his or her institution.

## THE FUTURE

How at the end of the twentieth century do we prepare for changes ahead? Our current situation presents us with substantial, but known, challenges. The future brings uncertainty. One of the most significant challenges we face is the telecommunications revolution. Its powers are extraordinary, since digitizing applies to sound, image, and text, as well as to data. And the revolution is gaining speed. Developments continue to be announced monthly. As formerly separate technologies converge, we may be on the cusp of needing new forms of collegiality. The multiplicity and instantaneousness of response and exchange that telecommunications permit could compensate for the absence of face-to-face contact. Alternatively, they could provide yet another reason for individuals to isolate themselves from each other—being on the Internet could provide yet one more excuse for not attending to departmental or institutional colleagues. We conclude the essay with a brief look at this and related prospects for our future.

## The Effects of Technology

With the growing distribution of multiple forms of learning through international and global networks and the increase in diverse modes of interactive communication, the spatially defined academic community appears at risk. The gathering of these new technological forces is a major threat to the enormous financial and personal investment of the academy in facilities and the familiar educational spaces facilities represent. Combined with increasingly unregulated and energetic forms of business entrepreneurship, the new technology may create such challenges to academic institutions that few will remain unaltered and some will disappear.

The impact of the telecommunications revolution on teaching is already potentially enormous. Multiple possibilities for enhancing classroom or laboratory instruction and for tailoring it to different student learning styles are at hand. Student control in the new technology is significantly heightened, for electronic storage accommodates quite different life and learning styles. Self-paced, self-selected learning will surely become more common. Learning has always in the end been self-education, but the technological revolution could radically redefine the role of the instructor as a distant midwife. Learning distributed off-campus will also increase. The home or the workplace could become the classroom. Ways to address what now can be an individualistic and isolated electronic experience will be devised, likely incorporating and expanding information technology developments such as groupware and other networked, collaborative learning products, perhaps together with periodic class meetings on campus or at other commonly accessible locations.

Will the Web rather than the classroom become the primary place for the dance of teaching and learning? It is hazardous to predict. The conservative nature of the academy makes it resistant to change. Yet not contemplating what the future may bring is equally hazardous. Some faculty and institutions will simply adapt new technology to current practices; others will see fresh structural possibilities. The speed with which this technology will be embraced is unclear. There is lethargy in some quarters, but already surprising speed in others. Increasing numbers of students enter college with sophisticated telecommunications skills and expectations. Younger students have grown up with technology. Older students may come from industry where careers now depend upon adept use of telecommunications. Faculty who disdain technology risk irrelevance and unprofessionalism, lacking hospitality and thoughtfulness. Institutions that do not respond may risk survival.

## Possible Scenarios

Three general scenarios for the future can be identified. One possibility is that the number and size of institutions of higher education will rapidly shrink as global electronic educational opportunities grow. Campuses will come under increasingly fierce financial competition within and beyond the traditional collegiate community. Many campuses will become service stations through which multiple learning modules are made available to students at a distance. Price will become an even greater factor in student choice. Attractive locations and pleasing surroundings will no longer provide institutions significant competitive advantages. People will no longer automatically look to local or regional institutions for educational services. Telecommunications will provide greater access but lesser community. The institution as a center of value will be further jeopardized. Campuses will struggle to remain as loci for collegia.

This new environment may liberate us from the insistent individualism that leads to self-indulgence and isolation. The intellectual transformation could generate an ethical transformation. More likely, though, it will augment and accelerate insistent individualism. The physical solitude of computer "interaction," combined with the control each individual has over the nature and circumstances of "dialogue" with others, will reinforce the cloistered and isolated self. Connections with others will be more apparent than real, more casual than constitutive of self. Institutions will appear more like work groups than collegia. Loosely connected bands of individuals without strong bonds of mutual interaction or mutual accountability, assembled and organized for specific projects or problems, will replace the collegium as the dominant form of institutional organization. Indeed, as contexts of intellectual and professional reciprocity, collegia will become increasingly difficult to recognize. What is the meaning of "colleagueship" for faculty whose relationality is effected through the Net? What links are analogous to the linkages of the local collegium? Whose standards are involved in the awarding of degrees? Where are the virtues of hospitality and thoughtfulness to be cultivated?

A second possibility is that the telecommunications revolution will prove to have minimal impact on educational institutions. Like the glorious future claimed for television and radio in earlier days, telecommunications will prove overrated. It may have already developed further than earlier fads, but its glamor will wear out. Electronic mail will overwhelm and exhaust users. Increasing carpel-tunnel syndrome will alienate others. The expense and effort of maintaining state-of-the-art equipment will strain institutions and the burden of attending ever more training sessions to learn the latest issue of application software will be seen as excessive. Common sense will win out and computers will be regarded as alienating machines. Traditional practices and values will prevail.

However attractive to traditionalists, this second scenario is unlikely. The telecommunications revolution has already advanced too far to be reversed. Industry and government seem irrevocably committed to the multiple advantages that the revolution has brought and entrepreneurs will provide educational services through telecommunications if campuses do not. Regulatory barriers against proprietary vendors are crumbling; various licensing and accreditation issues have already been addressed by some long-standing, respected programs and rapid progress is reported in others. Escalating tuitions will compel consumers to pursue these less expensive educational routes. In short, the revolution could call into question not only our practices, but many of the distinctions we presently take for granted, such as those between training and education or undergraduate and graduate work.

In the third scenario, most institutions will remain, but find themselves playing altered roles. Genuine community and personal accountability in what and how one communicates will continue to require physical proximity. We do not ordinarily acknowledge having "met" someone until we have been face-to-face and shaken hands, regardless of previous telephone conversations, network interactions, or exchange of correspondence. People must "work into" a collegium for truly competent and thoughtful education. They cannot simply subscribe one day as one might to an online discussion group. Nor, if it really is a community, can they leave by simply unsubscribing. Computer networks will not in and of themselves make people more hospitable or thoughtful. In fact, there are few personal consequences to acts on the Internet. Logging off in a huff is quite different from storming out of a committee meeting. And "flaming" seems much easier on networks than in person. By contrast, the obligations one owes others in the construction of conceptual dwellings or in the dance of teaching and learning are not incidental matters.

Yet there will be significant changes in this third scenario. Most campuses now pay insufficient collegial attention to pedagogy. The telecommunications revolution will spark renewed and revived attention. Widespread and creative collaboration among some faculty will identify innovative classroom and laboratory strategies and tactics. New and invigorated academic communities will quickly follow. Significant distance learning will also occur, but a role will remain for the traditional residential institution. Assessment criteria will be considerably improved in order to indicate more clearly the value that residence living and learning can provide. Likewise, the revolution will liberate some academics for more productive exchange with colleagues. The Internet or its successor provides an extension of the library and laboratory, a vehicle for rapid dissemination and critique of findings, and a forum for endlessly varied discussion groups. Freed from the constraints of the local situation, able to interact freely with scholars elsewhere, faculty can then turn their attention to the home collegium refreshed and energized by electronic dialogue with those at a distance. Especially for those isolated by geography or campus politics, telecommunications will rejuvenate.

Philosophical support for this third position may be found in Whitehead's observation decades ago that "personal interviews carry more weight than gramophone records." Technology has far outstripped what now seems a quaint illustration. But the philosophical point is that "the sense of reality can never be adequately sustained amidst mere sensa, either of sound or sight. The connexity of existence is of the essence of understanding" (Whitehead 1958, 45–46). We recall the earlier argument on the importance of the englobing reality from which professional and technical reason abstract. It is in this englobing reality that the felt evidence for values and for the affective domain rests. Does electronic connectedness provide sufficient "connexity?" Does near-instantaneous electronic communication constitute sufficient presence to each other? Do discourse and interactivity effected electronically abstract too much from primary experience or can they provide adequate glue for the collegium? Is the new commons of the Internet to replace or to supplement the agora, forum, classroom, or senate meeting?

It is too early to answer these questions. The telecommunications revolution could radically strengthen the togetherness or presence to each other in teaching and scholarship that we call the collegium. It could further fracture an already fragile entity. Or it could, in fact, come to constitute that community. At least part of the future will turn on what members and leaders of each local collegium are prepared to make happen.

## CONCLUSION

This book is not calling for some unreachable academic utopia. It *is* calling for change. The images and behaviors that flow from the model of the autonomous self are neither logically nor practically necessary. They are not rooted in unassailable first principles or practical requirements. Indeed, they seem to be incomplete, distorted versions of the logically prior and more practically satisfying model of the relational self. Likewise, the concepts of power and community associated with insistent individualism find correction and a more adequate context in the power and community marked by relationality. Human nature obviously permits both models and their associated concepts. The argument of the book is that the second set is far more inclusive and satisfying, and—with the collegial ethic of hospitality and thoughtfulness—far more fitting to the academy.

Three features of our collective experience undergird this entire project— the indispensability of our engagement in reason, the inescapable confidence in the existence of a reality in large degree beyond us, and the unavoidable presupposition of the meaningfulness of intellectual activity. First, an indispensable part of all conceptual dwellings is their rational foundation. We feel constrained to present our arguments in ways that avoid self-contradiction and that appeal to recognizable evidence. Even those who wish to deny the possibility of true statements outside the boundaries of their interpretive communities must cast their positions in ways that invoke the very standards they wish to deny.

Second, in all our work we presuppose the existence and intelligibility of a reality to a significant degree external to us. Even the act of communicating with others conveys this reality. Our very discourse presupposes the existence of a reality beyond and independent of our discourse. For instance, demanding proof of the reality of an external world is accomplished only through a public language. To argue against metaphysical realism actually presupposes and exemplifies it. The point is not that we can transcend our language, or secure some superior, extralinguistic standpoint. It is rather that in anything we do to affirm or deny that external world, we presuppose its existence. Our actions point to this antecendent, necessary commitment as a condition of their intelligibility and are affirmed in our primary experience.

Third, we also dwell in the unavoidable presupposition of the meaningfulness of our intellectual activity. It is employed even in efforts to repudiate it. The cynicism into which we may fall is muted by this fact that all our activity presupposes its significance. The degree of this significance may be in question. Our conviction may not be robust, or even conscious. The activities may disappoint or backfire; but success and failure alike have meaning. Nothing can be undertaken without the inescapable confidence that reality not only permits it, but that there is sense in undertaking it.

In the end, this is the trust of which Whitehead speaks, the trust "that the ultimate natures of things lie together in a harmony which excludes mere arbitrariness . . . . that in being ourselves we are more than ourselves . . . . that our experience, dim and fragmentary as it is, yet sounds the utmost depths of reality." Surely, this is the trust of every teacher and scholar, however rarely we step back to reflect upon it. "It springs from direct inspection of the nature of things as disclosed in our immediate present experience" (Whitehead 1967, 18). In all we undertake, we presuppose the intelligibility of reality, our ability to know it, and the meaningfulness of our endeavors. This trust supports the value and worth of our lives. There is an ultimate hospitality behind, beneath, and throughout all that we do—we cannot consistently think or act otherwise. This is the framework within which we live and think, construct conceptual dwellings, and perform the dances of teaching and learning. We engage this framework even in denying it. It is the ultimate answer to the malaise and cynicism in which we might otherwise dwell.

# BIBLIOGRAPHY

*AAUP Policy Documents and Reports.* Washington, DC: American Association of University Professors, 1995.

Adams, Hazard. *The Academic Tribes.* Second Edition. Urbana: University of Illinois Press, 1988.

Allan, George. "Process Philosophy and the Educational Canon." *Process Studies* 20/2, (summer 1991): 89–101.

Anderson, Charles W. *Prescribing the Life of the Mind: An Essay on the Purpose of the University, the Aims of Liberal Education, the Competence of Citizens, and the Cultivation of Practical Reason.* Madison: University of Wisconsin Press, 1993.

Anderson, Martin. *Imposters in the Temple: American Intellectuals Are Destroying Our Universities.* New York: Simon and Schuster, 1992.

Association of American Colleges. *Liberal Learning and the Arts and Sciences Major. Vol. 1: The Challenge of Connected Learning.* Washington, DC: Association of American Colleges, 1991.

Astin, Alexander W. *Academic Gamesmanship: Student-Oriented Change in Higher Education.* New York: Praeger Publishers, 1976.

Barber, Benjamin R. *An Aristocracy of Everyone.* Ballantine Books, 1992.

Barzun, Jacques. *The American University: How It Runs, Where It Is Going.* New York: Harper and Row, 1968.

Bellah, Robert N. et al. *Habits of the Heart: Individualism and Commitment in American Life.* Berkeley: University of California Press, 1985.

Bennett, John B. "The Dean and the Department Chair: Toward Greater Collaboration." *Educational Record* (winter 1990): 24–26.

———. "Husserl's *Crisis* and Whitehead's "Process Philosophy." *The Personalist* (summer 1975): 289–300.

Bennett, John B. and Elizabeth Dreyer. "On Complaining About Students." *AAHE Bulletin* (April 1994): 7–8.

Bennett, John B.and David J. Figuli, eds. *Enhancing Departmental Leadership*. Phoenix: American Council on Education and Oryx Press, 1993 (1990).

Bennett, William J. *To Reclaim a Legacy: A Report on the Humanities in Higher Education*. Washington, D.C.: National Endowment for the Humanities, 1984.

Berquist, William H. *The Four Cultures of the Academy*. San Francisco: Jossey-Bass, 1992.

Bess, James L., ed. *College and University Organization: Insights from the Behavioral Sciences*. New York: New York University Press, 1984.

Bledstein, Burton J. *The Culture of Professionalism: The Middle Class and the Development of Higher Education in America*. New York: W. W. Norton and Company, 1976.

Bloom, Allan. *The Closing of the American Mind: How Higher Education Has Failed Democracy and Impoverished the Souls of Today's Students*. Foreword by Saul Bellow. New York: Simon and Schuster, 1987.

Boice, Robert. *The New Faculty Member: Supporting and Fostering Professional Development*. San Francisco: Jossey-Bass, 1992.

———. "Coping with Difficult Colleagues." In *Enhancing Departmental Leadership*, edited by John B. Bennett and David J. Figuli, 132–138. Phoenix: American Council on Education and Oryx Press, 1993 (1990).

Bok, Derek. *Beyond the Ivory Tower*. Cambridge: Harvard University Press, 1982.

———. *Higher Learning*. Cambridge: Harvard University Press, 1986.

———. "Reclaiming the Public Trust," *Change* (July/August 1992): 13–19.

———. *Universities and the Future of America*. Durham: Duke University Press, 1990.

Botstein, Leon. "A Mirror on Higher Education: An Instructive Look at Choosing College Presidents." *Change* (March/April 1992): 48–51.

Bowen, H. R. and J. H. Schuster. *American Professors: A National Resource Imperiled*. New York: Oxford University Press, 1986.

Boyer, Ernest L. "Creating the New American College." *The Chronicle of Higher Education* (March 9, 1994): A48.

———. *College: The Undergraduate Experience in America*. New York: Harper & Row, 1987.

———. *Scholarship Reconsidered: Priorities for the Professoriate*. Lawrenceville, New Jersey: Carnegie Foundation for the Advancement of Teaching, 1990.

Brann, Eva T. H. *Paradoxes of Education in a Republic*. Chicago: University of Chicago Press, 1979.

Bromwich, David. *Politics by Other Means: Higher Education and Group Thinking*. New Haven: Yale University Press, 1992.

Brown, William R. *Academic Politics*. Birmingham: University of Alabama Press, 1982.

Bruffee, Kenneth A. *Collaborative Learning: Higher Education, Interdependence, and the Authority of Knowledge*. Baltimore: The Johns Hopkins University Press, 1993.

Brumbaugh, Robert S. "Some Applications of Process and Reality I and II to Educational Practice." *Educational Theory* 39 (fall 1989): 385–390.

———. "Whiteheadian American Educational Philosophy." In *Process in Context: Essays in Post-Whiteheadian Perspectives*, edited by Ernest Wold-Gazo. New York: Peter Lang, 1988, 57–67.

———. *Whitehead, Process Philosophy, and Education*. Albany: State University of New York, 1982.

Cahn, Steven M., ed. *Morality, Responsibility and the University: Studies in Academic Ethics*. Philadelphia: Temple University Press, 1990.

———. *Saints and Scamps: Ethics in Academia*. Revised Edition. Lanham, Maryland: Rowman and Littlefield, 1994.

Callahan, Daniel and Sissela Bok, eds. *Ethics Teaching in Higher Education*. Plenum Press, 1980.

Chait, Richard. "Providing Group Rewards for Group Performance." *Academe* (November/December 1988): 23–24.

Clark, Burton R., ed. *The Academic Profession: National, Disciplinary, and Institutional Settings*. Berkeley: University of California Press, 1987.

———. *The Higher Education System: Academic Organization in Cross-National Perspectives*. Berkeley: University of California Press, 1983.

Coates, Ken. "It is Time to Create an Open System of Peer Review." *The Chronicle of Higher Education* (June 23, 1995): A40.

Cole, Jonathan R., Elinor G. Barber, and Stephen R. Graubard, eds. *The Research University in a Time of Discontent*. Baltimore: The Johns Hopkins University Press, 1994.

Coles, Robert. "The Disparity Between Intellect and Character." *The Chronicle of Higher Education* (September 22, 1995): A68.

Creswell, John W. et al. *The Academic Chairperson's Handbook*. Lincoln, Nebraska: University of Nebraska Press, 1990.

Crimmel, Henry H. "The Myth of the Teacher-Scholar." *Liberal Education* 70/3 (1984): 183–198.

Damrosch, David. *We Scholars: Changing the Culture of the University*. Cambridge: Harvard University Press, 1995.

DeNicola, Daniel R. "The Emergence of the New American College." *Perspectives* (spring and fall 1994): 63–78.

Dill, David D. et al. *What Teachers Need to Know: The Knowledge, Skills, and Values Essential to Good Teaching*. San Francisco: Jossey-Bass, 1990.

Douglas, Mary. *How Institutions Think*. Syracuse: Syracuse University Press, 1986.

Dziech, Billie Wright and LindaWeiner. *The Lecherous Professor*. Second Edition. Urbana: University of Illinois Press, 1990.

Eble, Kenneth E. "Chairpersons and Faculty Development." In *Enhancing Departmental Leadership*, edited by John B. Bennett and David J. Figuli, 99–106. Phoenix: American Council on Education and Oryx Press, 1993a (1990).

———. "Communicating Effectively." In *Enhancing Departmental Leadership*, edited by John B. Bennett and David J. Figuli, 23–29. Phoenix: American Council on Education and Oryx Press, 1993b (1990).

Fairweather, James S. *Faculty Work and Public Trust: Restoring the Value of Teaching and Public Service in American Academic Life.* Boston: Allyn and Bacon, 1996.

Gabelnick, Faith, Jean MacGregor, Roberta S. Matthews, and Barbara Leigh Smith. *Learning Communities: Creating Connections Among Students, Faculty, and Disciplines.* San Francisco: Jossey-Bass, 1990.

Gardner, John W. "The Individual and Society." In *On the Meaning of the University,* edited by Sterling M. McMurrin, 52–62. Salt Lake City: University of Utah Press, 1976.

Geertz, Clifford. "Blurred Genres: The Refiguration of Social Thought." *The American Scholar* (spring 1980).

Getman, Julius. *In the Company of Scholars: The Struggle for the Soul of Higher Education.* Austin: University of Texas Press, 1992.

Giamatti, A. Bartlett. *A Free and Ordered Space: The Real World of the University.* New York: W. W. Norton and Company, 1988.

Graff, Gerald and Michael Berube. "Dubious and Wasteful Academic Habits." *The Chronicle of Higher Education* (February 17, 1995): B1–2.

Green, William Scott. "The Disciplines of Liberal Learning." In *Strengthening the College Major,* edited by Carol Geary Schneider and William Scott Green, 101–112. San Francisco: Jossey Bass, 1993.

Greenberg, Milton. "Accounting for Faculty Members' Time." *The Chronicle of Higher Education* (October 20, 1993): A68.

Gustafson, James M. "Human Confidence and Rational Activity: The Dialectic of Faith and Reason in University Life." *Cresset* (September 1988): 5–10.

Hauerwas, Stanley M. "The Morality of Teaching." In *The Academic's Handbook,* edited by A. Leigh Deneef, Craufurd D. Goodwin, Ellen Stern McCrate, 19–28. Durham: Duke University Press, 1988.

Hill, Patrick J. "Multiculturalism: The Crucial Philosophical and Organizational Issues." *Change* (July/August [23/4] 1991): 38–47.

Hirsch, Deborah. "Translating Research into Practice: The Impact of the Hidden Curriculum in Teaching Morals and Values." *Journal for Higher Education Management* (winter [3/2] 1988): 45–51.

Huber, Richard M. *How Professors Play the Cat Guarding the Cream: Why We're Paying More and Getting Less in Higher Education.* Fairfax, Virginia: George Mason University Press, 1992.

Husserl, Edmund. *The Crisis of European Sciences and Transcendental Phenomenology.* Translated by David Carr. Evanston: Northwestern University Press, 1970.

James, William. *Pragmatism.* Buffalo, New York: Prometheus Books, 1991 (1907).

Jensen, Ejner J. "The Bitter Groves of Academe." *Change* (January/February 1995): 8–11.

Kadish, Mortimer R. *Toward an Ethic of Higher Education.* Stanford: Stanford University Press, 1991.

Katzenbach, Jon R. and Douglas K. Smith. "The Discipline of Teams." *Harvard Business Review* (March/April 1993): 111–120.

Keller, Catherine. *From a Broken Web: Separation, Sexism, and Self.* Boston: Beacon Press, 1986.

Keller, George. *Academic Strategy: The Management Revolution in American Higher Education.* Baltimore: The Johns Hopkins University Press, 1983.

Kerr, Clark. *The Great Transformation in Higher Education: 1960–1980.* Albany, New York: SUNY Press, 1991.

———. "Knowledge Ethics and the New Academic Culture." *Change* (January/February 1994a): 9–15.

———. *Troubled Times for American Higher Education: The 1990's and Beyond.* Albany, New York: SUNY Press, 1994b.

———. *The Uses of the University.* Cambridge: Harvard University Press, 1963.

Kerr, Clark and Marian L. Gade. *The Guardians: Boards of Trustees of American Colleges and Universities.* Washington, DC: Association of Governing Boards of Universities and Colleges, 1989.

Kimball, Bruce A. *The 'True Professional Ideal' in America: A History.* Cambridge, Massachusetts: Blackwell, 1992.

Kimball, Roger. *Tenured Radicals: How Politics Has Corrupted Our Higher Education.* New York: Harper Perennial, 1991.

Kuhn, Thomas S. *The Structure of Scientific Revolutions.* Second Edition. Chicago: University of Chicago Press, 1970.

Kultgen, John. *Ethics and Professionalism.* Philadelphia: University of Pennsylvania Press, 1988.

Laney, James T. "Through Thick and Thin: Two Ways of Talking About the Academy and Moral Responsibility." In *Ethics and Higher Education,* edited by William W. May, 49–66. New York: ACE/Macmillan, 1990.

Langenberg, Donald N. "Team Scholarship Could Help Strengthen Scholarly Traditions." *The Chronicle of Higher Education* (September 2, 1992): A64.

Lawrence, Nathaniel. "Nature and the Educable Self in Whitehead." *Educational Theory* (July 1965): 210–216.

Lenn, Marjorie Peace. "The Globalization of Accreditation: Trade Agreements and Higher Education." *The College Board Review* (July 1996): 6–11.

Limmerick, Patricia Nelson. "Dancing with Professors: The Trouble with Academic Prose." *The New York Times Book Review* (October 31, 1993): (3)23–24.

Livezey, Lois Gehr. "Women, Power, and Politics: Feminist Theology in Process Perspective." *Process Studies* 17 (summer 1988): 70–75.

Long, Edward LeRoy, Jr. *Higher Education as a Moral Enterprise.* Washington, D.C. Georgetown University Press, 1992.

Loomer, Bernard. "Two Kinds of Power." *Process Studies* 6/1 (spring 1976): 5–32.

Lovett, Clara. "Listening to the Faculty Grapevine." *AAHE Bulletin* (November 1993): 3–5.

Lucas, Ann F. *Strengthening Departmental Leadership: A Team-Building Guide for Chairs in Colleges and Universities.* San Francisco: Jossey-Bass, 1994.

MacIntyre, Alasdair. *After Virtue.* Notre Dame: Notre Dame University Press, 1981.

————. *Three Rival Versions of Moral Enquiry: Encyclopedia, Genealogy, and Tradition.* Indianapolis: University of Notre Dame Press, 1990.

Markie, Peter J. *A Professor's Duties: Ethical Issues in College Teaching.* Lanham, Maryland: Rowman and Littlefield, 1994.

————. "Professors, Students, and Friendship." In *Morality, Responsibility and the University: Studies in Academic Ethics,* edited by Steven M. Cahn, 134–149. Philadelphia: Temple University Press, 1990.

Massy, William F., Andrea K. Wilger, and Carol Colbeck. "Overcoming 'Hollowed' Collegiality." *Change* (July/August 1994): 10–20.

May, William F. "Professional Ethics: Setting, Terrain, and Teacher." In *Ethics Teaching in Higher Education,* edited by Daniel Callahan and Sissela Bok, 205–241. Plenum Press, 1980.

May, William W., ed. *Ethics and Higher Education.* New York: ACE/Macmillan, 1990.

McDonald, Kim A. "Too Many Co-Authors?" *The Chronicle of Higher Education* (April 28, 1995): A35–36.

Mills, C. Wright. *The Sociological Imagination.* New York: Oxford University Press, 1959.

Moore, Mary Elizabeth Mullino. *Teaching from the Heart: Theology and Educational Method.* Minneapolis: Fortress Press, 1991.

Oliver, Donald T. and Kathleen Waldron Gershman. *Education, Modernity, and Fractured Meaning: Toward a Process Theory of Teaching and Learning.* Albany: State University of New York Press, 1989.

Palmer, Parker J. "Community and Commitment in Higher Education." An Interview with Russell Edgerton, *AAHE Bulletin* (September 1992a): 3–7.

————. "Community, Conflict, and Ways of Knowing." *Change* (September/October 1987): 20–25.

————. "Divided No More: A Movement Approach to Educational Reform." *Change* (March/April 1992b): 10–17.

————. "Good Talk About Good Teaching: Improving Teaching Through Conversation and Community." *Change* (November/December [25/6] 1993): 8–13.

————. *To Know As We Are Known: A Spirituality of Higher Education.* San Francisco: Harper and Row, 1983.

Pelikan, Jaroslav. *The Idea of the University: A Reexamination.* New Haven: Yale University Press, 1992.

————. *Scholarship and Its Survival: Questions on the Idea of Graduate Education.* Princeton: The Carnegie Foundation for the Advancement of Teaching, 1983.

Pettit, Lawrence, K. "Problems of Ethics in Higher Education." *Educational Record* (summer 1990): 34–38.

Plater, William M. "Future Work: Faculty Time in the 21st Century." *Change* (May/June 1995): 23–33.

"Professor Accused of Double Dipping is Fired." *The Chronicle of Higher Education* (April 21, 1995): A20.

Professor X. *This Beats Working for a Living: The Dark Secrets of a College Professor.* New Rochelle, NY: Arlington House, 1973.

Rich, John Martin. *Professional Ethics in Education.* Springfield, Illinois: Charles C. Thomas, 1984.

Rorty, Richard. *Contingency, Irony and Solidarity.* New York: Cambridge University Press, 1989.

Rosovsky, Henry. *The University: An Owner's Manual.* New York: W.W. Norton, 1990.

Rothkopf, Arthur J. "College Rankings: Increasing Accuracy, Improving Accountability." *The Chronicle of Higher Education* (September 7, 1996): B5–6.

Roy, David. "The Value of the Dialogue between Process Thought and Psychotherapy." *Process Studies* 14 (fall 1985): 158–174.

Schilling, Karen Maitland and Karl L. Schilling. "Professors Must Respond to Calls for Accountability." *The Chronicle of Higher Education* (March 24, 1993): A40.

Schneider, Carol Geary. "Enculturation or Critical Engagement?" In *Strengthening the College Major,* edited by Carol Geary Schneider and William Scott Green, 43–56. San Francisco: Jossey Bass, 1993.

———. "Toward a Richer Vision: The AAC Challenge." In *Strengthening the College Major,* edited by Carol Geary Schneider and William Scott Green, 57–70. San Francisco: Jossey Bass, 1993.

Schneider, Carol Geary and William Scott Green, eds. *Strengthening the College Major.* San Francisco: Jossey Bass, 1993.

Schoen, Donald A. *The Reflective Practitioner: How Professionals Think in Action.* New York: Basic Books, 1983.

Schulman, Lee S. "Teaching as Community Property: Putting an End to Pedagogical Solitude." *Change* (November/December 1993): 6–7.

Schurr, George M. "Toward a Code of Ethics for Academics." *Journal of Higher Education* 53/3 (May/June 1982): 318–334.

Schuster, Jack H. "The Context of Scholarly Communication." *The Serials Librarian* 17 (1990): 15–23.

———. "Whatever Happened to the Faculty?" *Teaching Excellence: Toward the Best in the Academy* 3 (1991–1992): 1–3.

Schwehn, Mark R. *Exiles from Eden: Religion and the Academic Vocation in America.* New York: Oxford University Press, 1993.

Searle, John R. "Is There a Crisis in American Higher Education?" *Bulletin, American Academy of Arts and Sciences* (January 1993): 24–47.

———. "Rationality and Realism, What Is at Stake?" In *The Research University in a Time of Discontent,* edited by Jonathan R. Cole et al., 55–83. Baltimore: The Johns Hopkins Univesity Press, 1993.

———. "The Storm Over the University." *The New York Review of Books* (December 6, 1990): 34–42.

Secor, Robert. "Recapturing Departmental Community: A Tale of Faculty Morale, External Pressures, and Departmental Collaboration." *AAHE Bulletin* (February 1995): 3–6.

Shils, Edward. *The Academic Ethic.* Chicago: University of Chicago Press, 1984.

Shore, Paul. *The Myth of the University: Ideal and Reality in Higher Education.* Lanham, Maryland: University Press of America, 1992.

Sloan, Douglas. *Faith and Knowledge: Mainline Protestantism and American Higher Education*. Louisville: Westminster John Knox Press, 1994.

Smith, Page. *Killing the Spirit*. New York: Viking Press, 1990.

Solomon, Robert and Jon. *Up the University: Recreating Higher Education in America*. Addison-Wesley Publishing Company, 1993.

Sorcinelli, Mary Deane. "Chairs and the Development of New Faculty." *The Department Advisor* 5 (fall 1989): 1–4.

———. "Satisfaction and Concerns of New University Teachers." *To Improve the Academy* 7 (1988): 121–133.

Stecklow, Steve. "Cheat Sheets: Colleges Inflate SATs and Graduation Rates in Popular Guidebooks." *The Wall Street Journal* CCXXV/66 (April 5, 1995): A1, 8.

Stimpson, Catharine R. "Some Comments on the Curriculum: Can We Get Beyond Our Controversies." *Change* (July/August 1992): 9–11, 53.

Sullivan, William M. *Work and Integrity: The Crisis and Promise of Professionalism in America*. New York: HarperBusiness, 1995.

Taylor, Charles. *The Ethics of Authenticity*. Cambridge: Harvard University Press, 1991.

Tierney, William G. *Building Communities of Difference: Higher Education in the Twenty-First Century*. Westport, CT: Bergin and Garvey, 1993.

Tompkins, Jane. "The Way We Live Now." *Change* (November/December 1992): 13–19.

———. "Teach by the Values You Preach." *Harpers Magazine* (September 1991): 30–35.

Veysey, Lawrence. *The Emergence of the American University*. Chicago: University of Chicago Press, 1965.

Weaver, Frederick Stirton. "Academic Disciplines and Undergraduate Liberal Arts Education." *Liberal Education* (1981): 151–165.

———. *Liberal Education: Critical Essays on Professions, Pedagogy, and Structure*. New York: Teachers College Press, 1991.

Weick, Karl E. "Contradictions in a Community of Scholars: The Cohesion-Accuracy Tradeoff." In *College and University Organization: Insights from the Behavioral Sciences*, edited by James L. Bess, 15–29. New York: New York University Press, 1984.

Weingartner, Rudolph H. *Fitting Form to Function: A Primer on the Organization of Academic Institutions*. Phoenix: American Council on Education/Oryx Press, 1996.

———. *Undergraduate Education: Goals and Means*. Phoenix: American Council on Education/Oryx Press, 1993.

Wergin, Jon F. *The Collaborative Department: How Five Campuses Are Inching Toward Cultures of Collective Responsibility*. Washington, D. C.: American Association for Higher Education, 1994.

Whitehead, Alfred North. *The Aims of Education and Other Essays*. New York: Macmillan, 1929.

———. *Modes of Thought*. New York: Capricorn, 1958 (1938).

———. *Process and Reality*. Corrected Edition. Edited by David Ray Griffin and Donald W. Sherburne. New York: The Free Press, 1978.

———. *Science and the Modern World.* NewYork: The Free Press, 1967 (1925).

Wilshire, Bruce. *The Moral Collapse of the University: Professionalism, Purity, and Alienation.* Albany: State University of New York Press, 1990.

Wilson, Daniel J. *Science, Community and the Transformation of American Philosophy: 1860–1930.* Chicago: University of Chicago Press, 1990.

Wilson, Everett K. "Power, Pretense, and Piggybacking: Some Ethical Issues in Teaching." *Journal of Higher Education* 53/3 (May/June 1982): 268–281.

Wingspread Group on Higher Education. *An American Imperative: Higher Expectations for Higher Education.* The Johnson Foundation, Inc., 1993.

Wong, Frank F. "Primary Care Education—A New American College Model." *Perspectives* (spring and fall 1994): 13–26.

# INDEX

*by Kay Banning*